PORTRAIT

* * * * * * * * * OF * * * * * * * * *

AMERICA

Essays from Esquire Magazine

PORTRAIT

OF

★ ★ ★ ★ ★ ★ ★ ★ ★ ★ ★ ★ ★ ★ ★ ★ ★ ★ ★

AMERICA

Essays from Esquire Magazine

Preface by
Lee Eisenberg

Foreword by
Phillip Moffitt

BONANZA BOOKS
NEW YORK

Originally published as Esquire's The Soul of America.

The text was previously published in the June 1985 issue of Esquire.

Copyright © 1985 by Esquire Associates
All rights reserved.

This 1989 edition is published by Bonanza Books,
distributed by Crown Publishers, Inc., 225 Park Avenue South,
New York, New York 10003, by arrangement with Charles
Scribner's Sons, an imprint of Macmillan
Publishing Co. Inc.

Manufactured in the United States of America

Library of Congress Cataloging-in-Publication Data

Portrait of America : essays from Esquire magazine / preface by
    Lee Eisenberg ; foreword by Phillip Moffitt.

        "Previously published in the June 1985 issue of Esquire"—T.p. verso.
        Reprint. Originally published: Esquire's the Soul of America.
        New York, Scribner. 1986.
        ISBN 0-517-68136-6
        1. United States—Social life and customs—1971-   2. National
    characteristics, American.   I. Eisenberg, Lee, 1946-
    II. Esquire.   III. Title.
    E169.04.04E77   1989
    973.92—dc19   89-498
                                                                   CIP

ISBN 0-517-68136-6
h g f e d c b a

Contents

Place Bound

Although this book, which began as an *Esquire* special issue, was conceived, planned, and published on the nation's most crowded island, it bears—for better or worse—very few fingerprints of native New Yorkers.

To begin at the beginning. The idea that eventually grew into "The Soul of America" started with Esquire contributing editor Geoffrey Norman, who was born in Virginia, educated in Alabama, and now lives in Dorset, Vermont. As a writer, Norman is on the go a lot, and he maintains his keen eye wherever his assignments take him. One day a couple of years ago he stopped off in New York for an editorial conference. He had regionalism on his mind.

Geography, he offered, was still the prime determinant of American character. "For example," Norman said, "a rich man in Alabama is more comfortable talking to a poor man in Alabama than to another rich man from, say, Boston." Norman then talked about trucks, allowing as how the pickup of choice in New England is different from its opposite number in the Deep South.

So, too, are the people who drive them, the kind of jokes these people laugh at, and what they wear as their Saturday-night best.

The conversation roamed widely. An editor who grew up in Miami told of the particular influence that place had baked into her values. Another colleague, from Dallas, argued that Texas politics were unlike any other. Somebody else, a Pennsylvanian, spoke about the activities of volunteer firemen: how firemen in Maine hold an annual lobster boil, while those in Louisiana fry mullet, while those in North Carolina barbecue pigs. All, including the bingo, for a good cause.

If there was anything startling about this conversation, it was that it was all *still true*—true at a time when so many of us assume that America is fast becoming one nation under Golden Arches. Even in the face of ubiquitous shopping malls, suburban sprawl, fast-food franchises, hotel chains, and network television, regional differences not only exist, they flourish.

Indeed, as someone speculated that afternoon, could the *threat* of sameness be triggering a reaction back to regional consciousness? The restoration of Charleston, South Carolina, for instance? The drivers born in Denver, Colorado, who attach special NATIVE license plates to their cars?

The meeting broke and everyone went for a beer. We thought we had something: a special issue dedicated to distinguishing East from West, North from South. But as the months went by, some kind of stubbornness—Yankee cynicism? southern pride?—kept pushing us further. A breakthrough came when we realized that we hadn't been talking about the differences among regions so much as the very essence of the American identity. That is, if there is such a thing as the American character, its soul lies in the sum total of values that exist distinctly in a multitude of places. But precisely *which* values, and *where?*

This is when the real work got started. For months we drew up lists of the qualities that we thought composed the American personality: materialism, powerseeking, frugality, love of risk, ingenuity, and on and on. Simultaneously we drew up lists of communities where these values are rooted or where they are perennially in bloom. In the end we settled on thirty or so destinations, our itinerary for the search for "The Soul of America."

The next step was to find the stories. From the start we were committed to a format not of essays but of reporting. It's one

thing to say that Houston is the capital of opulence, quite another
to tag along to some parties in River Oaks to meet people who
think nothing of ordering a $650 breakfast. Writers would write
about characters, phenomena, and issues of the moment. In short,
they would bring back living proof of the overwhelming importance and meaning of *place*.

The final and most critical phase was enlisting the wide
support of the writing community. As it turned out, "The Soul
of America" was an easy sell. If there is any universal truth about
writers, it is that they are place bound. In every sense. A writer's
place colors the voice with which he writes; his origins provide the
rooms, the streets, and the faces that his imagination works and
reworks into art. On the other hand, a writer likes nothing better
than to be bound for somewhere else: a new place with unfamiliar
rooms, streets, and faces, experiences in lively contrast to those
of his first and everlasting place.

In "The Soul of America" our writers had it both ways: some
explored new ground, others got to go home again. When their
assignments were over, they had a chance to reflect on the meaning of their own home territories.

William Kennedy grew up in Albany, New York, the city
wherein is set his brilliant trilogy, *Legs, Billy Phelan's Greatest
Game,* and *Ironweed.* Says Kennedy of the place: "It is an inexhaustible context for what I write. A city abundant in mythic
qualities, full of heroes, villains, and splendid citizens." For his
piece in "The Soul of America" ("Jack and the Oyster," page 3),
Kennedy stayed right there.

Growing up in Columbus, Ohio, Bob Greene ("A Few Words
with the Biggest Man in Dallas," page 153) felt the influence of
living "in the middle of the country, which helped make me go out
and find my own stories, to make me feel like the only writer around,
not part of the mob."

Tom Wolfe ("Proper Places," page 144) is a product of
Richmond, Virginia. Says Wolfe: "The main effect on my work was,
I suppose, the education. As far as a literature background is
concerned, almost any secondary school in Virginia was better than
the schools in New York or New England."

Growing up in and around Hollywood afforded an unusual
and, for Peter Davis ("The High and the Mighty Crowd," page 169),
useful benefit. "Being raised in the motion-picture community gave

me an almost obsessive curiosity about the difference between appearance and reality."

Douglas Bauer ("The Prime of Miss Jean Wilson," page 68) was raised in Prairie City, Iowa. He, too, observes a curious relationship. "My father is a grain farmer, and I think there's a great deal in common between farmers and writers. They're optimistic beyond any reasonable expectation."

A hamlet in the Catskills called Fleischmanns, in New York, was home to Joyce Wadler ("The Fine Art of Mountain *Tummling*," page 203). The town is part of the Borscht Belt, the subject of Walder's piece. "When I was seven," she recalls, "I could hear the sound of cha-cha lessons bouncing off the hills. Where else in the world do they bring you a dozen kinds of bread and rolls, juices, and coffee, then come up to you and say, 'Well, what would you like for breakfast?'"

Joe Kane ("Officer Hicks, Gay Cop," page 191) was brought up near San Francisco. He sums up the place in one word: "*Unique*. It made me want to write about subjects who were quirky. People in cracks and crevices. Not celebrities."

Lynn Darling ("True Blue," page 106) hails from all over: "I was an Army brat. As a girl I felt sorry for people who had to live in one place. Only in college did I begin to wish that I'd had a hometown. But moving around tends to develop the voyeuristic side of writing. You learn very early to notice things."

Just as place defines America, it also defines the American writer. From Kennedy to Darling, a theme emerges: the soul of the writer is composed of a love of myth, individuality, literature, illusion, stubbornness, humor, eccentricity, curiosity. These qualities abound in the separate pieces that make up "The Soul of America." And the editors of *Esquire* would like to thank each and every one of our contributors—wherever they're from, and wherever they're off to.

—LEE EISENBERG
Editor
Esquire

The Spirit of Place

Drive out of the Beaverhead National Forest, out of Montana and into Idaho, until you arrive at the Salmon River. Take a right and follow the river road until it comes to a small sign that says TO INDIAN CREEK GUEST RANCH. Follow the old logging road as it winds up the mountain. Along the way you will come across two fence gates that you will have to open and close behind you. At the end of that road you will find a small house belonging to the Briggs family—Jack and Lois and daughter Theresa—plus one guesthouse and three cabins, a pasture full of horses, and a barn to house them.

Briggs is a man who supports himself by sharing the place he loves—the Idaho mountains—with visitors. He gave up a dry-cleaning business in Salmon for the less lucrative but more satisfying experience of living with nature. Since he has come here Briggs has grown as sensitive to his environment as the black bear and rattlesnakes you encounter when traveling with him on horseback along the Bitterroot Range trails. He can hunt through the brambles and, without any clues, find bushes laden with delicious wild raspberries too delicate to be picked for market. His sense of place is nothing he talks about; it is something he feels. His are values rooted against the flow of time and passing fads.

Briggs is a man who is not imposing himself on his environment—he is integrated with it. To observe his interaction with nature is to observe a life cycle that nourishes itself. Those who, unlike Briggs, do not have their own sense of place must always seek nourishment for the spirit or be in danger of having it wither away.

Consider another man—this one an urbane magazine editor who is as different as can be from the man in Idaho in his speech, daily concerns, and intellectual interests. He, too, is at one with his place, his urban environment. He can feel it, taste it, and flourish within it. He is a hunter within his ecological structure, pursuing visions with huge bursts of energy. His sense of place nourishes him as he hikes the trails of museum corridors and meditates on the sounds in concert halls. He reports that it took twenty years for his roots to take hold in this urban ground, because he was so distracted by his drive for success that he didn't give himself time to come to terms with his environment. Yes, he hates the crime, the poverty, the dirt that mars the landscape, but like the man from Idaho, he can show a visitor a hundred small places of delight. He belongs to this environment; his values are inseparable from it, and together with thousands like him he is part of the landscape, the conscience, the soul of this country.

They are the lucky ones. The connected ones. Some rich, some poor, most in between, and of all age groups. They are everywhere: in beach towns and rural communities, on city streets. They have in common that which makes them different. They live with the grace that comes from possessing a sense of place. It is their identification with their community and their country that forms the core of our national character.

We are a nation of individualists—mobile, iconoclastic, and determined to put above all else our right to personal choice —yet despite the tension caused by radically differing individual values, we hold together as a nation. We do so through community—communities of family, of friends, and of those with common values. Each of these bonds is forged primarily in the context of place. It is a bond first created in childhood and made so strong in some that it can be carried intact from city to city throughout adult life. It is also a bond so strong that the members of the community may themselves change while the community identity continues, with new arrivals adopting the values of the place.

Not all of us are among the fortunate who possess this sense of place. Nor does everyone with a sense of place always manage to live in physical proximity to it—witness the transferred executive miserable with Manhattan life or his urban counterpart feeling isolated in the hills of Arkansas. For those temporarily displaced, in time an opportunity to move elsewhere will present itself, thereby correcting the imbalance caused by this propensity for moving about.

It is eye-opening to watch how those who are temporarily deprived of proximity to their place of identity cope with their situation. An executive who loves the ocean and the salty marshes of South Carolina but finds himself landlocked chooses to live on a lake, despite its distance from the office, just to be near water. A schoolteacher in Washington, D.C., returns to his beloved Mississippi Delta each summer and plans to retire there. A group of exiled San Franciscans discover they've all chosen the same little seacoast town in Connecticut because it feels just enough like northern California to satisfy the longing in their West Coast hearts.

Everywhere I travel I find countless such examples of people making adjustments and making them work, finding a sense of belonging and passing that on to their children.

Those without a sense of place are on an endless journey of uneasy living in one locale after another. They are always dreaming of and searching for the one place that will provide the opportunity of belonging and give the days of their lives a feeling of context. These wanderers are the unlucky ones, the disconnected ones, and wherever they go they are dependent on others for a sense of cohesion in life. It is as though they are always visitors wherever they live, observing and existing within a social structure but never becoming part of it.

It is astounding to me that America at this time can be so

populated with these wanderers and still have its underlying values remain strong, that the country can somehow accommodate
the cost to the community of the apathy and anger of these
people without a significant rending of the social fabric.

Explore any major city, and its disaffected are easily visible
on the street. Yet cities are flourishing. Wander through the
California beach towns, and the disaffected, while more blended
into the landscape, are there as well, yet these towns retain a
wonderful sense of community.

I travel a great deal throughout America, and I find these
wanderers everywhere. I cannot say why it is that so many never
find a sense of place. God knows, it is not for lack of looking. They
are willing to start over, make major sacrifices, if they could just
find a place where they felt they belonged. It seems to me that
most of the displaced start the search first by trying to find the
right part of the country, then the right community, and finally
the specific place.

The exceptions are those traveling in the fast lane, the ones
who will check out only the hot spots such as Aspen or Santa Fe
or Austin. When I encounter these fast-lane travelers supposedly
settled down—running a restaurant or an art gallery or "doing"
real estate—I am struck by how many are called to these locations
thinking of them as a possible home, and how few actually stay.

I suspect that discovering a sense of place requires a change
of attitude toward oneself and toward life. Somehow one has to
become a person willing to have roots, willing to surrender op-
tions, in order to be able to give oneself over to the identity of
a particular place.

This is a time of boundless ambition. People are consumed
by a desire to acquire more of everything, and this makes for
complicated lives. To give oneself over to a sense of place is to
choose a more simple life and accept that all one will have is what
place can provide. It also means giving time to the experience of
place at the expense of ambition.

It is no accident that young American adults place so much
emphasis on finding the right house or apartment—and have so
much trouble actually finding it. So often the motive for this
search is dissatisfaction. They lack a sense of belonging yet are
confined to their current area. Having no knowledge of what they

seek, they confuse the need for place with the need for the perfect abode. If only such abodes existed!

When I encounter those who are rooted in their sense of place, they are not necessarily the ones with the most attractive or stylish homes. Rather, their homes are infused with the spirit of belonging, of relationship to the community, to the local environment. In their homes there exists an intimacy, and the dweller *shares* with a visitor his or her dwelling place. Such a person is of that dwelling, and that dwelling is of a greater sense of place.

For the wanderer, a home is not really a home at all, but a dwelling where the owner is only a visitor, as if it were a temporary shelter or a hotel. Sometimes the dwelling is a home, but it exists as a retreat for the owner, a shelter isolated from the community, a barricade against the outside. Then there are those homes that reflect the place, be it a city or a woodland, and these are the homes where the spirit can really flourish, where a visitor is truly warmed, and where the owner can find solace for his own soul.

Today all of America is united by interstates, franchises, telecommunications, and endless standardization in business and education and health. Moreover, so many people have moved from here to there and then somewhere else that we are now thoroughly mixed as a population. Yet the sense of place that is unique flourishes beneath the surface.

Talk to a child growing up on Chicago's North Side, or a child growing up in a Minneapolis suburb or a Kentucky mountain village or a small town in Texas, and he or she will relate stories, impressions, and encounters that are unique. And these experiences are helping to shape these children into the adults they will become.

It is so easy for the adults of today, particularly those who draw little or no comfort from a strong sense of place, simply to miss these differences and see only sameness. But there are thousands and thousands who are becoming more acutely aware of the differences and are moving their families to a place for just such a reason.

I believe that in the future America will seem to be more and more the same all over, but it will be only a surface sameness, as we will continue to maintain our underlying differences.

Most places change; they are different, and what makes them so is not static. The small but flourishing cities around modern urban areas that are becoming America's corporate headquarters come to mind, as well as the cities and states now being settled by new waves of immigrants—Miami with Cubans and Latinos, California with Vietnamese, Texas with Mexicans. These new population waves will create new riches of difference —they already have, in fact—and it is a good thing.

We Americans have been able to tolerate one another's differences because we feel a security in our strong sense of place. To me, this is the magic elixir of America. It is a natural resource that has carried us through the social and economic upheaval of the last twenty-odd years, and it will be tapped again and again as we face further economic change and environmental conflicts. Our capacity for tolerance will continue to be the cornerstone of the national character.

As we face that future, what will take care of our values, make us feel like one country? Not government or other institutions, but the seemingly unrelated acts of love and caring of millions of individuals, always expressed in the context of community and of place.

—PHILLIP MOFFITT
President and Editor-in-Chief
Esquire

PART 1

TENACITY
AND
LASTING
TRADITION

ALBANY, NEW YORK
Craftsmanship and Professional Pride

WISDOM, MONTANA
Stubbornness and Persistence

PENDLETON, OREGON
Frontier Spirit

WALL STREET, NEW YORK
High Finance

Jack and the Oyster

William Kennedy

You could say that the world is Jack's oyster because the oyster is Jack's world. You could say that Jack is the pearl in Albany's oyster, as one headline writer already did. You could say that the oyster created Jack's world, or that the oyster creates a world of jack. Somebody once called the oyster a succulent bivalve. An Albany columnist wrote frequently about the oyster and never forgot to mention that it was a succulent bivalve. Every once in a while he might have said that the oyster was the quintessence of bivalent succulency, but no. Somebody else once said that the oyster was sexually ambivalent, that God told it to go fertilize itself and it did. The Albany columnist never wrote about that part of God's handiwork. Ambivalent bivalvency he might have called it, but no.

Jack, and this is true, has been shucking oysters for eighty-one years. No, you say. Well, that's the way things happen in

WILLIAM KENNEDY won a 1984 Pulitzer Prize for *Ironweed*. His impressionistic history of his hometown, *O Albany!*, was published in paperback last fall.

Albany. People go along doing things for eighty-one years and then the word gets around that they've been doing it and people say, No. What I say is, Go take your no and fertilize it. Jack *has* been shucking oysters for eighty-one years. When I saw Jack, he was recovering from pneumonia and was in a moment of hiatus. (*Huître* is French for "oyster"; *hiatus* is Latin for "gap" or "opening." For example: "The hiatus in Phutatorius's breeches was sufficiently wide to receive the chestnut"—*Tristram Shandy. Hiatus,* in a rare meaning, is also "a gaping chasm," as in an oyster after Jack has finished shucking it.)

Jack also shucks clams. In 1984 it was estimated that he had shucked three million clams during his lifetime. Was that true?

"Who could predict that for sure?" said Jack.

Which did he open more of, clams or oysters?

"Clams. They seemed to go for the clams. But I'd say it was close to even."

What of the method?

"When you open the oyster you take it off the top shell and put it on the bottom shell and they come out a whole lot cleaner."

Do you always know the top from the bottom?

"Oh, sure. The bottom is round, the top is flat."

And clams?

"Only one way to open a clam. From the top."

Jack opened a clam for me one night in late 1984 in the kitchen of his restaurant at 42 State Street in Albany. His hair was pure white, he wore his horn-rimmed glasses and had his apron over his collar and tie as he picked up the clam knife, palmed the clam (Jack shucks righty), flicked the knife into the clam's hiatus-to-be, beveled the doomed mollusk in palm, swung the knife this way with the first deft stroke, then entered the blade deeper into the violated chasm, rebeveled the now twained shell, raised the top half on its hinge, and revealed a clam—from the Old English *clam* or *clamm,* corresponding to the Middle High German *klam,* and to the German *klamm,* meaning "to cramp, fetter, constrict, or pinch," which is certainly what life was doing to that clam before Jack freed it into eternity for me with his clam knife—and revealed, as I was about to say, the most magnificent clam I have ever seen. Jack could have searched through a sugar barrel full of clams and wouldn't have found another with such a sunburst of pure clamency, untouched by the knife, a paragon of hemisected, unviolated abundancy, its liquor intact on the half shell, redolent, as one might expect, of the divine odor of clam juice.

How had Jack opened, protected, framed the perfect clam?

"Like everything else. Practice."

I did not eat the clam that Jack opened. I regret that. If I had, I could now say that I ate the most beautiful clam in North America, admittedly a clam claim difficult to prove. But let us here set that clam aside, as did Jack, and get back to Jack and the oyster.

Jack is Jack Rosenstein, now ninety-one, born at 21 Broad Street in the South End of Albany on June 5, 1893, to Isaac and Rebecca Rosenstein, late of Russia. Isaac was a cigar maker ("Very good cigars, no brand. Them days you didn't need a brand"). Jack went to work as a newsboy at age seven in 1900, working the corner of Maiden Lane and Broadway in front of Keeler's European Hotel, "225 rooms, 35 with bath, Gentlemen Only, Known From Coast to Coast." Jack remembered Sunday mornings he'd be there calling out "New York or Albany paper" (the proper newsboy pronunciation is PAY-pee), and the drummers who had been up all night (Keeler's never closed) carousing, after a week of selling their wares, would yell out at Jack: "Get away from there. We wanna sleep." And Jack would nod and call out, "New York or Albany paypee."

When Jack was nine, somewhere in 1903, the owner of Keeler's took meaningful notice of him and gave him a job running errands. Jack got to know the hotel, especially the kitchen, from which he would run orders of oyster fries and oyster stews to private homes. He sometimes, after eleven at night, delivered to the Tenderloin, when that Albany attraction was partially situated on Dallius Street, an old South End thoroughfare named for a seventeenth-century Dutch cleric.

"There was two five-dollar houses in them days," said Jack.

"Davenport's?"

"Right. Davenport's."

"Read's?"

"Lil Read's was a two-dollar house. Stanley's was a five-dollar house."

"Wasn't there a Creole place on Dallius Street too?"

"That was farther down."

The proprietresses would say, "Give fifteen, twenty cents to the boy," and Jack saved that change, the beginning of his $400 fortune, about which more later. Then one night one of the oystermen at the hotel didn't come to work, and Jack was put at the oyster and clam counter with the two other oyster openers.

"I can see all the oysters piled up, and all you kept doing was opening them and opening them. The boss took a likin' to me, and so they put me on the night shift, working oysters [clams also]. That's where I got the practice. Oysters I was a little slow on, but I opened them very good."

Is it harder to open an oyster than a clam?

"To some people it is." But not to Jack. "My training there made the big difference."

There were three oystermen working during the meal hours, with chutes where they threw the empty shells. Some of the oystermen broke oysters, then clandestinely threw them out. The boss would go below after dinner, however, and inspect the baskets at the bottom of the chutes. "He never found a broken one in my basket. But he did in theirs."

Jack had learned about oysters and clams from the very same boss, the hotel owner, William ("Sheriff Bill") Keeler. "He used to put me in front of him. He'd say, 'These are your hands, and I'll teach you how to open them clams and open them good.' He told others I was the cleanest clam opener he ever saw, but he didn't mention it to me."

One day Bill Keeler called Jack in and asked him where he'd go on a week's vacation. "Them days you didn't know what a vacation was." Coney Island, said Jack. "Okay," said Bill, as Jack remembers it. "Your pay will go on. But say nothin' to nobody." Jack was getting five dollars a week. On Christmas Day, Bill gave him a five-dollar gold piece. "This is your Christmas," said Bill. "Say nothin' to nobody." After a while Bill called Jack into the cashier's office. Bill was big and stocky, had a large moustache, and wore a black skullcap, a unique garment in Albany. It had a hook above the center of the forehead to which Bill could raise and affix his spectacles when he so chose. In the office Bill asked Jack: "How much they payin' you?" Jack mentioned the five dollars, and Bill said, "I'm raisin' it two dollars, but I won't put it in your envelope. I'll pay you out of my own pocket." Because grown men, the oystermen Bill had brought up from Crisfield, Maryland, where people really know how to shuck oysters, were only getting twelve dollars a week.

Bill Keeler knew about oysters because at age thirteen in 1854 he went to work in the oyster and fish business. Then in 1864 he and his brother John opened an oyster house at 85 Green Street in Albany. Bankers, farmers, editors, bootblacks frequented Keeler's, two hundred at a time, for the famous oysters—raw, stewed, fried. This was the advent of the oyster age in Albany, and it wrought significant change in the city's way of life. Success on Green Street with fries and stews led the Keeler brothers to open, in 1884, at 56 State Street, the restaurant that would exist until 1969 and prevail as one of the great four-star restaurants of this country: Keeler's State Street. It was an American-style restaurant, but it continued in the tradition established in 1838 by Delmonico's, the pioneer French restaurant in America. That is to say, it offered a highly diverse and often exotic menu, well organized by subject, superbly cooked to gourmet taste, splendidly served in elegant surroundings, and with all gustatorial whims and perversions catered to in the extreme.

Bill went off in 1871 to become an Albany alderman, street commissioner, and sheriff but retained the partnership with his brother until 1886, when they split. Bill went over a block to Maiden Lane and Broadway and opened his own restaurant, which soon became Keeler's European Hotel (for men only), and it was such a success that Sheriff Bill eventually bought half the square block and built a place that became a cynosure of the good life, the sporting life.

In time the hotel included a bowling alley, pool and billiard rooms, a barber shop with four baths, private dining rooms upstairs where families might dine or where hanky-pankers might pank privately. A restaurant for ladies was added, but the ladies were not allowed to stay overnight. Bill built a lake to furnish ice for his guests, bought a poultry farm to keep his kitchen stocked, and bought an oyster bed in Lynnhaven, Virginia.

The earliest menus I've turned up, one dated from March 12, 1897, and another from January 5, 1902, consist of four pages of dense, small-print listings (eighty-seven entries in 1902 on ways to eat clams and oysters: rockaways and rocky points, lynnhavens, bluepoints, littleneck clams). In 1838 on its pioneer menu, Delmonico's offered only five oyster dishes plus oyster soup. The oysters were menu headline items at Keeler's: LYNNHAVEN HALF SHELL 40–30 [cents], it read in 1897. OYSTERS NOW ON HAND was the 1902 banner, in type larger than the name of the hotel's.

The pattern continued at Keeler's State Street after Bill Keeler's hotel burned down. In 1932 and 1944 oysters were the main attraction: BLUEPOINTS, 45 CENTS, it read, the same price both years.

Politicians and celebrities came in great flow to Keeler's Hotel. (Jack couldn't remember any of them. "I was never interested in that. I was in the kitchen.") They consumed oysters by the barrel—five thousand oysters, three thousand clams signed for by Sheriff Bill in a three-day period in October 1914; that is, eight thousand mollusks in thirteen barrels, at a total cost of eighty dollars, or about one cent apiece wholesale.

"Nobody else handled them like Keeler's," said Jack. Other places had insufficient turnover on oysters, and sophisticated Albany oyster eaters demanded they be served fresh, as they always were at Keeler's—three oystermen working as fast as they could to answer the demand. A few years ago Jack estimated he could open fifteen clams in a minute, twelve oysters in two minutes. He works with a stabber, a long knife that was brought to Albany by the Crisfield oystermen. For anybody who has tried to open an oyster for the first time, six a minute seems like Olympic speed.

Alas, it's nothing of the sort. The oyster-opening record, according to Guinness, is held by Douglas Brown, who on April 29, 1975, at Christchurch, New Zealand, opened one hundred oysters in three minutes and one second. Guinness lists and knows no clam-opening record, which is almost shameful. But my guess is that it would be at least double the oyster figure. Clam eating, on the other hand, is laggardly. The record is 424 littlenecks, out of shell, in eight minutes, or fifty-three per minute, by Dave Barnes at Port Townsend Bay, Washington, on May 3, 1975. This compares with the oyster-eating record—held by Ron Hansen of Sydney, Australia—of 250 oysters, out of shell, in 2:52.33, or 87.0413 oysters per minute. My theory is that clams need a bit of a chew, but that the silky oyster slides swiftly and sleekly down the gullet.

I have not a whit of doubt that Jack could have established the speed record in his youth had that been his goal. There are unplumbed depths to Albany people: the road not taken. But Jack had another ambition: he wanted to become a waiter. *"Ah,"* said Sheriff Bill, "so you want to rob the customers, too." And so Jack went to work nights, a dollar a day plus the nickel and dime tips. By 1913 his fortune had climbed to $400, and with a fellow oysterman, Bill Evans, who knew oysters but had no money, he opened an oyster bar and wholesale delivery business to other restaurants, up the hill from Keeler's Hotel, on Lodge Street. Jack and Evans didn't get along; so Jack left and opened a hole-in-the-wall restaurant—four tables, a kitchen, and a marble oyster bar —back down the hill at Beaver and Grand streets.

Jack married Jane Millerstein from Troy in 1916 and began to prosper. Jane was cashier, Jack counterman. When a customer came in, Jack would take the order, call it through a partition— "One oyster fry"—then run into the kitchen and cook it. He took over a piano store next door and broke through the walls to expand. He took over a coal company that closed, put in private dining rooms, expanded his menu, and by 1937 employed seven waiters, five cooks, two checkers in the kitchen, an oysterman, and was selling eight hundred to one thousand oysters every other day. That year, '37, an Albany bank offered Jack the mortgage on a failed restaurant at 42 State Street, a block over from where Keeler's Hotel used to be and a few doors down from John Keeler's restaurant at 56 State. Jack moved in and has been there ever since, now seating 140 in the dining room, a bar adjacent where you wait for a table, banquet rooms upstairs; and during August, when transiency is at its peak, Jack's Oyster House serves five hundred meals a day, not including banquets. Jack's sons, Arnold and Marvin, run the place, and Jack's grandson, Brad, is apprenticing.

Photographic blowups of the town when Sheriff Bill was a presence adorn the walls. Jack was always a physical presence, working eight, ten hours a day until pneumonia and other ills hit him, and when we met he was sitting out front in his black suit and red tie, longing for last year's pep and yearning to get back to the kitchen with his apron and stabber. "I'd love to get in there. It runs good, but it'd run a whole lot better if I was there."

Jack used to go on vacation to Miami Beach, stay a month. "But it got monotonous sitting around doing nothing." So he quit vacations. "All I did was take care of my business. I always wanted to be here, never wanted to be away."

Jack's life embodies the golden platitude that America is a republic of equals, the land of opportunity. But even during America's incipient time Jefferson spoke of our "aristocracy of merit," and that seems closer to the truth of what Jack reveals to us. Bill Keeler and Jack Rosenstein, like the Walrus and the Carpenter—Bill with his big moustache, Jack with his tools—led a parade of oysters out of the nineteenth century through most of our own century, and Jack's sons are keeping the parade going toward the twenty-first.

We know that some things changed along the parade route. Bill Keeler's sons turned the hotel's Broadway dining room into a cabaret, the first in Albany, and an orchestra and entertainers played to turnaway crowds. "The crowds, you'd have to see it to believe it," said Jack. "But the old man didn't like it. Didn't care for that kind of business."

So Bill Keeler retired, and in 1918 he died in Virginia, nearer, my oyster, to thee. His hotel burned on the morning of June 17, 1919, and a fireman lost his life, but more than a hundred guests got out safely. The hotel had had a small fire in an earlier year, and an employee called Bill Keeler at home to tell him. "Why call me?" said Bill. "Why don't you call the fire department?"

I told Jack I was trying to personify the value he represented, and I asked him what he thought was the key element of his life's work. "That it's been done right," he snapped back.

I ate a dozen oysters while we talked, bluepoints, which Jack always loved best, except maybe for rocky points, which are larger, and there is therefore more of them to love. Did Jack love oysters the way I did?

"No, I never ate them. I can eat a clam, but I don't care for them much either. But I can't eat an oyster. I tried to cultivate a taste for them, but I couldn't."

"Yet you and the oyster," I said to Jack. "You were partners all your life."

Jack laughed at that. "That's right," he said.

"Did you ever think about what the oyster means? What it is?"

"Nah. Never did."

Nevertheless, there goes Jack, there goes Bill, walking up from Maiden Lane and Broadway—up to Lodge Street, and then down to Beaver and Grand, and then over to State. A hundred million oysters are following their trail, or is it two hundred million? Well, it's a lot.

> *"It seems a shame," the Walrus said,*
> *"To play them such a trick.*
> *After we've brought them out so far,*
> *And made them trot so quick!"*
> *The Carpenter said nothing but,*
> *"The butter's spread too thick!"*
>
> *"O Oysters," said the Carpenter,*
> *"You've had a pleasant run!*
> *Shall we be trotting home again?"*
> *But answer came there none—*
> *And this was scarcely odd, because*
> *They'd eaten every one.*

"The question now with oysters is," said Jack, "will you be able to get them? It's hard to get oysters, but that's the business. Will you get them?"

Bearings

ALBANY, NEW YORK

Population: 111,000
*Henry Hudson was searching for China in his ship the
Half Moon when he reached the site of Albany on
September 19, 1609.*

*In 1653 Dutch poet Nicasius de Sille said of Albany,
"They all drink here, from the moment they are able to
lick a spoon."*

*Before 1854 many of Albany's citizens disposed of
their garbage by throwing it in the street, where it was
eaten by free-roaming pigs. Eventually the city ended the
practice by rounding up fifteen thousand pigs.*

*Nelson Rockefeller's South Mall complex cost $1.9
billion to build and is reputed to be the largest marble
project in the history of the world. William Kennedy
wrote that it was designed to whisper "Nelson . . .
Nelson" for all eternity.*

Fenced In

Geoffrey Norman

S pokane Ranch is seven miles east of the Big Hole battlefield, where in 1877 a band of Nez Percé was attacked
by an infantry troop and some civilian volunteers. The Indians
slipped away, after winning the battle in a war they already knew
was lost. Eight years later the first Rutledges arrived in the valley,
coming from Illinois for the land and the life. Fred Rutledge is
still here, still ranching, the fourth generation. His son, Jerry, is
here, too. They run one of the biggest operations in one of the
most beautiful parts of Montana.

The valley runs north and south. The continental divide
marks the western limit of the valley, and the Beaverhead Mountains form the eastern border. The valley is about fifty miles long,
and the largest town is Wisdom, which consists of a post office,
two or three saloons, a fuel supplier, a café, a trading post, a town
square, a brick schoolhouse two stories tall, a church, and a few

GEOFFREY NORMAN chooses to divide his time between Vermont and the Gulf coast. He
tried the city once but feels more at home on the range.

other anonymous buildings where the people of Wisdom live and work. There is no movie theater. No bank. The nearest town with conveniences of that sort is Dillon, about sixty-five miles away.

This is cattle country, and beautiful country for it: so grand that even on a late January day when it is twenty below zero you want to ride through it with your car windows rolled down, the better to take it in. You can see for miles, and the only signs of human occupation are the occasional abandoned log buildings that were once used as homesteader shacks, the long, straight fence lines that look like razor scars on the snow-covered earth, and the beaverslides of hay piled high as a house. You have to search to pick out even one occupied ranch. If you have a feeling for country and space, then this looks like something close to paradise.

Raising cattle is the only good reason for being here, though. You can't farm this country. For three or four months out of the year you can put cattle out on the grass, and for the rest of the year you can feed them on the hay you grew and cut while the cattle were grazing. The early spring is calving time, and in the late fall you sell your yearlings. The bulls are turned out in July, right after branding. To an outsider, it is a life that is as seductive as the country itself.

But what Mr. Fred Rutledge, who has been in it all his life, says about the cattle business is this: "It's not worth a shit, Jeff. And it never has been. But I believe it is the worst it has ever been right now." And then he gives you a smile of absolute good cheer.

It has been a tough day. The colder the day, the more important it is that you get feed out to the cattle. Even in Montana, it just doesn't get very much colder than thirty below, which it was this morning at daylight in the Big Hole Valley. But when Fred Rutledge and his son and their four hired men went out to feed the cattle, they had a small problem. The people who supply Spokane Ranch with diesel fuel had filled the tanks with number-two-weight oil, which is thick enough to freeze in extremely cold weather. Rutledge had about a quarter of a million dollars' worth of tractors in the barn, where they wouldn't do him any good, and no telling how many head of cattle out on several thousand acres of snow-covered range. (You don't ask a man how many head of cattle he is running or how much land he is running them over, but I would estimate that Rutledge has somewhere around three thousand animals in his herd.)

"What a hell of a mess," Rutledge says, "what a hell of a damned mess."

Working on machinery is no rancher's idea of happiness, under any circumstances. Working on machinery when it is twenty below is plain misery. Your hands are numb, and the metal is magnetically cold. Skin binds to steel. A small flange can open a nasty, numbing cut. Fingers lose their sense of touch, and you drop tools and small parts into the dirt and snow. You can't blow your nose without getting diesel oil all over your face.

"This ranching is sure the life, now, isn't it?" Rutledge says about midmorning, when one of the tractors finally turns over, and he sends a hired man out on it to feed a few hundred hungry cattle a couple of miles away. "Man just can't get enough."

Rutledge is looking toward the corral, where his Belgian workhorses are standing close to one another, blowing three-foot trails of blue vapor. "We might have to pull out the sleds," he says. "Get the hay out to them behind horses. Just like in the old days." He spits, and it is plain that he doesn't find the prospect one bit romantic. And the prospect of spending the rest of the day answering a bunch of idiot questions about the lure of ranching doesn't much appeal to him, either. "Come on back this afternoon," he says, "after we've got these tractors running—if we do get 'em running. I'll buy you a cup of coffee and tell you what you want to know. But just now, I'm a little busy." No offense. Cold as it is, I'm delighted to drive back into Wisdom, find a booth at the café where I can spread out my notebooks, draw a cup of coffee, and reflect on the cattle business and the irresistible hold it has on the people who are in it.

It doesn't make any economic sense. You don't have to be a banker to know that. The live-weight price of calves has gone down since 1979. It is now about seventy cents a pound. Then it was a dollar. The price of everything else—including number-two diesel that will freeze in your crankcase—has gone up. The price of ranchland did go up for a while—a fact that has gotten a lot of farmers and ranchers into mortal trouble. But that just means, in strict accounting terms, that when a man like Rutledge tallies everything up at the end of the year, his return on investment would make any capitalist weep.

It would be altogether typical for a large-scale rancher who owns land with a market value of two or three million, and machinery worth a quarter of a million to sell his calves at the end of the year, pay off his help, settle up with the bank, and clear maybe twenty or thirty thousand. If he were a publicly held corporation, T. Boone Pickens would be out buying the stock. And the first thing he would do, once he had control, would be to fire the old management that couldn't make a 4-percent return on an investment at a time when banks are paying 10.

All this doesn't even take into account the rancher's own labor. That's free.

Then, of course, there are the bad years that every farmer or rancher has to expect. Those are the years when the first hard snow comes in late October and the weather doesn't let up until May. And then, once summer does come, it is so dry you can't work up a spit. So your calves don't gain the weight they should, and it takes all kinds of supplements, which are expensive, to get them up to the five hundred pounds buyers want before they'll ship them to Iowa or Kansas to finish them on corn in a feedlot.

And then there is the infernal cycle, which works like this: Cattle prices are low, let's say, since they almost always are. Farmers whose main line is not cattle won't have any real incentive to buy a few and put them out on unused pasture. Some farmers who do specialize in beef will go out of business, and others will cut back on the size of their breeding herd to save money. This means fewer calves, and eventually something like a shortage of beef occurs. The price begins to go up. The ranchers who are strictly raising cattle begin to make a little money. Then that fellow who grows beans and wheat decides to put out a few steers. And the speculators lease some range and put some cattle on it. Production goes up.

Pretty soon there is a glut again, and the price goes down. The people who came in late get wiped out. The rancher who has been in for a long time merely sighs and keeps on working and figures that in a few years it will turn around again . . . if he can hold out that long.

Then there is the government. Cattlemen are probably the

least-subsidized segment of American agriculture. There is no floor under beef prices. No payment-in-kind program. But like just about everyone who makes a living from the land, they have to borrow money to make it through the year. When they borrow, they have to pay the money back with interest. And interest debt is piling up on ranchers. Especially the ones who went into debt to buy land in the late 1970s, when inflation made land look like a bargain and the price of an acre of good range could double in about five years. But in the last three or four years the price of land has fallen—in some cases almost as fast as it once rose. The people who bought land still owe the money—and the interest— but their equity has gone down. A lot of them have had to come up with more money—like market players meeting margin calls —and money is one thing that no farmer or rancher has in surplus. So people are going broke—so many that they are starting to take some banks and production credit associations (institutions specializing in farm loans) down with them.

Finally, there is the memory of what the government did the last time it had a chance to help out cattlemen: not one damned thing. Prices were going up in 1978, after the cycle had bottomed. Cattlemen were thinking about settling up with the bank and maybe even springing for some new equipment. But inflation was on the minds of the men in government, and a Jimmy Carter operative named Barry Bosworth decided that American cattlemen could not be allowed to make indecent profits at the expense of the average housewife and so forth and so on. So he relaxed the quotas on imported beef—the one protective arrangement the cattleman enjoys. The price of live cattle dropped overnight. The government had chopped the top of the cycle cleanly off. No rancher doubts that it could happen again.

So why do it? Why stay in the business at all?

A day or two before I met Rutledge, I asked that of P. J. Hill, a man who had grown up on a cattle ranch in the dry, vacant country of eastern Montana and who had left, finally, for the University of Chicago, where he took a Ph.D. in economics.

"It's not the money," Hill said, smiling. (Cattlemen are the best people I've ever met for smiling about their own misfortunes.)

Then what?

"Well, you know, it is a legitimate way to put on your boots and your hat and be outside when you're working."

And you aren't tempted, ever, just to quit it? Sell out and get a job in town?

"No," Hill said. "In fact, that's probably your worst fear. That you'll have to quit and go get a job in town, even though you probably wouldn't work as hard. Every now and then, when I was growing up, some family, neighbors of ours, wouldn't be able to make it. And when they left, you'd hear people saying, 'Well, I can understand why they had to do it. But I just hope they'll be happy doing something else.' But from the way they said it, you knew that ranchers didn't really believe it was possible to be happy doing anything else.

"When I was in graduate school, on a Ford Foundation grant, I'd have to fill out these forms every now and then. When I'd get to the blank about 'career plans,' I'd just write in 'cattle rancher.' Then, when I got my degree, somebody came around and asked me where I planned to work. What he meant was, 'Which teaching position do you think you will take?' I told him I was going back to the family ranch in Montana, and he couldn't believe it. I told him I'd been putting it on those forms every time one came around, and he told me he thought I'd been joking."

Hill eventually found a faculty job that lets him spend half the year teaching but still get back to the family ranch for calving and roundup and branding.

But what about the cycle, and all the economic uncertainty of ranching? Doesn't that just wear you down?

"Most ranchers I know just don't think about it."

That sounded impossible.

"No. You worry about the weather, maybe, but you don't worry about those other things. They're out of your control. You just figure what the right-size herd is for your spread, and that's how many animals you run. Then you just do the best you can. There's something very fatalistic about it. But there's something to be said for that, too. It actually relieves you of a lot of worry."

That made sense.

"There are hardships. Nobody lives in a mansion. When I was growing up, we didn't have running water or indoor plumbing, and neither did our neighbors. A couple of them still don't.

For nine months of the year my mother and I and the rest of the kids lived at a place in town, while my father stayed out on the ranch. It was just too far to drive every day to go to school. So we saw my dad on weekends. That was one of the hardest things."

What about the good parts, if there are any?

"Oh, yeah. There are a lot of those. I guess the best of them would be in June, when you're having roundup. And you get some neighbors to come over and help. Winter is over and the grass is growing and the calves are all on the ground. The weather is just beautiful, and everyone feels great being outside again. That's the most hopeful time, too, because you don't sell your yearlings until fall, and you think maybe this will be a good year. That's a great time. One of those times when you can't imagine doing anything else."

It still didn't seem like one of those times when I drove back out from Wisdom to the Spokane Ranch to talk to Fred Rutledge again about the cattle business. He was down near some corrals where he had a few hundred calves that weighed about four hundred pounds each—Angus-Hereford crosses, mostly, which he said did "about as well as anything else we've found out here. Some of those exotics, the Simmentals and Limousins and Charolais, will gain a little quicker, but they have more trouble calving. And we can't afford much loss during calving season. And anyway, hell, nothing gains very fast in this kind of weather, eating the hay we give 'em. We'll be lucky to get a pound a day. In the summer, when we put 'em out on grass, that's when we get our fast gain. They can put on two pounds a day then. Course, in one of those feedlots, eating corn, they make three easily."

He put away some vehicles and other things that needed to be put away for the night. Then we went up to the house, where his wife was waiting.

"Don't have time for coffee," she said. "That cook will be wanting us any minute."

She went on ahead of us to the cookhouse. I'd been invited to stay for supper, almost without it being said. Rutledge, his wife, son, daughter-in-law, four hired men, cook, and I all sat at a big table. The talk was about the winter, as the potatoes and the greens and the platter full of hamburgers made their way around the table. Rutledge told me that the man I was sitting next to had been with him for forty years. "Too many more days like today, though, and he may not finish out this winter."

Which reminded him of what another hired man once said, after a day much like this one. "We were still using horses back then. Pulling the hay out to the cattle on sleds. We'd been at it all day, and Lord, it was miserable. Like today, only with some wind. After we'd finished up, this fellow looked at me and said, 'Mr. Rutledge, you know winters like this is hard on horses and hired men.' "

Everybody at the table laughed.

After supper I heard more about the ranching life. None of it milk and honey. Then, when I was about to leave, Rutledge told me I ought to come back in the summer. "We can do a little fishing then, if you like to fish. That's the time to see this valley. In the summer. Everything looks a lot better then. But to tell you the truth, even on a day like this one, it doesn't look that bad."

I believe I understood what he meant. And why he is still in that valley, one hundred years after the first Rutledge came out to raise cattle on what was then still an open range and just past being Indian country. It isn't the kind of thing you can understand when somebody tells you. But it does come to you when you're standing there. Then, it is undeniable.

Bearings

WISDOM, MONTANA

Population: 150
The Lewis and Clark expedition arrived at the area around the Big Hole Valley in 1805; they named a river they found here Wisdom, in honor of Thomas Jefferson.
John Evans, a sheepman, grazed his sheep in the valley in 1878, and Joseph Ketchum wintered cattle there in 1880. In 1882 Ketchum's men told one prospective settler, "You can't live in a place like this. You'll starve." He stayed nonetheless.

*In 1910, with the invention of the beaver slide, a
device for stacking hay, ranching became commercially
viable.*

*An average ranch in the Big Hole Valley has fifteen
hundred head of cattle; the bigger ranches run from five
to fifteen thousand acres. It takes four or five men to run
a five-thousand-acre ranch, with one or two extra at
calving time and more at haying time. The first snow can
come before Labor Day.*

———

The Blue-Ribbon American Beauty Rose of Rodeo

Ken Kesey

My father took me up the gorge and over the hills to my first one thirty-five years ago. It was on my fourteenth birthday. I had to miss a couple of days' school plus the possibility of suiting up for the varsity game that Friday night. Gives you some idea of the importance Daddy placed on this event.

For this is more than just a world-class rodeo. It is a week-long shindig, a yearly rendezvous dating back beyond the first white trappers, a traditional powwow ground for the Indian nations of the Northwest for nobody knows how many centuries.

Is it just the result of geography? A place pointed out by the blade of the Umatilla River slicing green through the eastern Oregon brownlands, the protecting hills and the moisture collaborating to toss together an interesting salad in the middle of an otherwise drab table of sagebrush and stickers? Is this what makes it an American landmark?

KEN KESEY is writing a book about Pendleton with his friend Ken Babbs, who collaborated on this piece.

Search along the rims: chiseled petroglyphs tell stony tales of heroes and hunts. Tribes meet in the fall to pound pemmican and dry salmon, prepare for winter. In the afternoon, races and wrestling. In the evening, stick games, story dances.

In the 1700s, explorers. Then pioneers. Then settlers tired of the Oregon Trail, this is fur damn piece enough by gadfrey! Then ranchers and stock, riders and roundups. Finally the wheat farmers draw lines, and more lines, gathering space, creating a county.

Umatilla County. Two million acres. Drained by McKay Creek, Birch Creek. Out of the Blue Mountains. Towns. Hermiston, Stanfield, Echo, Adams, Helix, Athena, Milton-Freewater. And, as county seat, the biggest little city north of Reno—Pendleton, Oregon.

In 1865 the county seat was Umatilla Landing, where the Umatilla River meets the Columbia. Point of departure for pack trains bound for placer mines in Idaho. In 1868 the railroads push inland; kills the river trade. Umatilla Landing dwindles in size and importance, becoming barely a ghost port. Farsighted go-getters sign petition demanding county seat be moved to Pendleton. Shoot, the only saloon in the territory is located there, stands to reason the county business oughter follow suit. Even build a courthouse to accommodate it. But them dang Umatilla Landing diehards block the action with legal bullroar. Ghosts they may be, but they ain't turnin' loose the reins long as they can help it.

So. Nighttime. Soft-shod horses carry furtive go-getters across Goodwin's Bridge along the river, over the moony prairie, to Umatilla County Courthouse. Steal the county records and the county seal, hightail 'er back home to Pendleton. Naturally the county bureau-rockacy has to follow. Cain't run a county 'thout a saloon and county records, can ye?

Forty-odd years later that same go-get-'em spirit prompts a half dozen citizens to put on the first public roundup. Nineteen ten. The previous year there'd been a bucking event at the Fourth of July baseball game, and it had enjoyed considerable popularity. Seems the local boys could handle high buckers a bunch better'n hot grounders. So the half dozen go-getters become the NFEA, the Northwestern Frontier Exhibition Association. Roy Raley, the first president, is in charge of composing the initial program.

Keep it simple. Start with a parade, follow through with riding, racing, and roping, end up with steer and bronc busting.

Shares are sold ten dollars each, one per man. Six officers, a board of nine directors, 250 businessmen and ranchers. Thirty-two hundred dollars' worth of stock and they start planning it out. Keep it simple but make it hop. Three events ready or on at all times. Say, what about sham battles? Shoot-outs between soldiers and Indians? Whoa mule on that. I ain't gonna be shot at even with fake bullets. Fair enough. We'll stick to true stuff, roping and bulldogging and bronc riding. Folks *know* them critters is the real article.

So. Build bleachers, corrals, temporary stables. Quarter-mile running track, three-foot rail fence around it. Set up ticket booths, see how it goes. Well, it goes. And how it goes! Nobody coulda ever reckoned the size of that crowd. Forty-five hundred and sixty paying spectators, net profits of three thousand greenbacks on the barrelhead!

Day after the show the shares zoom from ten dollars to fifty, seventy-five. A hundred! Whoa mule again. We didn't go to all this nuisance just to make money. Let's keep it clean of the filthy green. No profiteering. Fair enough. Then here's what: let's everybody donate their shares to the city of Pendleton. And dig deeper for next year, a bigger arena, stands covered against the cruel sun and the possible rain. Plant a nice park by the river for picnickers, buy a field where the Injuns can put up their tepees. And permanent stables, real chutes. Let 'er buck!

Thus is Round-Up Park, bought, built, and deeded to the city. The burgeoning NFEA pays one-dollar-a-year rent, works to put it together for next year, and not a man jack of them to make one red penny offen it. A planning committee agrees on three essentials for the show: thrills, spectacle, and laughter. Thrills provided by the contests. Spectacle by picturesque background of Indian village, cottonwood grove, crowds of cowboys in colorful clothes making great dusty teeth-rattling cavalry charges across the arena right down the throats of the audience.

Laughter we'll leave to accidental incidents. Clowns, wild-cow milking, *some* thing . . .

But the *main* thing . . . is that everyone in town participates. Two weeks before the event, decorate your shop, trim your beard, paint your wagon, groom your best saddle pony, and get into your pearl-buttoned foofaraw. Broadbrimmed hat, horsehair band, with just the right feather. Top-creased brim rolled with just the right tilt. Shirt bright with a touch of embroidery, long cuffs, tight-fitting. Chaps, though you maybe never went brushpopping after a maverick through the sticker trees in all your life. Boots stitched sharp, tops slitted front and back, heels and insteps high to keep from slipping out of the stirrups. Spurs, dull-pointed, brightly jingling, shanks down. Or up.

Bandanna for the last lilting touch, like a personal gawdy banner to march beneath, yup-*ho!*

The Westward Ho! Parade. Folks gathering from everywhere, far and near. Samy Jackson, former owner of the Pendleton newspaper, has become publisher of the Portland, Oregon, *Journal.* He has organized a tour train, the Round-Up Special, tickets to include food and drink, poker chips, passes to the rodeo and the Indian Happy Canyon Show at night, plus side-spur parking near the arena all day. City dudes and their delicate lady friends can sit right in their gambling cars and view the parading panorama of the Old West blending into the New.

The governor in a polished Pierce-Arrow, mayor in a buckboard. Round-Up committee in a Conestoga wagon what was drug all the way from Independence by matched oxen sebenty year ago. Haywagon floats, tableaux of hairy trappers skinning beaver, pioneer mothers churning butter, Indian men and WCTU women pounding drums. Oxcarts chuck wagons six-line skinners stagecoaches and goat carts. Young braves on painted pintos, old squaws on fur-heaped travois.

Downtown. Main Street. Nineteen eleven. Hot *dog.*

First prize is displayed on a specially woven Pendleton Woolen Mills blanket, at the corner of First and Court streets, in the window of Hamley & Company. A beautiful saddle, handtooled from horn and cantle to skirts and tapaderos. Studded and inlaid with silver medallions. *Hi-yu-skookum,* say the Indians. Very good saddle. Waiting for the first world-champeen cowboy *ever* to ride in and win it and ride out.

Traditional rivalries, man and animal, cowboys and Indians, and coloreds. Yes, coloreds. The two favorites for the prize saddle are Jackson Sundown, a forty-five-year-old nephew of Nez Percé war chief Joseph (and the original "Red Rider" of legend); and "Nigger George" Fletcher, a local cowboy famous for riding the baddest outlaws on four feet to a standstill *backward*. In fact, as many as eight thousand black cowboys helped blaze the western trail. Nat Love, Deadwood Dick. Broncobuster Jesse Stahl. Bill Pickett, inventor of steer wrestling . . . barrier drops, a big steer calf comes kyoodlin' out of the chute . . . "Rope 'im, Bill!"

But Pickett, galloping hot after the critter, realizes he's clean forgot his damn lariat rope. Says a quick prayer in the saddle: I ask no special favors, Grandfather, no powers above normal men. Only that I might throw this beast without a loop. Pass Your hand over me, and let Your winds run easy, amen.

He's riding a fast little spotted mare called Chico, comes alongside the steer lickety-split. Jumps, catches the horns, and sinks his teeth into the animal's tender nose just the way he's seen bulldogs do it . . . fangs the calf to the ground and trusses him tight with his piggin' string. Rodeo crowd likes that plenty, so does the rodeo committee:

"By gosh, we'll put that in the show—call it bulldogging!"

Men, animals, cowboys, Indians, coloreds, and wimmin. *Uh-huh*, wimmin. I bought a trap, hid it in the weeds, brought that mushrat to her knees. Mercy me, did you see them cowboys ride! Them warn't jist cowboys, ma'am. That one were a black man; that other one were a red man; that un there? That there's a ma'am, ma'am.

Better make 'em wear skirts, then, black and divided, ankle-length. Underneath, bloomers. Hateful things, the cowgirls know. Especially in the relay races. Gotta switch horses in midrace, the change station right in front of the grandstands. Lorena Trickey switches with such fervor she pops her bloomers belt, hobbles to the other horse, pink lace around her ankles. Can't straddle the saddle, so she shucks 'em clean.

Busted a belt, and the whole stand's like to bust a gut laughing. *There's* one of them accidental incidents. Lorena doesn't give a rip, goes ahead and wins the race.

Oh, the seasons and the stories that gather in this little salad bowl in the Oregon brownlands. Spicy and juicy, to the rim and overflowing. Here's a last little taste, another tale about another Pendleton hero stout of heart and strong of tooth.

World wrestling champion Frank Gotch comes through town to take advantage of the Round-Up crowds. His strength is ballyhooed on billboards all over town, along with the challenge that his manager will pay to any local strong boy that can stay in the ring with Gotch for fifteen minutes without being pinned *one hundred dollars cash!*

Everybody knows that the strongest man in Umatilla County is an Indian called Motanic. Bite a silver cartwheel in half, he can. Straighten out a horseshoe. Strong, but sulky. Dark . . .

Motanic is something of a mystery, wandering as a youth from tepee to tepee. Staying with a family or a tribe until he gets moved on. Eating huckleberries and grasshoppers to stay alive. Meets an orphan pup and they ramble together, sleeping tight against each other for mutual warmth.

Sleeping, Motanic hears a voice call him into the forest. He sees an eagle, and where she perched he finds an arrow with the tip chipped from moonstone. Voices sing behind him and in front, powerful songs of a fierce future coming. He comes out of the trance and realizes he's lost and it's very cold and dark. He prays until a lonesome wail drifts to him through the pines. His dog. He follows the sound back to the camp and bed.

Lying there, he realizes he's found his *weweyekin,* his animal familiars, his two spirit guides: the eagle who called him to the woods and the dog who called him back. And they have awakened him to his power. He's bad, bad, and nothing human can best him.

So Motanic grows up into dissoluteness. Fighting, drinking, gambling, and whoring. And his strength is renowned. He may be a heller, but the cowboys around town agree he's the man to dethrone the champ. Remember the time Motanic picks up a 350-pound Yorkshire boar and throws the protesting porker into the back of a buckboard? Anyone can throw a mean hog twice his weight bound to be able to throw the champ. Whaddya say, Motanic?

"I can throw any Indian in Oregon, but I don't know anything about this man Gotch or this pinnin' two shoulders to the mat."

"That don't matter. We'll show you how, we'll *train* you."

There's a picture in the paper of the champion doing road-work in tights. The ladies sew the challenger a pair out of BVDs; the fellows take him for long runs in the hills:

"Gonna have to get me a automobile. This guy can outrun a horse."

The night of the match Matlock's Opera House is packed with red men and white. Gotch and Motanic meet in the center of the mat. No strangleholds, the ref says. Self-conscious in his long johns in front of all these people, Motanic blinks his huge brown eyes in confusion. Never hear of stranglehold. Ref says fifteen-minute time limit, pin to win or until one of you hollers Uncle. Motanic blinks; never hear of no Uncle. That's how you give up, the ref says, by hollering Uncle or pounding the mat. Whoever pounds the mat loses. Ready? Rassle!

Motanic charges. Grabs Gotch under the armpits, hoists him aloft, holds him a moment (not near heavy as a hog), then sets him gently back down on the mat and turns to walk away. The cowboys are stunned silent, but the Indians are war-whooping like Indians. They know that according to all the time-honored rules of civilized Indian wrestling, Motanic's won. Superior strength and balance made evident, the battle is over. Just like wolves. No need to keep chewing each other up.

But Gotch is not an Indian or a wolf. He is a white barbarian. As Motanic walks back to his corner Gotch nails him from behind with a vicious hammerlock. Motanic goes down. Gotch hangs on to the hammerlock and puts on a head scissors for good measure. They roll groaning on the mat. Gotch suddenly lets out a horrible howl. Motanic's got his teeth buried in the champ's butt, and he won't let go.

Gotch howls and curses, turns loose the lock. Motanic still won't let go. Gotch pounds the mat in agony. The referee tries to pry them apart. The champ's manager and handler rush the center of the ring with hoe handles. Motanic's cowboy seconds pull their six-guns. The crowd masses against the ropes. Police whistles scream. The cops separate the factions and hustle the wrestlers to their dressing rooms.

"Why the hell didn't you just pin him, Motanic?" the cowboys want to know. "You was the stronger man . . ."

"You say make him pound mat. He pounded mat."

"But why'd you keep on biting him?"

Motanic, confused and hurt, pulls a blanket around his shoulders. "Why he keep on twisting my arm?"

He is disqualified and dejected, scorned and alone. He hears a dog wail outside and goes to the dressing-room window. "Leave me," he tells his *weweyekin.* "I am done with you. I am done with this way of mean living forever."

Throws off his old life like a moth-eaten blanket and takes up the Bible. He never gets his hundred bucks, but he does get a position in the church, a reward for his victory over the dark pagan forces. You can find his pictures in the local history books —level-browed, gentle-eyed, strong-jawed . . . Parsons Motanic, teaching the Good Book to his own variegated gathering in the Pendleton Sunday-morning outskirts.

So it is more than just geography, then. Perhaps it began with geography, back in prehistory, but it has become more. It has become a spiritual gathering place. Those ancient salmon dries, these stories and ceremonies and celebrations, the stomp dances and the punkin rollers, the old-fashioned back-lot bucking contests before a couple dozen idlers, and now the modern harvest festivals that every year attract forty, fifty thousand excited spectators plus millions of *Wide World of Sports* viewers across the nation . . . all twining together, blossoming full into that Blue-Ribbon American Beauty Rose of Rodeo—the Pendleton Round-Up.

This is more than just the way the river runs.

Bearings

PENDLETON, OREGON

Population: 14,350
Lewis and Clark reached what is now Pendleton in 1805,
and a fur-trading expedition organized by John Jacob
Astor arrived in 1812, but the area was not settled until
1843, when Dr. Marcus Whitman and his bride Narcissa

brought a thousand settlers in 110 wagons with 1,300 head of cattle. Whitman was later killed by Indians.

By 1864 Pendleton consisted of a stage-stop hotel and fewer than five residences.

An early settler wrote of the virtues of Oregon's citizenry: "They were all honest because there was nothing to steal; they were all sober because there was no liquor to drink; there were no misers because there was nothing to hoard; they were all industrious because it was work or starve."

Pendleton secured its claim to the Umatilla county seat by stealing the county seal and records from Umatilla Landing. The first business performed there was to issue a liquor license to a local establishment. Today there are fifty-six establishments that serve liquor.

Many of Pendleton's main streets are named for Confederate generals, the result of an influx of southern immigrants after the Civil War.

Next to its rodeo, Pendleton is most famous for the Pendleton shirt.

The first sighting of a "flying saucer" was reported by one Kenneth Arnold on June 25, 1947, in the Pendleton East Oregonian.

Capitalism's Main Street

Michael M. Thomas

Most of us have a picture of the place, an image that is part of the collective national consciousness: the compact forest of buildings, all height and no space, perched on the tip of Manhattan, threatening to unbalance the island, to capsize it and send it tumbling like some perverse Atlantis to the bottom of the harbor. It looked that way in Westermann's 1852 bird's-eye view of lower New York; it looked that way to the writers of the WPA Manhattan guidebook; it looks that way now, only the forest is taller and denser. As with most things that change on Wall Street through the years, the differences are really only of degree.

Despite certain new pretensions, it is hard to call the financial community a real community. The values that Wall Street monumentalizes are hardly those we celebrate on Main Street. Apartment buildings have recently appeared on the fringes of

MICHAEL M. THOMAS is the author of *Green Monday* and *Someone Else's Money*. A former partner at Lehman Brothers, he lives in New York.

the district, grocers and dry cleaners have gone into business, a hotel has been built; there are, we are informed by the traffickers in life-style, people who go "uptown" on Saturday nights to nearby SoHo or TriBeCa, where they drink deep at the revivifying well of fad. In a way, it's fair to see these hardy settlers as prototypical American pioneers striking out on their own, choosing to live above the store, collecting into the nexus of a new, true community. The fact is, however, that these are mostly refugees driven south by the unspeakable cost of uptown space, bid up to inconceivable heights by the new Visigoths, the stockbrokers, traders, and merger experts—ironically from Wall Street itself—who have driven out the old inhabitants. The point of the exercise on Wall Street is to make money to put on display elsewhere, preferably uptown, in the splendid apartment buildings, extravagant shops, and arrogant restaurants of the Upper East Side.

The Street—as it is known to its familiars—is rooted in the national awareness, but for none of the reasons that *places* customarily are, not for its appearance or the character of its street life, not like, say, Trastevere or Kensington or the Left Bank, or —in Manhattan—Greenwich Village or Harlem. It is a place essentially devoid of architectural distinction or historical presence; Wall Street will never have its Chartres. Indeed, a number of its proudest, most typical institutions have long since fled uptown. Its street life is Manhattan-ordinary: descendants of the kings of Benin urging passersby to "check out" the latest hauls in wool scarves and batteries; runners scoring nickel bags of dope in the desolate spaces of Jeanette Park (actually a concrete escarpment with a few gloomy, beleaguered trees); a street cuisine offering everything from knishes to dim sum. Nothing exceptional here, nothing different from what one finds on any Manhattan sidewalk.

As for history, there's no money in it, so it's left to the people who guide or take weekend walking tours to know that Wall Street was where the Dutch constructed a wall in 1653 to keep out the English, that George Washington was inaugurated where the Subtreasury Building (now Federal Hall National Memorial) stands, that the Equitable Building, constructed in 1915 at 120 Broadway, so appalled the New York citizenry with its light-blocking mass that new zoning ordinances were passed; but of course, as architectural critic Paul Goldberger reminds us, "greed was a fresher idea back in 1915 than it is today."

Sunshine or shadow, yesterday or tomorrow, it's all the same to The Street, which lives indoors, on the telephone, and for today. Inside there's nothing really striking either, except to tastes enchanted by uproar. Nothing's been allowed to linger past the point of absolute utility. Once upon a time, one could point to the indescribable pandemonium of the Stock Exchange trading floor as a sort of wonder of the modern world, but much of the business has moved off the floor, "upstairs," as they say, and the noisy organized confusion has been replicated half a dozen times in the trading rooms of the big firms: Shearson Lehman, Merrill Lynch, and, most impressively, Salomon Brothers, where vast jumbles of circuitry are populated by electronically activated puppets.

A case could be made that history was once respected here. Until about ten years ago, The Street's business was still split up and parceled out by its principal proprietors as a compact among gentlemen, some real, some would-be. There were as many unspoken rules in force as there were stipulations and regulations set down in cold type by the powers that were on The Street and in Washington. As seems true of much of American life, the way things were on Wall Street in, say, 1970 was on the whole more similar to what we know of 1870 than to 1980. Deals were still done on handshakes; firms were smaller; a bit of nineteenth-century archaism—a touch of wrought iron and mahogany—impressed the customers and distracted them from the fact that the yachts they had been promised were moored at their brokers' docks. Available technologies were relatively primitive, and they enforced a pace more human in scale. Today, after a decade that has had the evolutionary effect of a millennium, those ways seem remote, back in an age, perhaps golden, when Adam delved and Eve span.

Yet was it golden? Was greed "a fresher idea"? I doubt it. Wall Street is always changing and yet is ever thus, because Wall Street is by, for, and about greed and efficiency and, above all, change.

Now, these may be good things or bad things, but they are, beyond all question, central and essential American passions. The Street so, well, splendidly incarnates them that it has acquired an extraordinary presence in the soul of the nation, probably the most readily identifiable monument on the skyline not only of our self-awareness but also of the world's sense of America. Wall Street is both a real place and a symbol. It is both Niagara Falls and Zenith, Yosemite and East Egg, because it is both a district of our character and our landscape, and not the best of either.

The cravings that The Street celebrates are, I suspect, instincts that we find less than wholly admirable, even if they do deliver the goods. The words "Wall Street" are spoken even by zealots in a tone that mingles apology with contentiousness, as if those who've found the pot of gold at the end of the rainbow are mildly abashed, and yet displeased, to find the vessel slightly tarnished. Wall Street is about having everything all ways—and now! No American place buries its dead so grandly and forgets them so quickly, which is understandable when the prevailing view of life is as a series of discrete transactions.

And perhaps it is. Richard Whitney, all jowls and chin and firm purpose, strides onto the Exchange Floor in 1929 and bids for Steel in an effort to quell a panic and keep the game alive; within a few years, Whitney is sent to Sing Sing for misappropriation. The only occasion to which The Street ever truly rises is its own; the point is to live to fight another day, when there'll be fresh money on the table.

Thus those who mourn "the old days and ways" are deceived by their memories; their keenings are mere pointless howlings after the unrecoverable. Wall Street is us, and the changes we lament are of degree and equipment: there are newer and fancier and deadlier bows and arrows, but they are aimed by eyes and drawn by arms unchanged for eons. Man hasn't altered much in a million years, but look how far the maintenance of the human machine has come, and would we turn back the clock on that? So it is with The Street. The computer has made possible a variety, volume, and velocity of financial transactions unimaginable with the machinery of the past. The calculator and slide rule I used twenty-five years ago were nothing more than fancy abaci, different only in degree from their Oriental ancestor; the computer employed by my modern Street counterparts is, I suppose, different only in degree, too, but what a degree! The machine I used, a somewhat primitive Monroe desk-top calculator, was dependent on me; today the direction of that dependency has reversed. The Street works now to machine time and machine habits. Machines need no sleep, hence the imminence of the twenty-four-hour marketplace, which promises rates of volume and velocity and levels of profit that ten years ago would have seemed ridiculous.

It's a nice marriage, this mating of the machines and The Street, and intellectually convenient too. Machines are neither moral nor, other than mathematically, judgmental. By reducing everything to pure numbers, they make the magic even more glittering, they speed up the proliferation of new and seductive forms of wagering. In the old days there seemed to be something more to the game than simple win-lose. The Stock Exchange's public-relations rallying cry, "Own Your Share of America," hinted of higher verities: thrift, proprietorship, common cause. One saw behind the stock certificates, the shadowy forms of mills and factories, things being made, earth being mined, jobs and enterprise. It's somehow different now, yet The Street still towers to the very roof of our sense of what this country's all about, because it dances to tunes formed from the profoundest chords of our national soul, tunes to which the essence of the country must inevitably vibrate. In my working lifetime, Wall Street has essentially recapitalized commercial America from an equity-rich industrial capitalism owned by individuals into a highly leveraged investment game board dominated by fiduciary institutions and their brokers. All in the name of action, which requires no special place or trappings, no philosophy other than that the game must ever be afoot.

The endurance of The Street is its strength and its wonder. Other American commerces are brought low by new technologies and new competitors. Clouds lower over the steelmaking valleys; assembly lines lie halted and silent; buzzards circle above the copper pits of the West; crowds gather by Iowa courthouses to watch the auctioning of family farms; on the Texas plains, stacked drilling rigs rust in the spring drizzle. And yet Wall Street goes from strength to strength.

Why is this? I think it is because The Street has the greatest product ever devised for one man to sell another. The product is action. Gambling without sin, the apotheosis of church-social bingo. And The Street's mission is to bring the product, in an increasing, tempting profusion of forms, to an ever-purer, which is to say more perfectly fungible, arbitrageable state, to bring it ever closer to the perfect randomness of the roulette wheel, where everything is purely a matter of money.

But action isn't much beyond itself, which is perhaps why at a time like the present, when the nation is totally obsessed with money, Wall Street seems so unpeopled, so impersonal, uniform, gray. Other than to connoisseurs of acquisitiveness who like a smidgen of sliminess in their high finance, there's little in the way of personality; the action has largely been entrusted to legions of bright young things doing what the computer tells them.

All America knows The Street's symbols, the bull and the bear, which are as potent and vivifying for our imaginings as the Statue of Liberty or Uncle Sam. Yet, like Bellow's Sammler eyeing his papers, I find myself wondering, are these the right symbols, the right animals? Wouldn't the shark be more appropriate? Not because it is by instinct the most rapacious of animals; not because through centuries of cataclysmic change it has retained its primitive form, although these match up well with The Street. Most fitting of all, though, is that it is said of the shark, and it is true of Wall Street, that it must keep moving or it will die. To keep itself in BMWs, The Street must ever invent one new game, then another, and then when the string appears played out, reinvent the whole thing—as it now seems to be doing with the recapitalization of industrial America.

I go to Wall Street very seldom now. The place is full of memories, some good, some bad, but not the sort of recollections one has on returning, say, to Greenwich Village or cruising down Park Avenue of a December evening with the Christmas trees alight. Not memories of places where love turned up, or one good night or ten bad ones were drunk away, or youth and foolishness had their hour. Not any of that unbankable stuff, because Street memories are strictly cash-and-carry, fleeting inward grins and grimaces recalling a few thousand made here, lost there. Not much in the way of fragments to put away against one's ruin. Now and then I'll walk by the eccentric building on William Street that housed my old firm for nearly a century. It's an Italian bank now. Tragic, I think, how awful. It reminds me of the Italian shoe stores that are running riot on the avenue nearest where I live. The sad thought lingers only for an instant, however. It was getting and spending then, and it's getting and spending now. The name above the door doesn't really matter, since it's more of the same. After all, this isn't a *neighborhood*, this is Wall Street. No one lives here. Or perhaps everyone does, which comes to the same thing.

Bearings

WALL STREET

Wall Street follows the line of a wooden barrier put up by the original Dutch inhabitants to protect themselves from Indians and Englishmen. Much of the land that comprises the financial district was originally rented from the king of England by Trinity Church for one peppercorn a year.

On May 17, 1792, twenty-four brokers met and signed the Buttonwood Agreement, by which they agreed to give one another preferential treatment. The title referred to a tree where they met to conduct business in warm weather. In cold weather they traded in the Tontine Coffee House.

The New York Stock Exchange was organized on March 8, 1817. Members could be fined for absence or for not wearing hats.

The stock ticker was introduced in 1867, revolutionizing the business.

Before the 1929 crash, stocks listed on the New York Stock Exchange were worth $90 billion; in 1932 they were worth $16 billion.

Securities listed on the Exchange today are worth $1,721,926,000,000. Six of the eight largest accounting firms, a third of the largest law firms, ninety Fortune 500 companies, six of the ten largest banks, and all of the three hundred top brokerage firms are headquartered in Manhattan.

A phrase often heard on The Street is, "To know and not to do is not to know."

———

PART 2

LOYALTY
AND
COMMON
PURPOSE

SALT LAKE CITY, UTAH
Rectitude

CAMDEN, SOUTH CAROLINA
Southern Loyalty

BOSTON, MASSACHUSETTS
Yankee Thrift

ATLANTA, GEORGIA
Enlightened Practicality

BLOOMINGTON, INDIANA
Sports Mania

PITTSBURGH, PENNSYLVANIA
Family

God's Hotel

Jane Howard

Okay, let me get my bearings. I'm looking west from the window of Room 1028, on the top floor of a "grande dame, a great lady," as its manager refers to the newly renamed Westin Hotel Utah. By the tub hangs a one-size-fits-all terry-cloth robe; by the sink are three kinds of fancy soap; on the pillowcase of my downturned bed each night is a foil-wrapped chocolate mint. But these things, and the fact that the window can actually be opened, are not what make this hotel special. What makes it special is its history—it was called "the most perfectly arranged hotel in the United States" when it was opened in 1911 by the Church of Jesus Christ of Latter-day Saints and others—and its location, at the exact center of what Salt Lake City's chamber of commerce president says is "a community of real, authentic achievers, with an infectious belief that we are sent to this earth to prove ourselves. What we amass here we take with us when we go."

JANE HOWARD, who was born in Springfield, Illinois, writes frequently about Middle America. She is the author of *Margaret Mead: A Life.*

When he talks about going he doesn't just mean skiing, which, as I write, hundreds of people are doing in the Wasatch Mountains, a forty-five-minute drive away. Since today is not smoggy, the mountains are visible and beautiful. So is the Union Pacific Depot, an admirably restored nineteenth-century relic a few blocks away, still in daily use by Amtrak. Just this side of the depot, beyond Symphony Hall and several other burgeoning hotels, is Triad Center, part of a $1.25-billion construction project financed by two brothers from another get-up-and-go theocracy: Saudi Arabia. Triad Center has a skating rink, a trolley line connecting it with the heart of town, several high-rise office buildings with 2.5 million square feet of space to rent, a shopping mall full of boutiques, and four restaurants. It will also have a Hyatt-Regency Hotel. It hopes to be Rockefeller Center. It isn't.

But the most arresting sight from the window of Room 1028 is just outside: a golden angel twelve feet tall, blowing his trumpet. The angel's name is Moroni, and he stands on the topmost turret of the Mormon temple, on Temple Square across the way, which has more annual visitors than Yellowstone National Park. This city would not exist had Moroni not appeared in a series of visions, beginning in 1823, to a perplexed upstate New York youth named Joseph Smith. Following Moroni and doing God's complex bidding, Smith established the Church of Jesus Christ of Latter-day Saints (LDS), who now number nearly six million worldwide. Brigham Young, who took over after Smith's assassination, led the early Mormons across the continent to Salt Lake City, which to them was Zion, in 1847. It has been called the largest religious migration since the time of Moses.

Young had a flair for real estate, and so have his successors, who own much of Salt Lake City, including this hotel. Last year they voted to turn over its operation to the Westin Hotel Management Corporation. The phrase "Westin Hotel Utah" did not at once trip off the tongues of telephone operators, but they learned, and so did the rest of the staff, as stationery and menus were changed, and a man from Housekeeping was sent around every morning with a fancy W stamp—the Westin logo—to press onto the finely strained sand of the twenty-odd "sand urns," as spittoons are now called, in the hotel. Numerous improvements have been made, but one tradition remains inviolate. The LDS still won't allow the sale of liquor in the hotel. It can be drunk, but not sold.

Tom Hosea, who came from Cincinnati to manage this hotel for Westin, calls his new job "another fun challenge" but admits that the alcohol policy is "an uphill selling situation" and "a unique marketing problem." Other hotels in town, even the Marriott, which is owned by a Mormon, are not governed by the Apostles of the LDS and gladly offer spirits to individual guests and businesses meeting in their public rooms. Hosea and his people spread the word as best they can that you can purchase alcohol at other places all over town, bring all you like of it to the hotel, serve it to clients, drink it in your room, or pay a $2.50 corkage fee to have it served, with a flourish, in the Roof Restaurant. Nor will you be thought disloyal if you ask the concierge to show you the menus of fifty-five other restaurants in the vicinity, several of which are nominally "clubs" that can be "joined" in a silly rigmarole that permits "members" to order all the drinks they want.

One day the ebullient wife of a lapsed-Mormon physician takes me and four other women to a merry lunch at the New Yorker Club, which I leave persuaded it must be the town's best restaurant. The next noon I become an instant member of the club at the Oyster Bar, where I drink wine as my orthodox Mormon guest, Peggy Fletcher, tells me, sipping water, of her worries about her city and her faith. "What we ought to value are the differences," says Fletcher, who edits the independent Mormon publication *Sunstone*, "but we don't; we value similarities. We edit out the eccentricities—the quirky habits that make us us. What would heaven be with no eccentrics there? And is the church so seduced by growth that ten years from now this city will look no different from Denver or Phoenix?"

So far, in spite of the protrusions of the Khashoggis and other developers all over town, Salt Lake City continues to hold its own: I know I'm someplace distinctive, outside the hotel and in it. There's a special air, as if everyone here, even gentiles (as nonbelievers are called), led his life the way the Mormon hymnal suggests that its anthems be sung: Earnestly. Reverently. Resolutely. Energetically. And familially. Eternity, for devout Mormons, is a sort of ultimate family reunion, not only of all the baptized relatives they have encountered in this life but of all who have gone before, ever. Their duty is to trace each twig of their family trees as far back as they can, with the help of the LDS Genealogical Library, behind the hotel, and to marry early so as to get a good start "bringing spirits into the world."

All over town, statues with titles like *First Day of School* remind passersby of the joys of family life. Many hotel employees work with their relatives. Tristyn Bowman met her husband working here; so did one of her sisters, two of whom work as part-time banquet waitresses, as does their mother. "In the banquet kitchen," she says, "you yell, 'Mom!' and half the women in the room turn around. Banquet food—especially the hotel's famous hard rolls—is surprisingly good."

So are breakfasts in the Grill, Falstaffian enough to suit William Howard Taft, who declared that the hotel ranked with any in the world when he visited in 1911. Scott Matheson, Utah's outgoing governor, said his greatest pleasure in office was sneaking over to the Bowl and Basket on Fridays for clam chowder. Nelson Styles, who has worked for the hotel since World War II, counts it an evening lost when he has no occasion to serenade a guest at the Roof with his special rendition, owing much to Paul Robeson, of "Happy Birthday to You." After dinner you can retire, if you like, to one of nine Heritage Rooms, furnished with antiques, or to one of forty-four rooms reserved for, and exclusively tended by, nonsmokers. Someone at the desk in the lobby will be glad to chat with you, of ski conditions or of genealogy, in Thai or Spanish if need be ("They're like, shoot, therapists," says Tristyn), if at 3:00 A.M. you should be wakened by funny beeping sounds outside.

The beeping sounds turn out to be traffic signals telling the blind when to cross the streets. Nobody jaywalks. Shoppers, emerging from malls that smell of fudge, wait patiently for lights to change, clutching parcels. What is in them? Maybe Jots and Tittles: The Trivia Game for Latter-day Saints, from the Deseret Bookstore. (*Deseret* is the Mormon word for "honey-bee," which is what Utahans in general and Mormons in particular are supposed to be as busy as.) Maybe something from ZCMI, Zion Cooperative Mercantile Institution, the oldest department store west of the Mississippi, where you get a discount on a new coat if you bring your old one in to donate to the needy. Maybe embroidery supplies; as the Mormon Handicrafts Center behind the hotel suggests, this is a very big town for sewing.

"You'll notice that the girls' rooms are bigger than the boys' rooms," says the Mormon lady leading the tour of Beehive House. Brigham Young, Joseph Smith's successor, built Beehive House to settle into in 1854. "The girls' rooms are bigger," she goes on, "because girls spent more time at home. The boys were expected to be out more, working for the church." How many children did Young have? She isn't quite sure. How many wives had he? She says twenty-seven, but others say forty. Polygamy, which was outlawed in 1890, is nobody's favorite subject. Most people's favorite subject is the sanctity of the family.

Having identified their ancestors' ancestors, devout Mormons next must qualify them for eternity by means of proxy baptisms and marriages called sealings. These sealings take place in the Mormon temple, from whose turret Moroni blows his trumpet. Being a gentile, I am not allowed inside the temple. Neither are a lot of Mormons. Mormons can't go in, even for their own children's weddings, unless they have "taken out their endowments," which means making sacred vows concerning everything from tithing—giving 10 percent of their income to the church—to wearing special underwear known as "garments," thought to ward off harm. Temple weddings are regarded as much more binding than ordinary ones, which they can either replace or supplement.

Most of this and much more I learn at the Visitors Center, also on Temple Square, where beaming volunteers whose name cards identify them as "Sister" and "Elder" So-and-so are delighted to tell the Mormon story, with the help of brochures, murals, dioramas, and space-age audiovisual displays. Tourists are also welcome at Sunday-morning performances and Thursday-evening rehearsals of the Mormon Tabernacle Choir, in a building with such flawless acoustics that a dropped pin can be heard from 230 feet away.

Margarita Gonzales was married, to the same man for the second time, in the temple. Margarita, who is thirty-seven, tells me something of her story when she comes into Room 1028 to change my sheets. The oldest of her six children is a law student, just back from his two-year missionary service in Lagos, Nigeria. Her second son studies political science at Berkeley, and the next child, still in high school, wants to be a stewardess. Margarita was converted in Mexico, where she was born and first married, and loves her weekday work in this hotel and her Sunday duties at the Relief Society in one of the Spanish-speaking "wards," or parishes, of the LDS: "I teach fifty womans every Sunday how is good neighbor, good mother, good wife, how you should spend the money."

Heartening though it is to walk down such unfailingly cheerful hotel corridors and streets, something in me longs for a jolt of wickedness. Can it be that I'll find it at Triad Center, at the private club called Café Vicieuses Rumeurs ("Vicious Rumors")? Certainly the place tries to look racy, with mannequins on a balcony wearing sequined red dresses, as if they were ladies of the night, and a church confessional transformed into a telephone booth, outside of which is a shoeshine stand: a shapely hostess in a short skirt kneels at the feet of a male patron, shines his shoes, lights his cigar, and accepts his tip, which is all she works for.

"Have the pizza," suggests someone at the next table. "It's awesome." As a matter of fact it is pretty good, and the waiter who brings it, a musician by vocation, needs no persuading to tell of his own spiritual odyssey. At age eighteen he was the black sheep of his strict Mormon family. "I went through a rebellious phase," he says. "I did a lot of questioning for a while, but I came up with the right answers." The answers included divorcing his first wife, petitioning the church to have that union "unsealed," and marrying another woman. "I feel very sealed to my kids," he says, "but not their mother."

This waiter and husband and father, having survived his rebellion, appears to be a happy man. He makes me think of the schoolroom of the Beehive House, where Brigham Young's children learned to read and write and paint. A picture on an easel there has the legend "The children are happy. They are kind to each other. Grandpa is watching the children."

"In a way, if I were any good at sewing," I said, "I'd have liked to have been one of Brigham Young's children. Their lives must have been so free of ambiguity."

"My life's free of it now," the waiter says. "You know *Fid-*

dler on the Roof, the line that goes 'Everyone knows who he is and what God expects him to do'? That's the way I feel, now that I've made the loose ends fit, now that I'm rectified."

"Don't listen to him," says a waitress who stops by the table later, who has overheard my talk with her colleague. "He wears garments."

Another vicious rumor, maybe. Time to head back toward the hotel. On the way I stop only at the Tabernacle, where enraptured-looking couples on dates hear the choir practicing: "Now the battle o'er/Now the triumph is won."

I feel pretty righteous and safe, walking under the crystal chandelier in the lobby, into the elevator. I feel as if the angel Moroni were watching over me. Which from the window of Room 1028, he is.

Bearings

SALT LAKE CITY, UTAH

Population: 169,000
When Brigham Young first saw the valley of the Great Salt Lake, he said, "This is the place." Said Harriet Young, one of the women in his expedition, "Weak and weary as I am, I would rather go a thousand miles further than remain in such a desolate place." She stayed.

Today Salt Lake City is 56-percent Mormon and 1.5-percent black.

Most Mormons pay more to the church each year in tithes than they pay in either state or local taxes. The church's annual income has been estimated at $1.5 billion, which would make it one of the 250 largest corporations in the U.S.

Of church founder Joseph Smith's 112 revelations, eighty-eight concerned economic matters.

Salt Lake City puts a higher percentage of its children through high school and college than any other city in the U.S. The city's divorce and cancer rates are among the lowest in the country.

The city has been called the Stock Fraud Capital of the World; the Mormon ethic of trusting fellow Mormons apparently makes them easy marks for swindlers.

The Great Salt Lake is biologically dead.

Tour of Duty

Guy Martin

L et me tell you first about Hancock, in Chattanooga, Tennessee, a long time ago. Hancock was the bugler, the clear, ringing heart of the Baylor School. We had others, but Hancock made them all sound like they were out in the quadrangle beating a chorus of farm animals. Even Hancock's worst enemies, including the Colonel and his staff, stood in awe of his chops. Hancock spoke to us each day with precision and grace: *You will wake, you will stand, you will march, you will eat, you will sleep, you will live to the code.*

There are many Faustian methods of survival in a military school, and Hancock's was singularly so. He made a deep fetish of military pomp. He decorated his blouse with cords and Korean War ribbons that the authorities constantly had to strip from his chest. He wrote ornate, prayerful poems extolling cadet life. He

Like his father before him, GUY MARTIN was a cadet at the Baylor School in Chattanooga Tennessee. He has contributed articles to *Esquire* regularly for the last five years.

bent the wire in his garrison hat to form an SS officer's peak. The Colonel astutely determined that this zeal in fact bordered on voodoo and so refused to give Hancock, who was the star of the Drum and Bugle Corps, a shred of rank.

At the same time, for the same reasons, Hancock cloaked himself in the mythology of suffering, the ancient low-down blues. He made a weekly pilgrimage, in uniform, to the record shops along Ninth Street, Chattanooga's black mecca, where he would ferret out Chess reissues. He cajoled sympathetic blacks into buying him pints of Ripple. He bought a dobro and taught himself to play slide with the instrument lying flat on his lap, the way the best bluesmen did. While most cadets juked to the saccharine harmonies of Motown, raw burning strains of Blind Lemon Jefferson issued from Hancock's cave.

The Colonel was always on the lookout for new marching tunes, and the news was that Hancock had composed a winning tattoo. The D&B rehearsed it for a week, then unveiled it at drill. It was marchable, all right, but it had this queer, demonic cheeriness, something a madman might whistle as he stomped a litter of kittens to death. I can't remember who recognized it first, or if word was somehow leaked, but I do recall the brigade marching down the hill to this music and a number of cadets *chuckling.*

Tah tah *TAH* ta/Tah tah *TAH* ta
Tadala, tadala, *TAH TAH TAH!!*

The D&B played furiously on until the realization hung, perfectly diabolical, in the air: the corps of cadets from the Baylor School was marching to the theme song from the *Captain Kangaroo* show.

And we kept on marching to it. No one explained the provenance of the tune to the Colonel on that day or apparently on any other, because I watched my younger brother march to it some years later. This is the most important part of the history of Hancock's tattoo; the secret wasn't broadcast or bandied about, it was adopted as a parallel, subterranean tradition. The cadets preferred to keep it that way. *That* was discipline—and a testament to the ability of the young southern male to play the double game. It was how we accepted the voice of sacrifice. It was how we made it sing.

Most southerners—rural, urban, or indifferent—have been brought up to feel they owe their lives to the land. Whether the feeling took, how it grew, what vestiges or perversions of it are left, is not the point. It is laid into a young life at every turn, instinctively, repetitively, a presence in each conversation, a hue in every perception. Part of it is the result of an almost completely agrarian way of life, even in the towns, until the middle of this century, but the greater reason is the overwhelming loss sustained by the region in the Civil War. One in four able-bodied southern males, including blacks, were killed or maimed. In the year after the war 20 percent of the budget for the state of Mississippi was spent on artificial limbs. And after offering up her sons, the South, where the lion's share of the destruction occurred, lay under the fist of the conqueror for a decade.

It was essentially this down payment, in blood, that consecrated the ground for the immediate survivors and created the debt for subsequent generations. We owe. Specifically, we owe *them.* This is not a normal debt in any respect. In the first place, it is rarely articulated and has never been paid, but instead is held aloft as a thing to which the young may aspire. Of course, this happens to any group of people who lose a war for their home; they must assimilate the loss, and they build the first monument to it in the minds of their young. For young men aged twelve and up this means much ritual loss, great sudden shearings of innocence, so that they come to a very early understanding of allegiance and honor, of how honor first means to learn to live with a wound.

Hard by the war's old scars in Virginia, Alabama, South Carolina, and Tennessee are the military schools. Some of them existed before the war, most notably those in Virginia, one of which, the Virginia Military Institute, supplied 247 fifteen-to-twenty-four-year-old cadets as cannon fodder in the Battle of New Market. But most of the schools were built late in the last century or early in this one, with Tennessee running second to Virginia in number. With the advent of World War I and the creation of the Reserve Officer Training Corps (ROTC) in colleges, military schools became a first stage in the conduit supplying officers to the Army. The schools retain that function today, though the majority of cadets do not go on to military careers.

Below the Mason-Dixon line military schools are not auto-
matically regarded as places where young first offenders must go
in order to stay out of jail. In the eyes of the region there is
something much more normal, even elite, about them. With all
due respect, northern parents who want to send their fourteen-
year-old to Andover or Phillips Exeter simply do not consider
sending him to Pennsylvania's Valley Forge Military Academy.
As one observer put it, the South is freely martial. The region
bears the usual signs of that, plenty of hunting and terrific college
football, but it has something more, in the feeling that it will at
some point be a privilege to take up a gun in service to this place.
Even that is not quite accurate, because one is not really offered
the gun but a kind of initiation into the cult of the gun, the gun
reduced to a discipline of manners.

Southerners have a necessarily corrupt, sidewinding view of
power because they lost power so completely once. They know,
the way any conquered people knows, that power is fragile, tem-
poral, vain. It is the seat of their skepticism but also of their
worship—for the strange truth is that southerners accept author-
ity with readiness and teach it as a moral absolute. Their insides
never have to agree with their faces. This is what makes them
such adroit and brutal politicians, what makes their writers obsessed with grotesques, what makes them such good soldiers.

Southern military schools derive sustenance from such nineteenth-century values, but they must survive in the twentieth.
They had to pick their way through the late stages of the Vietnam
War, and like the rest of the American military apparatus, they
did not have an easy time. Applications dropped as much as 20
percent in the early seventies, a devastating blow since most of
the schools had fewer than six hundred students. Schools closed
in Virginia, South Carolina, and Tennessee. The survivors began
to soften their stance a bit, admitting blacks and girls and in a few
cases abandoning their military programs entirely. There are some
left, and it seems they will be there for a good while.

Camden Military Academy in Camden, South Carolina, is a
strictly southern anachronism, though it is only thirty-five years
old. Tucked away in the sandy belt of the piedmont, it accepts
boys in grades seven through twelve. The cadet battalion is a

junior ROTC unit, but in terms of career planning the Army's presence is informal. Camden lives instead in the shadow of the Citadel, the venerable military college of the state, which means that though some Camden graduates plan to enter the Army, many of them see four more years of cadet life before they do it.

Camden is a private school in the most literal sense, belonging to a foundation run by its headmaster, Colonel Lanning P. Risher. Colonel Risher, a graduate of the Citadel, is the scion of a South Carolina family in the business of running military schools. Risher's father and brother, also Citadel graduates, owned and ran Carlisle, a now-defunct military school in Bamberg, South Carolina.

Colonel Risher is a lanky, middle-aged man with dark hair and a chiseled aquiline face. He swivels his chair in his sunny office and says, "Military education is a means to an end. Always. I have been fortunate enough to have a military education, and that is what we are in the business of providing here. They say education is a three-legged stool: physical, moral, and intellectual. Any two or any one of those things is not gonna do it. I don't care how smart an individual is, if his character is not strong, he will not contribute to society."

He pronounces it *karak-tah,* with affectionate disregard, as a man might who deals in this commodity on a daily basis. "You see, in a normal high school there are perhaps fifteen positions of leadership. Here there are eighty, at all levels, and it isn't just student government or sports. Basically we want to develop a young man so that he takes a little more responsibility for his own life and the life of others."

Colonel Risher and his assistant headmaster, Lieutenant Colonel C. R. White, feel very confident about the school and so do not care to accompany me on my rounds, assuming their presence might inhibit what some cadets would say. I do, however, pick up a guide, Cadet First Lieutenant Jay Harris, the battalion supply officer. Harris is a straightforward, well-spoken senior who plans to go to the Citadel and from there into an Army career.

Before beginning our barracks tours, Jay asks, "Sir, perhaps you could tell me who would you rather see, our more normal cadets or what I would call our strange and remote units?" We settle on a philosophy of half and half.

The first tour begins after dinner, in C Company barracks, where Lieutenant Cecil and Cadet Sergeant Major Hill have decided to ignore study hall. These boys are seniors and have the sureness that attaining rank confers. Lieutenant Cecil, sleepily smoking a cigarette, has just come in from a date. He says he's not going to college in the spring—he needs a new challenge and plans to enlist in the Marine Corps, working his way up from the bottom.

Sergeant Major Hill says, "Any changes in this place first come through us. I mean, we want the honor code, and we wanted one written down with a lot more emphasis on it, because a lot of us are thinking about going into the military, specifically to the Citadel, and we need to be ready for that. But you see, although we want it stricter, I think the office feels if it were written down it could lead to cadets burning each other, and possibly to hazing. And the office doesn't want any hazing. So now we have a code, but it is just among ourselves."

The office, as Hill calls it, has even restricted military courtesy. It is not mandatory for underclassmen to salute their cadet leaders, although practically all of them do. Jay explains, "An underclassman can come to attention and salute me in the barracks only if he likes me. It is a sign of respect." But that is an officer's explanation. The savvy underclassmen use it time and again to curry favor, or simply to amuse themselves. They use it as a basketball player would set a pick, coming up behind an officer and snapping to attention, forcing him to turn and acknowledge them. They learn an infinite vocabulary of postures. They have a snide, smiling way of standing at attention for officers they hate, making their enemies enter a transaction of respect.

The maggots, as the seventh, eighth, and ninth graders are known, come to attention whenever Jay and I walk into their rooms. Then they explain how and why they are in trouble. They are extremely forthright, because military misdeeds result in military justice, the most public form of redress, and they quickly learn to wear their transgressions. Maggots customarily pile up huge loads of demerits simply by existing. Up to a certain limit, each demerit is worked off by sitting at one's desk for a half hour ("serving a confinement"). Beyond that, cadets may be required to march for the same amount of time, with a rifle, on the penalty pad (a TBW, or "tour to be walked"). For some offenses, TBWs are the automatic punishment. Both confinements and TBWs must be served during free time.

At Camden the notion of honor has been pressed into this system on a parabola of offenses that result in specific penalties, formally set down on a schedule of demerits in the student handbook. What are seen as honor violations—cheating, making a false official statement, engaging in conduct unbecoming a cadet and a gentleman—ride high on the curve, drawing as much as a hundred demerits (fifty hours of sitting or marching) or even dismissal. These are cataloged on the schedule of demerits with the more quotidian crimes—failing to know one's rifle serial number, sleeping on guard duty, fighting, drinking. The theory is that cadets come to regard honor and its maintenance as a daily task; but there is something in the cadets that holds honor violations apart. The penalty for drinking may be the same as for cheating, but to get caught drinking is often a laughing matter, part of a game. Cheating is seen rather flatly as a weakness.

There are *kinds* of honor. All cadets share a general kind of honor they usually pin on the school, the very light honor, the stuff in the air. Then there is a tighter, more tense honor among specific groups within the community, among officers, for example, whose unspoken code it is not to punish one another for certain minor offenses that would draw automatic penalties if an underclassman committed them. It's commonly perceived as a perquisite of rank, but because the code is tacit, the line between acceptable and unacceptable behavior is at best hazy and at worst completely invisible. There is a different but no less difficult kind of honor among cadets who are friends. As underclassmen, when neither boy has much at stake, it is relatively easy to cover or to accept punishment for something a friend has done. As they rise through the ranks, especially if they rise to different levels, they must be careful not to jeopardize each other by counting too much on the friendship. In this sense honor means to live with a threat. A cadet's life at school depends on how he embraces it, or whether he can embrace it at all.

Jay introduces me to the infamous Cadet Mundy as he

strains to finish a week without, in cadet parlance, "getting burned." Mundy bears a huge load of demerits, so many that it is physically impossible to serve them. If he can go the week without receiving a single mark, the commandant will reduce his load by half. Mundy stands up from his desk, where he has been crouching for some reason with the lights off. He has an agile Levantine face, the face of an otter, and approximately one thirty-second of an inch of black hair covering his head, like an Iraqi prisoner on display in Tehran. Jay says, with some pride, "Sir, this is our Mundy here, *definitely* a strange and remote unit. We call him The Geek, because that's what he looks like. At ease, Mundy."

Mundy smiles at this and Jay says, by way of biography, "Mundy here has been caught doing just about everything, serving confinements in trees, falling through ceilings . . ."

"Now, sir, that wasn't my fault. How was I supposed to know that was a live wire when I grabbed it?" Mundy turns to me. "You see, sir, I'm a monkey, I'll climb anything." To prove it, he jumps on his bunk and from there negotiates a toehold on the top of the doorframe, a solid piece of 5.4 climbing. He smiles and jumps down. "See, this was the first trouble I was in. So we heard there was some old boxes or something up inside the roof of the gym, maybe some treasure, so we went in there and I grabbed a live wire and got shocked and fell through the ceiling and hit a water fountain and rolled off and hit a box or a table and then rolled off that and hit the floor."

Jay says, "I thought you were up there playing Dungeons & Dragons."

"Well, we *were* fightin' with persimmons . . ."

"Which one of you was it that was playing a lot of Dungeons & Dragons and started believin' a little too much in the characters? Who was it I heard was into devil worship?"

Mundy says, "Look, it wasn't *me* . . ."

Mundy has a plan. Although he is within millimeters of being kicked out, he wants to stay at school. He has been left back two years in the civilian world: though he is old enough to be in the tenth grade, he's in the eighth. He wants to attend summer school for the next two years to catch up with his class at Camden. Then, he says, he wants to enter the Navy as a bosun's mate. That failing, he and his buddy Crowe will go exploring for hire. "Just like," Mundy says, breathless with possibilities, *"just like Indiana Jones."*

We leave Mundy's room for Rogers's. Rogers is deeply into biologicals. During the introductions he professes not to know how many demerits he has, but under pressure he finally admits to "somewhere around seven hundred." Rogers is fat and happy, a little eighth-grade Buddha. His roommate, a long-suffering boy named Covington, is just on his way out. He raises the mattress to his bunk and takes out a pair of drumsticks.

Jay asks, "Covington, why do you keep your drumsticks under your bed?"

Cutting his eyes at Rogers, Covington says sullenly, "Sir, I am trying to learn to play the drums, but Rogers keeps taking my sticks and beating on the wall. Then the CO comes in and takes the drumsticks away."

Covington is also plagued by fights. "How many fights you been in this year so far, Covington?"

" 'Bout thirty, sir."

Rogers laughs. Jay walks over to the desk and picks up a glass vial corked with foam. At the bottom of the vial is a greasy beige substance. "Rogers, this is dis*gust*ing! How long have you been growing this?"

"Some weeks," Rogers says, barely able to contain himself. "It comes from science class. It's s'posed to attract flies, but . . ." He looks doubtfully at it.

Jay tosses it back on the desk, where it clatters against a stack of books. Rogers gives a start. Two things begin to wrestle on his face: a desire to become famous by getting caught, and a desire to have the project work. Then he says, "Sir, I don't think it would be too good to break that. It might smell up the room."

My last conversation at Camden is with Ian Baucom, last year's battalion commander, a figure of some controversy among cadets even today. Not many of his former subordinates, today's battalion staff, bear him goodwill; they refer to "last year" with a certain coolness, they tell me time and again that *this year's* staff, under Cadet Lieutenant Colonel George Washington Pagan, really has it together. By that they mean esprit de corps is high, which in this instance is a gauge for the degree of trust,

58

or mistrust, they accord one another. At Camden the battalion commander is the hinge between the administration and the cadets, the man who sets the tone of the dialogue between them. Ian's tenure was divisive at best, not because he acted like a bastard or a stooge, but because he chose to make a few very tough moments even more difficult. Ian is currently a student at Wake Forest University, and he is back, looking a little out of place in mufti, for a holiday visit to Camden. We have breakfast together.

He says firmly, "I never question what I did here. Military schools deal in moral absolutes, and I was confronted with the question, is it honor to turn in a friend at military school? I had to turn in a lot of my friends last year, one in particular, because what they did was wrong according to the strictures of the academy. And for those nine months I was confident that I not once failed to do what I perceived as my duty. I felt that I had done the right thing. It hurt, it hurt a lot.

"I wonder, if moral strictures had been flexible, if they had been subject to give and take, well, what I would have done. I haven't resolved that yet. At a place like Camden you're confronted with one set of rules everybody plays by, and then you move out of here into a place where everybody is playing for themselves. The first thing you realize is that you're not inherently better than everybody else. And the second thing is, you can't judge everybody by your set of rules. I still think the sacrifice I made was good, and the friend I hurt most said later he respected me for it. But I still don't have him as a friend.

"You've got to recognize the potential for more than one system of values. But having a system of your own, I don't know, it helps you realize that there are *facets* of good. Like, maybe a crystal with a lot of facets, so that if you're looking into it, maybe somebody else is looking into it from another facet, but you're really looking at the same thing."

Breakfast is over and the cadets stand dismissed. As they file out past Ian at the faculty table near the door, most of them recognize their former battalion commander. Two boys stop to shake his hand, then they are swept with the crowd out the door.

There are many different ways of becoming a soldier. At Marion Military Institute in Marion, Alabama, they've honed it to a science over the past century and a half. A total of 175 admirals and generals began their military careers here. Of the 315 ROTC programs in the nation, Marion ranks ninth in production of second lieutenants. Forty-two Marion seniors sought appointments to service academies last year; thirty were successful.

In addition to its high school, Marion offers a junior college program, which has in fact become the school's main business over the last ten years. Today Marion is heavily influenced by its ROTC affiliation and has survived the vicissitudes of time by emphasizing a schedule of study that makes reserve or National Guard second lieutenants out of high school seniors in two years (as opposed to four). This, and the strong record of service-academy prep, gives a rather cool, regular-army tone to the place. Since there are only six military junior colleges in the nation, Marion, which has also become coeducational, draws cadets from all over the country. It is a paradigm of how a military school survives by filling a larger and more current national need.

Captain David Seaman, Marion's very busy ROTC recruiter, has just returned from another trip "throwing the net out" in Alabama high schools for Marion's early-commission program. He explains, "We tailor recruiting to fit different parts of the country. In the Northeast somebody's momma might get worried if we sold the aggression, the more competitive side of the Army. For example, if she were to see a picture of an individual running, shooting, and communicating in a field of battle. So for *her* we sell the job, the educational opportunities, and the travel. But here we're in the Southeast, which is historically an intensely patriotic part of the country, and the mommas don't worry about Johnny having to carry a gun. We just don't have that problem."

Marion's faculty is made up largely of retired military men, some of whom began their careers here. For the most part, these men feel very chipper these days, if a little suspicious. The country has turned in their favor, they have been delivered from the civilian lashing of a decade ago. They are middle-aged but relatively young and have retired to Marion to impart knowledge. One sees a strange and very broad kind of knowledge in the pictures lining their walls and in the ribbons on their blouses: a NATO tour in Brussels, a "helping hand" mission in the Sudan, a dash across some hot, swarming MACV base in South Vietnam.

One of those 175 flag officers who graduated from Marion is currently its president, Major General Clyde W. Spence Jr., U.S. Army—Retired. General Spence is a small, white-haired fellow with a deep voice and a strong, can-do set jaw. He stands athletically straight, rather like Johnny Carson, and he smokes cigarettes like Johnny Carson does, with the same sort of slight but charming disappointment in himself.

"I have to say I think it's very simple," the General says. "The attraction of the people in this part of the country to the military has to do with their feeling for the outdoors. Look at our boys here, they've grown up around guns, they are exposed to these things at an early age. We've got access to twelve hundred acres over here, and one of the most popular activities in the school is the hunting club. They love it. They love the bivouacs, the rappelling off towers, the out-in-the-field camaraderie, the adventure of it."

He stops. "But," he says, popping the word out like a rifle shot, "we have a right to expect academies to develop good value systems and character traits. We can never escape the responsibility for that, because we can do things in a school that we can't do at home. That is, we can put them in positions of leadership among their peers. Young people want responsibility and will do as well as they can with it. I'll guarantee you that they learn more leadership here in a year than they do at West Point. Things are less rigid. And there is this simple fact: if they can lead and motivate a platoon of ninth graders, they can lead any soldier in the U.S. Army."

Until this year the ninth and tenth graders at Marion lived in a sort of moral no-man's-land, exempt from judgment by their peers. They reported directly to the commandant, Colonel Ralph Livingston, for their punishment, while their elder partners-in-crime were charged with much more serious honor violations for the same offenses by a student board. The premise of Marion's code is quite simple: a cadet must not lie, cheat, or steal. The theory was that thirteen- and fourteen-year-olds didn't realize what they were doing when they violated the code. As it turned out, they knew *exactly* what they were doing, and they knew they'd be punished less severely for it. This year they've been brought, very gingerly, into the system.

The General says, "We are experimenting with an honor
council made up of representatives from each class, with, of
course, the knowledge all along that I am the final arbiter of all
punishment. The council has faculty sponsors to make sure that
due process is observed, that all the evidence is made available,
that they have wrestled with the proper issues. I have to say that
all the cadets have been extremely responsible in working with
this. They take into account the relative maturity of ninth graders, and whether a deed has been done in a premeditated way or
in the heat of passion."

General Spence speaks precisely at all times, but when he
discusses matters of discipline or honor he enunciates with an
extra clarity. For Spence the process of instilling a sense of honor
in a young human seems not unlike surgery—one uses all manner
of trick knives and delicate knots that will dissolve as the tissue
heals, but the immediate problem is what to do with the patient
once the anesthetic wears off. Because it hurts.

The General says, "You know, at schools like the Citadel or
the University of Virginia they have a strong idea of honor. I
mean, you violate that honor code and *wham,* you are out of
there. That assumes a committed, aware attitude on the part of
the students, and frankly, we do an injustice to assume they have
a strong sense of honor when they come here. So we do not make
that assumption. We are here to instill those traits, not to act as
if they already have them intact."

Cadet Lieutenant Colonel John Patronis, brigade commander, is a rawboned football player from Quincy, Florida, a college
sophomore in the accelerated commission program who plans to
complete his education at Auburn before selecting an active unit.
He says he would like to be branched out into the infantry. He
is utterly unsentimental about how honor works.

"If you're gonna do something around here that's bad," he
says with a soft drawl, "then you had better be watchin' your back.
You learn quickly. You may want to do this or that at a certain
point, but you realize it's not just cuttin' up, you could forfeit your
career. You get to where before you do that bad thing, you don't
even think, you just don't do it. It becomes second nature.

"Now, there is another thing, you can use the honor system
against another person, you can get them to tell you things. Or

it can be used against you. You can make almost anything into an honor violation, which is a kind of dishonorable use of it."

Patronis says this with a certain edge to his voice, as if he's seen it happen but accepts it as one of the risks. He wears his rank comfortably, neither ignoring nor counting too much on the diamonds on his shoulders, and he seems to treat his idea of honor in the same way. He makes no bones about it: on a daily basis honor is a pain in the ass. Yet it is for him very much worth all the polishing, much like one's crossarms, without which the uniform would be just another suit of clothes. He votes strongly for bringing the ninth and tenth graders under the full weight of the code.

"There was the problem where they knew what they were doing wrong but they'd just go to the commandant to get written up, which was unfair. Now, under the code, we find they're taking themselves more seriously. I've always thought that having their minds probed was good experience. It makes them grow up." He shrugs and laughs. "Sometimes . . . you just want to take 'em up against the wall and shake 'em. They will do anything just to see how far they can drive you. But you have got to make adjustments. You try to earn their respect and then pull, and pull, and pull. They spill their guts out to you, the young ones do."

He's talking about basic ninth-grade fear—of the process, of the institution, of leaving home, of puberty itself. There is essentially no such thing as honor for a person under these pressures, but there is a weaning, an opening of the chest cavity so that something may be planted in it. It is both the promise and the danger of these places that so much of that work is done by one's peers, who have in turn just had it done to them.

Cadet Sergeant Major Kerry McCown, commanding officer of the Swamp Foxes, says he is at school and a member of this unit to perfect his basic infantry skills, in his opinion the highest form of service. The Swamp Foxes are named for the American Revolutionary guerrilla Francis Marion, after whom the town and the school are also named. They are the shock troops, the Special Forces of the school. They wear camouflage fatigues, jump boots, and black berets.

McCown is proudly steeped in Swamp Fox lore. "The unit was first formed here at the school in 1963, specializing over the years in hand-to-hand combat, mountaineering, patrolling, combat recon, raids, and ambushes. We have a strong emphasis on survival and guerrilla actions. We are airborne-, air-assault-, and Ranger-qualified, and we do some demolitions, to the extent that the Military Science three- or four-level student is allowed. We can play the role of opposing forces in war games. Our principal activity is teaching in the pit for FTX, which is a Field Training Exercise. The FTXs last from 2200 Friday to 1200 Sunday, and they are, if I may say so, sir, quite strenuous."

McCown is a paragon of excruciating military courtesy. Though he admits the war games he has played bear very little resemblance to the real thing, he carries every scrap of combat experience with unshakable pride. His ambition in life is to become an infantry officer. Among his fellow Swamp Foxes he feels a strong sense of honor.

"If I might also add, sir, what we try to do is keep a low profile. I mean, we do not like to Hollywood, sir, we do no type of Hollywooding at all. Now, for Parents' Day our demos are naturally *some* Hollywood, but basically we feel it detracts from what we do. Because one day we're gonna be called on to be there, and it's gonna be for real. People's lives will be at stake and we will burn right out if we have been Hollywooding all along. Because these are future officers out there, sir."

McCown and the Swamp Foxes are called on that very afternoon, but very few lives are at stake. They were asked to march in the town Christmas parade when another group backed out, which embarrassed them more than a little, being disposed against any form of Hollywooding. But it was even more bush not to march, so they stand in formation before the chapel, joking and griping before they march to town.

"Man, what're we doin' in a *parade?*"

Colonel Livingston, commandant of Marion, waits downtown for the parade. Colonel Livingston is a big man with a thin, broad mouth and deep-set dark eyes. He is responsible for the day-to-day discipline of the school, to most cadets a fearsome or at least highly unpleasant figure. Among adults he is subject to acute fits of philosophy. A graduate of the Citadel and a career Army officer, Livingston put in a long tour as a brigade executive officer in Vietnam. He has a big, soft speaking voice laced with a South Carolina accent.

The town square fills with people waiting for the parade. Livingston says, "We like to *think* that we are patriotic, or that we have a higher sense of mission, or a sense that the other folks don't. But it's not really true. We like to think that we have that tradition, and that is what the banners are for, and the ribbons for the engagements on this uniform. This is just a uniform like any other, no more, no less. And we like to think that means something, but it really doesn't. It's really like anything else, we *aspire* to tradition and to honor; maybe it's possible to attain it for a moment. But we don't really have it."

Anticipation grows around the little square as the steel helmets of the White Knights, Marion's crack drill team, can be seen gleaming down the street. Behind them marches the color guard, and behind that, as if to protect the colors from a rear action, come the Swamp Foxes. Colonel Livingston says, "*Ah*, that's nice, a full color-guard complement. See that little girl carrying the rifle?" He smiles, pointing out a dark-haired high school cadet marching on the near side of the guard, next to the school flag. "I just had to tell her she's restricted for two months." Then the colors, swirling, are abreast of us, and it takes some seconds to realize that Colonel Livingston stands silently at attention, saluting.

For years it was impossible to think of Hancock without arriving at the notion that he was dead. Even at school he seemed too advanced, too fast to live, and when he left, angrily, toward the end of his senior year, not many who knew him felt he had much time left. He was one of those primal beings the school somehow encouraged and cushioned but to whom the real world would have just one of two responses: it would exalt him or it would chew him up. Since there had been no news of Hancock the Famous, one assumed as a matter of course that he must have died gloriously.

I found him living as an enlightened hermit with his wife and children in Gainesville, Georgia, just a couple of hours from Chattanooga. He'd written a letter some time back, to a teacher at the school, mentioning events he authored in high belligerence some fifteen years ago, and he'd included his address on the envelope. It was odd to hear that the great unrepentant Hancock had written this letter, as if to settle an account, but it was profoundly unreal to find him living so quietly.

He understands instantly why I have come, as if we have an account to settle, too. He says, "I've just been sitting here, layin' low, wondering who would come by to talk. But all these years, it was like nothin' happened. Nobody came. I've been right here."

He looks the same, with the addition of a little weight. His dark-brown hair is still cut military-short; his narrow eyes hold themselves back behind the same wire-rimmed glasses. He explains rather proudly that by sculpting false teeth at a dentist's office he has put his wife through college and is only now finishing college himself. They have three children, one of whom, Heather, bundles down the stairs to ask her father when she has to go to bed. "Cuteness," says Hancock, delivering his first real curveball of the evening, "is gonna be the death of Heather."

His music has not changed, only deepened. Hancock plays a tape of Bertha "Chippie" Hill, a Twenties blues mama who really sets up a wail. Hancock uses her as a sort of starting gun for reminiscence. "I don't know," he says, "seems like Baylor really just taught you about the world, guys sneakin' around, and havin' to bribe people, to enter into illegal dealings. The thing is, if you've got that many, maybe three hundred boys with average or above-average intelligence, *and* no girls, *and* they can't go anywhere, well, hell. They'll be just *thinking* of ways to get some action.

"I hid a lot, it was where I learned to hide. I'd make a nest in the blankets in the tops of closets or under the beds; it's astonishing how small a space a human can get into when he really wants. I imagine it was like hiding from the Nazis. You'd hear the master key in the lock, and of course there'd be some cadets on the other side of the door who really wanted to stick it to you. But the thing is, we had just enough mental freedom to be wild. I mean, it was *fun* tryin' to beat 'em. And cadets were vigilant, my God. The game wasn't uncertain in any way, *those* were the guys you were gonna beat. It gave a focus to the rebellion."

Then Hancock begins to unload his litany of crimes, a sly, random stroll along the school's underbelly. He sabotaged pep rallies by leading cheers for Ho Chi Minh; he went AWOL in stolen canoes to the island in the middle of the river; he imported suitcases full of bad wine; he began the fad of planting smoke bombs and other Class D explosives on timed cigarette-fuses around campus. It was just this kind of work, Hancock says, no matter how extravagantly doomed, that going to military school required.

He says, "The other thing that was interesting, despite the regimentation, despite the heavy religious indoctrination: I've never met a more paganistic group of people in my life. I mean, boys more willing to do anything, anything *fundamental*. You learned how to motivate people. It was like bein' at war."

I ask him where he attends college. He says offhandedly, ingenuously, "North Georgia College in Dahlonega." A military school. "People come from all over to go there. It's got a good reputation academically, and I don't have to wear a uniform, because I'm a commuter. But the rest of the cadets, of course, do. I'm a junior now, and I like it pretty much. Been readin' Thucydides lately, the Peloponnesian War. You like Thucydides?"

I have a vision of him thirty or forty years down the road, the Perpetual Cadet, the Cadet Emeritus.

He says, "You know, I was always disappointed that Baylor didn't have a proper band, instead of the Drum and Bugle Corps. They shoulda got that glee club singing while they marched, that would have sounded strong. Hey, remember my dobro?"

He opens the case on the floor and brings out the pristine guitar. It is inhumanly beautiful, the perforated steel resonator shining under the strings like a small spaceship. The dobro has so much metal wrapped around it that it looks like a weapon, not an instrument. Picking up his bar and finger picks, Hancock says, "This is a little something I picked up since Baylor. Elmore James's 'Dust My Broom.' "

With that he rips into the music, lean and glancing, full of promise and failure and the fragile unguarded thing of males. It is like a sinew or a tendon, a cord that is strong in one direction but can be torn very easily by a blow from the side. If honor is a moment, or at best a series of moments, then this is one. Hancock plays the curving, strong-handed tune, his hands riding it like a wrangler on a bull while he sits bolt upright and unmoving, the picture of composure, pursing his lips a little, inclining his head like an old man.

When he finishes, the suggestion of a smile plays across his face and he says, "You know, one thing I never understood about my Baylor career. I am amazed they didn't give more rank to me, a cadet with as much experience as I had."

Bearings

CAMDEN, SOUTH CAROLINA

Population: 7,462
The Wateree Indians, the original inhabitants of what is now Camden, were one of the few tribes to permit a woman to be chief.

In 1730 King George II ordered a town to be built on the "River Watery."

During the Revolution the colonies lost nine hundred men in the Battle of Camden. Andrew Jackson, imprisoned here during the war, was scarred with a saber when he refused to black the boots of an English officer.

In 1862 Kershaw County property values were compiled for Confederate taxation as follows: real estate, $1,636,336; merchandise, $129,425; slaves (9,371), $4,552,110.

The town's biggest industry is textiles, but its biggest passion is horses. The Colonial Cup, with a purse of $60,000, is the richest steeplechase in the country.

The Prime of
Miss Jean Wilson

Douglas Bauer

Jean Wilson's job at Durgin-Park, 11:00 to 10:00, four days a week, is only her second as a waitress. She worked first at Sailor Tom's in Reading, a bustling seafood restaurant at the bottom of a hill, overlooked by the owner's enormous house, which he himself built, riding a high wave of sentiment, in the shape of a boat. After a short time Jean quit Sailor Tom's having perhaps caught the spirit of adventure working among the memories and icons of a life at sea. With a girlfriend, she drove to Cape Cod, all swash and buckle, looking for the lucrative work that always opened up at the height of the season. Except that it rained and blew unrelievedly that summer; very few people came to the Cape and many fewer than that got waitressing jobs. She came home, she says, "with my tail between my legs," and not until the end of summer did she find steady work, at Durgin-Park in Boston.

DOUGLAS BAUER was raised on a farm near Prairie City, Iowa. He has lived for two years in Boston, where he teaches writing at Harvard University and is working on a new novel.

And that's all there is—end of résumé—so that as I describe her moving among patrons and colleagues and the long rows of tables with economical grace, diner-thick plates lining her arms like overlapping scales, her humor keen and her temperament even, all the time alert as a young bird for a raised hand, an empty cup, you nod and say, "That good? And only her second job? Clearly she's a natural."

But for one more thing. Jean was extremely relieved when she got her job at Durgin-Park, a reprieve, as she saw it, from her summer's whim and a hard-won lesson on the wages of transience. So she started, eagerly and quite fittingly, on the morning after Labor Day—a very hot one, she recalls—in 1945. If this is just her second waitress job, it's also one she's had for very nearly forty years.

"I must like the work in ways I don't know. I must. I've been here forever. But I never ask myself the question 'Do you like it?' " Her thick black hair is cut mannishly short and in a kind of modified DA. The animate lines of her face seem dependently woven, as though if one were to come unraveled the entire facial pattern would come apart. Her bones, especially the strong planes of her nose and cheeks, give her the mien of an Indian on a coin. "It's what I do best, I guess. But all you need to be a waitress," she says, winking, "is a strong back and a weak mind, right?"

Maybe. But while she clearly has the former, her mind also holds several dishes at a time and is abundantly filled with wit and sense and recall. To work a job for forty years is on the face of it remarkable. But to work them here, at Durgin-Park, is something more than that. It's also precisely symbolic of the place and what its life has unwittingly come to stand for.

Durgin-Park occupies one of a row of shore-front warehouses in a part of Boston called Faneuil Hall. A duplicate row parallels it, three stories high, perfectly dentilated, both flanking the area's original building, a market house built in 1742 by an entrepreneurial colonist named Peter Faneuil. In the beginning, when bay waters lapped at the end of the buildings—a scene drawn on the front of Durgin-Park's menus—they were occupied by merchants selling meat, poultry, produce, and dairy products. Farmers brought wagons pyramided with foodstuffs into the market; men dressed in white aprons, broadly smeared with the juices of their commerce, unloaded the goods, dressed them, carved them, stacked them, and ultimately resold them. One can easily romanticize the sense and stir of the market at its peak: raunchy, high-tempered, a kind of muscular fraternity essential in its air. But who knows? Perhaps the air was nothing more than foully odorous and suspicious and the merchants and farmers strained in common sullenness to lift their heavy loads. In any case, at mealtimes their appetites were epic. Inevitably, a dining room opened to appease them.

The first hundred years or so of Durgin-Park's prehistory run vaguely, free of names and dates, though it's known that, on what is now its second floor, the market men came at dawn and noon. They sat down at long tables, families joined by common work and bottomless hunger. They ate a lot of food in very little time, served by women at least their equals in their total lack of decorum and gentility. Concern with ambience was unnecessary, irrelevant. The men were hungry, the dining room had food. Who had time, or need, for sweet solicitude? And so the overriding features that distinguish Durgin-Park were formed by the nature of its energetic origins. Customers placed elbow to elbow along long wooden tables. Enormous portions of beef, chicken, fish, baked beans, corn bread, Indian pudding. And its legendary waitresses, whose attitude, in one word, might best be called "abusive."

History is first specific in 1840, when John Durgin and Eldredge Park bought the dining room with a third partner named John Chandler. Both Durgin and Park were dead within a few years, but Durgin-Park remained in the Chandler family for still another century and was sold to James Hallett in 1945, the year Jean Wilson began. It was sold again in 1977 to the Kelley brothers, who, having owned Durgin-Park for only eight years, might be said, given its history, to have barely closed the fountain pen with which the deed was signed. Further, such a record places the individual history of Jean Wilson's life here in an even more impressive context: Durgin-Park has had four ownerships, and she has worked for two of them.

"It's true about the waitresses," she says. "Even when I started, there were some real raunches." It should be said immediately that Jean was never, is not now, any version of the blue-mouthed Durgin hashslinger. She is voluble, participatory, quick to say to a hesitant customer, "Let me mind your business for you," and proceed to recommend. But what she's known for, widely, is her kind, concerned efficiency.

She sits at a table, one among those that comprise her station, number nine, next to the wall by the entrance to one of the three dining rooms. She's claimed this station, presided over the same rows of tables, for as long as she can remember—her narrow streets of influence within the teeming township. "Old-timers like the idea of knowing where they're going to be working every day. I roll out of bed, I imagine my tables. It makes me feel good." The tablecloths in this room are, uniquely, white. Elsewhere in the restaurant they are red-and-white-checked. As in the other rooms, the walls are painted an unattractive yellow, the value of margarine, and trimmed in a deep brown. The floors are unfinished wood. Lamps in rows hang from low tin ceilings. There seem to be twice as many lamps burning twice as brightly as necessary. In keeping with Durgin-Park's philosophy of excess, electricity is served in prodigal abundance.

"Now, there's a *few* I wouldn't want to sit with myself, but most of the girls are real nice. It's like the signs you see when you come into a little town: 'We've got three hundred good citizens and a few old crabs.' Well, we've got a few old crabs. If we snap at ya, it's just because we get so busy."

"I'd like a doggie bag."

"What for?"

"What for? For these leftovers, what else?"

"You don't want a doggie bag. I mean, if ya do, I'll get it, but how often do you eat your leftovers, really?"

"Well . . ."

"Got a dog?"

"No."

"How often?"

"All right, forget it."

"You'll thank me, really."

"Thanks."

"You're welcome."

Jean speaks of her own accelerated apprenticeship with women who learned in the truly lawless days at the turn of the century. "When I started, we didn't even have numbers on our order slips so you could tell whose order was whose," she says. "If there's five roast beef and you're waiting for roast beef, you just made sure you got one. I was so innocent when I came here I blushed if the wind changed, and I couldn't figure out why *my* orders were taking so long. My customers waited a long time for their orders, until I learned to take care of myself."

It's 4:30 in the afternoon, a frigid January day in Boston. Station nine, and nearly all the other nineteen as well, is empty of customers. Between the hours of 12:00 and 2:00 the restaurant serves perhaps 20 to 25 percent of the roughly 2,500 meals it prepares daily. Now it is recuperatively quiet. Beyond the high arched windows at the end of the rooms, a steady snow falls. People tiptoe along the icy walks as though balancing on wires. Inside, the restaurant feels envelopingly friendly, warmed by an aromatic steam, very nearly intimate, not a word that usually applies.

"The place looks exactly like it did when I started. About the only thing different is the kitchen. All that stainless steel. Used to be there was just rows of tables and ladies washing dishes in huge tubs."

On the other side of the wall from where we sit stands the vast open kitchen of Durgin-Park. Strategically central, it dominates the dining space. Inevitably, after one has climbed the fifteen steps to the dining rooms, it is the kitchen one first sees and hears and feels, in the summer, like a Bessemer's blast. Gleaming planes of stainless steel. Capacious ducts of it, compartments high as walk-in closets. Dishes and glasses stacked in racks. Plates of beef, chicken, fish, crocks of beans and squash under infrared spotlights. Fifteen, seventeen, twenty waitresses at once, sliding past, around, over one another to get to their food and get it out.

"It's interesting," Jean says, "the way people work competitively in tight spaces. Especially, in the old days, if you were a waitress and you were tall and had a reach, you had no problem in the kitchen." She is perhaps five feet tall, and her arms are proportionate for a woman of that height. "I had to learn how to find *space*. You duck between the big girls, you slip right under their arms, snag your order, and *run*."

In ways both actual and metaphorical, the second-floor kitchen is the engine of the place. It sets its cadence (frantic), supplies its background music (clangorous to deafening), defines the ambience (plainly open, emphatically free of aesthetic airs). It is Durgin-Park's chief inconvenience and its prime attraction.

"Customers love the kitchen," says Mike Ferris, the restaurant's manager. "People come up to me and say, 'Why don't you air-condition this place?' I say, 'We'd have to close off the kitchen.' They say, 'Oh, you can't do that.' "

So, to summarize, if the pace is chaotic, the air is often stifling. If the tables are filled with parties of ten, twelve, some of them are placed considerable distances from the kitchen. If the hours are long, the floors are hard. And those lights, hanging low and glaring superabundantly, hit someone who stands five feet tall "right smack in the face."

"Probably the hardest part of working here is the food. It's heavy. You take your plate, which weighs a pound and a half or so all by its *onesies*. Then you put a two-pound slab of roast beef on it. You see what I'm talking about?" She gets up as she speaks and balances an imaginary order on her arm. "You have to carry it close in and lift with your arms and legs. You carry it out away from you, it's a stomach rupture right there."

Standing, Jean is remarkably bowlegged, but like the rest of her, this looks to be not the inevitability of forty years on her feet bearing roast beef but a feature of a shape absolutely born to do so. Head to toe, Jean appears a design of brilliant utility: very minimally hunched, her wide forearms gracefully curved, her gravity centered and low, she seems an accommodating human basin on which platters of food nestle securely. There's no verticality to her, no rigid surface; she's entirely receptive as she moves toward a table, cradling plates of prime ribs, the bones the size of boomerangs, and chops from the lambs of Brobdingnag.

"I'll take the roast pork."

"Sorry I didn't see ya sooner. I'm blind as a bat without my glasses."

"S'all right. I'll take the roast pork."

"I just got a complaint on it."

Clank! from the kitchen, as if amplified through speakers.

"Then the chicken livers."

From the kitchen, shouting up through a dumbwaiter to the third floor, where the food is initially prepared: "How long on those potatoes?!"

From the third-floor kitchen a reply, a gust of emphysematous weather: *"Grmmmph!"*

"What?!"

When Jean Wilson served her first prime rib in 1945, it cost $2.50. Pot roast, including bread, dessert, coffee, was ninety-five cents. Today, unaccompanied, it's $5.25, and Roast Prime Rib of Beef, the most popular item on Durgin-Park's menu, costs thirteen dollars. Whether the portions are the same as then or smaller (a favorite debate among customers with memories, or at least those who claim to have them), they are still, unarguably, almost comically, huge. Durgin-Park's prime rib remains remarkably priced, as does everything else, from Frankfurts and Beans ($3.95) to Three One-Pound Lobsters ($18.95), and the prices on the menu are certainly a reason 2,500 people open it daily.

But not the only reason. For the fame and lure of Durgin-Park draw purely on the notion of abiding Yankee thrift, and that is not so simple a concept as one might suspect. Attempts to define it often resort to freshly dusted aphorisms or to the thing exemplified.

"Women in Boston don't buy hats, they *have* hats," a friend of mine said recently, voicing her doubt about the lasting success of a newly opened arcade of exclusive shops in town, where one suspects a surcharge for the breathing of the air. My friend had Yankee thrift in mind, for her comment suggests that her Boston woman had *once* bought a hat, or had inherited a hat her mother had once bought, and that the hat has endured. Which means, furthermore, that its fabric is strong and was cut and sewn with care. And finally, my friend implies that the hat, worn season after season, is unelaborately styled to the point of indistinction and is seen as desirable in part for that reason. It is chiefly bought, that is, because a hat is the thing one puts atop one's head.

The ingredients emergent, then, are not only low price but

durable quality and unadorned practicality, and these elements in some integral mixture combine as Yankee thrift. What applies to this imagined Boston hat can be quite actually seen, and eaten, on a plate at Durgin-Park. The food here honors most of all its ancestral requirement of unalloyed *heft*, as Jean Wilson knows every time she lifts a dish. For the Puritan, food was fuel, little more, and the more of it per sitting, the better one could work. The stronger the fabric, the longer it will wear. The larger the portion, the longer it sustains. And if neither is fancy, they won't cost much at all. The idea that eating (or *any*thing, for that matter) might be recreative, leisurely, sensual, indulgent, was at least an ocean and an epoch away. You ate as you prayed—crowded together on hard wood, except that prayer went on longer, its helpings larger.

The value, admittedly, may be remotely rooted and highly abstract, but it's immediately recognizable on the walls, in the air, in the food at Durgin-Park. Take away any one of its elements—quality, quantity, price, austerity to the depth of discomfort—and the reason to come here no longer holds.

"We built a new dining room on the third floor," Mike Ferris says. "It's really nice. Dark wood, brass. Very quiet. It's the same menu, the same prices. But people go up there and they're uncomfortable. They come back down, saying, 'We want the noise. All the people. It's lonely up there.' So we made a private banquet room out of it."

And: "Lots of customers, especially the old ones, don't know how to act if a waitress treats them nice. And lots of people come in and say, 'Be sure we get a waitress who'll treat us mean.' "

"Oh! Look at this. I can't eat all this."

"You know, when I started coming here, these tables were filled with workers from the market. They could eat that much food."

"When was that?"

"Forty-five years ago."

"People had larger appetites then, I suppose. The kind of physical labor they did."

"No. People were *fat* then."

A week of inclement weather has passed. The view from each of Durgin-Park's windows is identically alive with a drapery of snow, with people stepping nimbly as though readying for a pratfall. Inside, the rooms are replicatively empty, the sense of intimacy exactly reproduced.

Jean prepares her tables for the evening meal, one aspect of her job that isn't as it always was. "Used to be, not so many came at night. If you ate out at night, it meant you had a lazy wife."

She holds bottles of ketchup, two in each hand. They appear in her grip as canisters of ammunition. She sets them down, then herself. A younger waitress passes her shoulder, touching it lightly. "Thanks for setting me up, Jeannie."

Jean winks. "One of my protégées. I'm the old hen now, the matriarch," she says. "Young people are smarter than we were. They know they can always pick up a waitress job. It's the most transient business there is, restaurants."

The value of things that last. One considers the particular longevity of Durgin-Park as it sits in Faneuil Hall, an area of Boston ambitiously "restored." While the restaurant went about its daily thriving business—serving the market's purveyors, the merchants, the bankers and lawyers from Boston's nearby business heart—the marketplace, itself outmoded, surely died. The warehouses emptied, the area decayed, its commerce now offered to sailors by whores. And so on.

Until developers, drawn to its extraordinary architecture, its location, and its history, brought it back to life with one of those fastidious reclamations that leave every brick looking inexplicably, simultaneously, authentic and brand-new. And true to the market's beginnings, or some would say with them perversely in mind, the dominant feature now of Faneuil Hall is Quincy Market, at its center, housing an imponderable number of booths and shops selling food. Gourmet peanut butter in several granular modulations. Greek popovers. Apple pies, pregnant to term. Spice booths, where fenugreek is as commonplace as pepper.

And all that time, across the way, Durgin-Park has uninterruptedly done business.

"A couple of weeks ago," Jean says, "a family came in. Man, his wife, two daughters. Beautiful girls. *Beautiful.* I used to wait on the parents, but they moved away, and I hadn't seen them in years. Well, the man looked at me and he couldn't believe it. 'Are *you* still here?' And I said to him, 'Yeah, I'm still here. Welcome home.' " She cocks her head slightly. "And it felt real good to be able to say that. To say, 'Yes. I'm still here.' "

Bearings

BOSTON, MASSACHUSETTS

Population: 560,847
Robert Gorges led a settlement party to the Boston area in 1622, but only one of them, clergyman William Blackstone, decided to stay. He built a cottage on the Boston peninsula and lived there alone for eight years. When John Winthrop's party landed in Charlestown, Blackstone invited them to stay on the peninsula, where they would be safe from wild animals.

In 1635 the first public school in the U.S., the Boston Latin School, was founded here; in 1639 the first printing press published Oath of a Free Man *and the first post office was opened, charging a penny a letter; in 1690 the country's first newspaper was published.*

In 1648 the city's first witch was executed.

Boston's penchant for baked beans developed because the dish could be prepared on Saturday, thus allowing the Puritans to observe the Sabbath strictly. The New England boiled dinner was created so the Brahmins could eat well on cook's day off.

Books banned in Boston include Leaves of Grass, Elmer Gantry, The Sun Also Rises, An American Tragedy, *and* Manhattan Transfer.

Boston has the highest cost of living of any major city. Because of the many churches and educational institutions, it is among the lowest in percentage of taxable property.

The greatest traffic jam in U.S. history occurred in Boston—downtown traffic was at a standstill for five hours.

Too Busy to Hate

Art Harris

"**M**y job," says Mayor Andy Young, "is to see that whites get some of the power and blacks get some of the money."

He applies the sole of his soft Italian loafer to the accelerator of the blue Cadillac Seville. Traffic finally begins to move on congested Peachtree Street. He jockeys the sedan around a caravan of semis hauling steel girders for the four new hotels rising from the tough red clay in reborn Atlanta, and roars off.

The mayor is in a hurry to make things happen in the Deep South's brightest urban jewel, proud to have the nation's second-busiest airport, a two-million-plus suburban population sprawl, and a sleek new $100-million rapid rail system to speed all those commuters to the South's undisputed center of commerce. Seven billion dollars in new construction resulted in one hundred thousand new jobs in 1984—enough to give Georgia the fastest personal-income growth of any state last fall.

ART HARRIS was born in Georgia, where his great-great-grandfather made swords for the Confederacy. He is the Atlanta correspondent for *The Washington Post*.

"And Atlanta is just taking off," says Andy Young, self-styled point man for a new southern-fried capitalism that promises to burn bright, but not with the fires of racial unrest that have held back cities such as Birmingham, Little Rock, and Miami. A century and a quarter since General Sherman torched it, Atlanta chooses to keep its peace by igniting the entrepreneurial spirit. It elects to call itself The City Too Busy to Hate. And with the same profit motive that begot Manhattan's "I Love New York" tourism campaign, Atlanta pitches for big business to pack up its mainframes and come on down. Frontier opportunism, biracial harmony, unlimited growth: these are the corporate siren songs Andy Young plays for prospective foreign and domestic investors. To locals he preaches the possible dream: Believe, hustle, share the wealth, and you will receive. A new message for the Eighties: Andynomics!

This crisp January morning he is off to consort with bankers and developers at a meeting critical to the city's immediate future. A new economic development chief must be chosen, a man who can keep commerce at its current breathless pace. He parks the Seville in front of the First National Bank building and sprints for the lobby. "Andy, daaaaahling!" A white Junior Leaguer offers her downy cheek for a kiss. He smiles, obliges, and spins to catch the elevator to a boardroom where a committee of business leaders awaits him. Coffee is served in dainty china cups as Young calls the meeting to order. The mood is convivial, but amid the civilities someone must lay the delicate issue of race on the table. A white developer clears his throat.

"We have an excellent black candidate," he says.

"No," says the black mayor, "I think he should be white."

Andy Young is doing for Atlanta what Reagan has done for America: he's making rich white people feel good again. He believes that someday such an unexpected priority will be toasted as wise by both races in this black-majority city—that his Atlanta will be remembered as a united city. For a century and a half, white leaders here had administered two communities, one white and one black. Still, somehow, Atlanta held together—through the racially violent sixties, the black political take-over of the seventies, and the recent traumatic series of murders of twenty-eight black children. Today racial harmony remains a mutual goal, but in booming Hotlanta, prosperity, not politics, is its greatest incentive.

In earlier days, peace—at least relative peace—was the legacy of a historic alliance between black preachers and white business. Though blacks had no real power, whites ran prospective candidates past black preachers such as the Reverend Martin Luther King, Sr., father of the slain civil rights leader, who died last fall at eighty-four. John Cox, who is fifty-five, remembers the tone of the dialogue when white politicians were invited to speak and face questions at the Hungry Club, an integrated YMCA lunch group founded in 1941. When Cox waited on tables at the club, *hungry* meant "knowledge" to the black membership.

"They [the whites] would say, 'Don't you think So-and-so is all right?' " he recalls. "But it was never 'Who do you want?' "

Still, people were *talking*. It was the only Deep South racial DMZ of its kind, says Cox, now a Delta Air Lines executive. "There was never any confrontation. Everyone acted like gentlemen. Maybe it was hypocritical—or you might call it 'southern manners.' "

That gentility was severely tested in 1961 when black students protesting segregation were jailed and Atlanta faced the same racial crisis that would leave other cities burning. Robert W. Woodruff, the late genius behind Atlanta-based Coca-Cola, summoned business leaders to his office and quietly demanded that schools be kept open at all costs. So to keep the lid on, white mayor Ivan Allen, Jr. proposed that the desegregation of downtown lunch counters and department stores coincide with the desegregation of public schools. That meant a five-month wait. And it was a black preacher—Martin Luther King, Jr.—who demanded black patience from his pulpit.

"I'm surprised at you," he railed, just released from jail on a trumped-up traffic charge. "I find people here who are not willing to wait another five months after waiting a hundred years. . . . If this contract is broken, it will be a disaster and a disgrace. If anyone breaks this contract, let it be the white man."

No one did, and the consideration was returned. Ivan Allen shrugged off the boos of whites as he dismantled the COLORED ONLY signs at city hall, tossed out the ball for the first integrated season of the Atlanta Crackers, hired black firemen, and granted black police the power to arrest whites. Still, when President

Kennedy beseeched Allen to endorse pending civil rights legisla-
tion, "Daddy" King begged him not to—not just yet—lest he
further antagonize Atlanta whites. (Allen did it anyway.) Both
sides understood: riots killed black people—and white business.

No one was more conscious of that than Robert Woodruff.
When Allen proposed that the first black guest be admitted to
the all-white Commerce Club, members sat mute until Woodruff
endorsed the motion. And when white businessmen seemed reluctant to attend a dinner in honor of the Reverend King's Nobel
Peace Prize, another top Coke official scolded, "Gentlemen, we
can't operate from a base where our town is reviled. Coke doesn't
need Atlanta. It's up to you whether Atlanta needs Coke."
Within twenty-four hours, tickets to the dinner were sold out.

By 1973 blacks had the voting majority, and white flight from the
city was a pressing concern. That year, with enough of the white
establishment behind him, Maynard Jackson, a lawyer, became
Atlanta's first black mayor. A bold, articulate man with the girth
of a sumo wrestler, he lost no time in flattening white business.
He earmarked 20 percent of city contracts for minority firms,
holding up $400 million worth of airport construction until whites
complied. He put white bankers on notice: failure to grant loans
and promotions to minorities would mean goodbye to $450 mil-
lion in city funds. The city of Atlanta would bank in Birmingham.
Birmingham. It was a well-aimed insult, and a very real threat. To
integrate the money, Jackson now reflects, he had to get tough.

Into this city of outraged white business rode Andrew
Young, son of a New Orleans dentist, an ordained minister, and
former aide to Martin Luther King, Jr. They knew him as the first
black elected to Congress from the Deep South since Reconstruction and as the firebrand American ambassador to the United
Nations for almost three years, where his fluent radicalese encouraged Third World nations. There he once called the Ayatollah
Khomeini a saint and secretly met with the outlaw PLO—a move
that cost him his job.

Elected mayor in 1981 on a platform of racial and economic
togetherness, Andy Young is championing underdogs again in
Atlanta. This time they are rich, white, and dominant in the
business establishment, but powerless at the polls. Biracial Atlanta

elected a pragmatist, a diplomat who understood the delicate mechanics of compromise.

It made sense in an evolving "New South." If Atlanta's leadership had been transformed, so had the cotton-patch visions of Dixie, from the downtown skyscrapers to the Big Chicken carryout on Highway 41. Tourists hunting for Tara will only find a theme-park Dixie at places like Aunt Fanny's Cabin, where black women dressed in slavery chic earn twelve dollars an hour serving up collards, fried chicken, and gospel songs to 250,000 visitors a year.

Suburbs overflow with yuppie carpetbaggers from Ohio and New York; office parks boast hundreds of foreign firms. Bagels can be bought as easily as biscuits.

All of these changes are borne with a mix of humor and stoicism, yet, according to one New South realist, political transformation was a serious blow to the white Atlanta aristocracy. Charlie Loudermilk, white millionaire founder of Aaron Rents, the nation's largest furniture-rental firm, found himself ostracized by the family blue bloods when he underwrote Young's mayoral campaign for $300,000. Yet he does not condemn them.

"You've got to understand their trauma," he says. "It will take the next generation to appreciate what's happened. Maybe it's too much for this one."

Of his own support Loudermilk insists, "I just felt Andy was the best candidate—and the right color—to lead a city that is 67-percent black. We're far ahead of Houston, New Orleans, or Miami. We've crossed fifty human-relations bridges that others haven't crossed. Can you imagine Andy Young accepting someone like me? A white, conservative Republican?"

"Nothing moves forward without the business community," Andy Young says to the knot of assembled dignitaries and workers on an Atlanta sidewalk. He grabs a jack-hammer, not a shovel, for this ceremonial ground breaking and positions it between his feet, pressing hard. Concrete shards fly on the site of a new office tower. Frowning, a black street vendor shouts at his mayor.

"We goin' to remember you when it's time to vote!"

Andy Young can't hear him over the din; his daily schedule leaves little time to check in with the street constituency. As a nearly full-time big-dollar diplomat, he is too busy hustling in

senate chambers and corporate boardrooms, touting the bottom-
line joys of racial harmony, courting dollars and jobs for his vora-
cious town. Andy Young: the new high priest of profits. He is
Atlanta's ambassador abroad, his pitch more fiscal than philosoph-
ical, as he travels from Lagos to Riyadh in search of investors in
his city's bright promise. He even comes home with petrodollars
from Third World leaders who remember the former ambassador's vocal support. "We owe him a debt even our grandchildren
can't repay," says one Saudi visitor. Back home, white businessmen can hardly believe it. Andy Young is playing *their* song.

"This may sound like heresy," he tells a group of liberal professors
and civil rights veterans, "but I see us gaining more under the
Republicans. We might even be in better shape now than four
years ago."

His audience is rigid with shock as the mayor preaches his
gospel: there *is* salvation through free enterprise; it's okay for the
rich to get richer—so long as their gain trickles down and "bubbles up to feed the hungry, clothe the naked, and heal the sick."

"I've made peace with capitalism," he confesses to the assembled, joining the heretical fold of black conservative leaders
who maintain that twenty years of liberalism has failed to ease
black despair. Of capitalism, the Reverend Mayor Young adjures,
"There's nothing better for coping with sin. It rewards people for
working hard."

On Peachtree Street there are loud amens. But in the black
strips of commerce centers like "Sweet" Auburn Avenue, in
places like Willie's Tavern and the Auburn Rib Shack, there is
seasoned skepticism.

"Andy can do more with white folks than a monkey can do
with a peanut," says black activist Hosea Williams. What he
wants to know is how the mayor plans to cure Atlanta's black
inner-city problems, second only to those of Newark on the poverty charts.

It's true that Young has upped minority city contracts to 35
percent, salted city hall with appointees, and designated a white
police chief to work with a black public safety commissioner. But
many blacks have yet to see the prosperity of Atlanta "bubble up"
in their neighborhoods.

"The secret of Atlanta," Young explained to questioning

black journalists, "is sharing the wealth. We've given out 230 contracts worth $130 million to blacks in the last three years. That circulates to beauty parlors, barber shops, gets young people off the street. That's why we don't have black people jumping up and down . . . like black folk in Jamaica or Miami."

But later he concedes, "Atlanta is overrated as a black paradise." He is sure, however, that conditions *will* improve along Sweet Auburn. Andy Young, in the tradition of black preachers before him, stresses the virtues of timing and patience. He is determined to dispel the serious white ill will inherited from the first black mayor, who squeezed downtown business in order to integrate the money. Guilt-tripping whitey has its limitations as a long-term strategy.

"For the last twenty years white males have been made to feel guilty by everybody," he says. "But you never get progress through guilt. You make people change by making them feel more secure."

Complacency is not something that Atlanta's mayor condones in his city's future leaders, black or white. This he stresses over a meal of prime rib and French Burgundy as he presides at a testimonial to the future of white business and black youth. Citicorp has bestowed generous grants on promising black students. Candles flicker beneath crystal chandeliers at the formerly all-white Commerce Club; waitresses in starched lace attend bankers and black leaders. As the young honorees, all of them poor, timidly experiment with the baffling number of forks, Young raises his glass and toasts Citicorp. He nods at the portraits of white leaders lining the walls.

"They just decided that Atlanta wasn't going to go like Little Rock. And out of that strategy, blacks and whites here set an example for the Southland: working together to share the growth and prosperity of the region."

Addressing the honorees, he is less sanguine.

"Politics doesn't control the world. Money does. And we ought not to be upset about that. We ought to begin to understand how money works, and why money works. . . . You're not going to get nine million folks in Ethiopia eating unless you get money into their economy. If you want to bring about what we preachers preach about—feeding the hungry, clothing the naked, healing the sick—it's going to be done in the free-market system. You need capital. You need technology. You need marketing."

The Reverend Mayor pauses, then delivers his final benediction.

"God bless you, the Lord has given you the opportunity to learn how to make money and to serve."

Bearings

ATLANTA, GEORGIA

Population: 427,000

In 1837 surveyor's assistant Albert Brisbane set the stake that marked the future site of Atlanta at the intersection of two planned railroads. By 1842, when the railroad was completed, there were six houses here.

The city was originally called Terminus, then Marthasville, after the daughter of Georgia's governor.

In 1856 the Atlanta city council denied a request by a black man to open an "ice-cream saloon," calling the proposal "unwise."

The Confederacy lost eight thousand men in the battle for Atlanta; at the end of the battle the city treasury contained $1.64.

Coca-Cola was invented here in 1886 and billed as the "Ideal Brain Tonic."

Atlanta became Georgia's capital in 1867 when the hotels in the old capital, Milledgeville, refused to let rooms to black delegates to the state's constitutional convention. Black representatives were ousted from the legislature in 1868.

In the 1960s Atlanta called itself The City Too Busy to Hate.

Atlanta has the country's largest and second-busiest airport, although 75 percent of the people who pass through it every day are on their way somewhere else.

The
Basket-Case State

David Halberstam

Bobby Knight and I are having lunch at Andy's Country Kitchen, which is some ten miles out of Bloomington. We are friends, unlikely as that may sometimes seem to him, to me, and to anyone who knows either of us, and he has volunteered to help me on my tour of Indiana. It is critical, he feels, that I dine at Andy's. The sign outside, slightly intimidating, says No Public Restrooms. Andy's special for this day is either the salmon patties or the chicken dumplings. Each comes with two vegetables. The price is $2.50. Bobby is delighted. "Better than the Carnegie Deli in New York," he says. "What does a sandwich cost there—nine dollars? Maybe ten dollars, am I right?" He competes, I think, even at lunch; Bobby wants to *win* lunch. Right now in his mind he is ahead at least $6.50.

DAVID HALBERSTAM is a Pulitzer Prize-winning journalist whose love of basketball is well chronicled, most notably in his 1981 book *The Breaks of the Game. The Amateurs,* his account of four scullers trying for the 1984 Olympics, was published by William Morrow in 1985.

The only other people at Andy's are three hunters, and they catch my eye as we catch theirs. They are not pleased to have people here as well dressed, as *alien,* as we are—sweaters, slacks, semiexpensive clothes. They eye us with palpable suspicion. Then they see Bobby. "Bobby Knight . . ." one of them says, " . . . okay." They are hard-looking men, more than just rural—settlers, really. For a moment I cannot think of precisely the right word, and only later does it strike me that these men are *untamed.* I see them and I think of men from those Civil War photos, severe and unbending, expecting little out of life, and rarely, therefore, disappointed by it. Slowly they begin a cross-table conversation with Bobby about hunting. The grouse hunting has not been particularly good, the weather has been too warm. Gradually they are relenting, and accepting him. As they leave, one of them comes over and asks for his autograph. I am stunned; they did not seem your typical autograph hunters. But then, given the culture of Indiana, which is the culture of small towns, and the importance of Bobby Knight in Indiana, for he is easily the most recognizable person in the state, the dominant figure in the world of Indiana basketball, it is not altogether surprising.

He and I are fascinated by the degree to which the sport has become the connecting tissue of the state. The feeling of the state, the nuance of it, he says, remains rural even now, although Indiana is a great deal less rural than it was twenty-five or thirty years ago, and the small towns are drying up. But, he notes, if people do not live exactly as they did thirty years ago, they still *think* as they did then. Even the city kids at Indiana University, he says, are not like city kids from other states. They are different —simpler, less spoiled, probably less sophisticated. There is no brittleness to them. It is as if they are closer to their past. Which is just as well for him, he suggests. The fans do not want their players to be too sophisticated. They want them to be like the kids they knew in high school. They want the kids to show that the game matters.

Indiana is not the only place where basketball has such a powerful hold: there is an area that runs like a belt through parts of Appalachia and into the South; it includes parts of West Virginia, Kentucky, Illinois, Ohio, and Tennessee. This is a section of the country that the American industrial surge never reached, and where the small towns, villages often, neither grew nor died; they just stayed there suspended between life and death. In an atmosphere like that, where so little meant so much, there was only one thing that male (and often female) children did, and they did it every day and every night, and that was play basketball. It was a sport for the lonely. A kid did not need five or six other friends; he did not need even one. There was nothing else to do, and because this was Indiana, there was nothing else anyone even wanted to do. Their fathers nailed backboards and rims to the sides of garages or to nearby trees. The nets were waxed to make them last longer, and the kids spent their days shooting baskets in all kinds of weather. This was the land of great pure shooters, and the true mark of an Indiana high school basketball player was hitting the open shot.

If a small town had a good player, the aficionados would start watching him play when he was in junior high school, and if, blessed event, the miracle had happened and there seemed to be more than one gifted player in the same grade, then the crowds for the junior high school games might be even larger than those for the high school. The anticipation of what might happen in three or four years was almost unbearable (although sometimes it petered out into bitter disappointment when a talented young player failed to grow physically). It was, said Bob Hammel, the sports editor at *The Bloomington Herald-Telephone* and a particular connoisseur of the sport and the state, like a basketball-crazed NBA city about to get the number-one pick in the draft. Friday night was almost a ceremonial event: it was high school basketball night. People did not go anywhere else; about the night there was a ritual observance. College and professional teams learned quickly to schedule their games on Thursdays and Saturdays.

A community's identity came as much as anything else from its high school basketball team. These were towns too small and often too poor to field football teams. (In the fifties, before a major statewide program of consolidation, there were some nine hundred high schools playing basketball and perhaps two hundred playing football.) Basketball became critical in determining a town's identity. It was what the state needed, for there was so little else to do in these small towns. In the days when all this took place, when the idea of basketball was bred into the culture, there was neither radio nor television; it became in those bleak years the best way of fending off the otherwise almost unbearable loneliness of the long and hard winters. There were few ways for ordinary people to meet with one another. The lights in a house went on very early in the morning, and they were turned off very early in the evening. Guests and visitors were rare. There was church, and there was basketball, gyms filled with hundreds, indeed thousands of people, all excited, all passionate. In a dark and lonely winter, the gym was a warm, noisy, and well-lit place.

Basketball worked in Indiana not just because kids wanted to play it but because adults needed to see it, needed to get into a car at night and drive to another place and hear other voices. So it began, and so it was ingrained in the customs of the state. What helped fan the flame was the instant sense of rivalry, the desire to beat the next village, particularly if it was a little larger. The town of five hundred longed to beat the metropolis of one thousand, and that metropolis ached to beat the city of three thousand, and the city of three thousand dreamed of beating the city of six thousand. If it happened once every twenty years, said Hammel, that was good enough. The memory *lasted,* and the photograph of the team members, their hair all slicked down, stayed in the local barbershop a very long time.

That helped create the importance of basketball in Indiana, but what crystallized and perpetuated it was the state tournament. It helps explain why this sport dominated the theology of Indiana as it failed to do in similar states. Outside of Indiana there were state tournaments, but they were divided into classes, usually A, B, and C—A for the large metropolitan high schools, B for the medium-size schools, and then the C for the small country high schools. Indiana was, and is, different. There is only one tournament. Big schools play against little schools. This not only focuses all the attention on a single competition, which strengthens the sense of unity within the state, but also allows the dream to live. In a thousand hamlets in an essentially rural state, the dream is that a tiny school with a handful of boys will go to the state finals and fulfill the ultimate fantasy—beating one of the big city schools, Muncie Central or Indianapolis's Crispus Attucks.

The entire state roots for this to happen again, as it happened once before, in 1954, when little Milan beat Muncie Central as Bobby Plump took the winning shot with three seconds on the clock. In an odd way the tournament summons the dream, and the dream unifies the state; when the dream happens, or at least almost happens, the state rests again comfortably in its myth, that this is still a simple and quiet rural life.

In truth, Bobby Plump and several of the key players on that team did not come from Milan: they were even more countrified than that. They came from Pierceville, about three miles away, a village that consisted of about forty-five people, and to them Milan was the big city, the place they went to if they were lucky and their parents went shopping on Saturday. Milan had a population of one thousand people, and sometimes on Saturday Plump's father would only say that they would go to town and do their trading. Mr. Plump would shop and go to the Odd Fellows, and then Bobby would be able to take in a movie and have something to drink at the soda fountain. Plump remembered feeling bashful and awkward every time he went to Milan, because it seemed so big.

Pierceville, by contrast, had only a grocery store, a service station, and a post office. There was one church, but no resident minister; instead, preachers came on loan from surrounding churches, or local laymen conducted the service. There was no such thing as a fast-food franchise or a movie theater. Gene White, who played on that team, didn't eat in a restaurant until he was thirteen years old, and the restaurant, naturally enough, was in Milan. Cities had restaurants. The Milan kids, White remembered, seemed snobbish at first, and better dressed with more expensive clothes, which probably meant that they bought a better brand of overalls.

This was southeast Indiana. It was all farm country, but the farms were small and the farmers scratched out a marginal living. No one owned very much land and no one ever had very much money; there weren't many people to make money from. In the Plump family, with six children, there was neither indoor plumbing nor a telephone. These were not lives of poverty, as an outsider might have thought; instead, they were lives of simplicity. They had all the basics but precious few luxuries. Growing up, Bobby Plump remembered, there was an unwritten rule that there were a lot of things you just did not ask for, because they could never be attained—like telephones. Bobby Plump wanted one so that when he called a girl he didn't have to walk over to his neighbor Glen Butte's house. Some of the boys' fathers had to travel a considerable distance to hold jobs. It was, in fact, a classic slice of small-town rural life. None of these boys owned a car; their mobility limited, the one thing they could do was play basketball each day.

Of the fathers of the boys who grew up in Pierceville, Plump's worked at the small pump factory in Lawrenceburg, Gene White's father drove a school bus and ran a feed mill, Glen Butte's father drove a truck and farmed, and Roger Schroder's father ran the family general store. It sold groceries, canned goods, clothes, and indeed became the first store in the area to carry television sets. It was also the place where everyone hung out. Mr. Schroder had put two benches in the front of the store, and that was where people came and sat and talked. The store took the place of a local paper, serving as the community's source of information. That made the Schroders the most prosperous of the Pierceville families. The other boys assumed that though they would not go to college, Roger would, because his older sister was already in college. Plump once asked his father if he could have gone to the university without the championship season, which brought a scholarship. "You're the youngest of six kids," his father reminded him, "and I couldn't afford it for them, and I don't see how I could have afforded it for you."

Even by Pierceville standards Plump, whose mother had died when he was five, was painfully quiet. "Bobby's so shy," Gene White's mother once said, "that he won't even ask for a second piece of cake when he wants one." It was as if he could only express himself through playing basketball. They all had baskets in back of their houses. Plump's was somewhat under ten feet, and the court was limited by a concrete back porch that extended into the court and cut down the potential range of their shots. Schroder's was better, ten feet, even with a level court, albeit filled with gravel, which made ball handling hard (though by working on gravel, they were better ball handlers when they finally put the ball on wood). They played every afternoon, and then at night they strung a 300-watt bulb on an extension cord along the house above the basket, tied it to a shovel handle, and used tin sheets to reflect the light down on the court. That allowed them to play until 10:00 during the fall and winter, and until midnight during the summer.

They had grown up together, playing basketball every day. When they were in junior high school they had a good team, and in the eighth grade they lost only one game. After that, people in the Milan coffee shops began to pay attention to them, asking questions about how the team was doing. They had arrived. In their sophomore year in high school they began to sense just how good they were. That year Herman "Snort" (so named for his temper) Grinstead was still coach. There was a moment that season when, angry over their indifferent play and an embarrassing 85–40 loss to neighboring Osgood, Snort kicked seven players off the team and played his sophomores. Eventually he would allow two of the best players back. With the sophomores playing, Milan had beaten some of its toughest rivals. Because of that, there was a sense in the town that they had something. All the players were good, they could all shoot, they could all handle the ball, and they were all unselfish with it. Everyone, particularly Plump, had exceptional speed.

It was becoming increasingly clear that their success was not a fluke. None of them was big: Gene White played center at five feet eleven, but he was smart and had the knack of making opposing centers do exactly what he wanted them to. In their junior year they were even better. In a typical small-town power struggle, Snort Grinstead had been fired. He had bought new uniforms without authorization; there was no money in the athletic budget for them. Snort offered to pay for the uniforms himself, but it was too late. He was let go, and Marvin Wood was hired.

Wood was twenty-four, by his own description an Indiana farm boy who had grown up in a town of seven hundred, his background remarkably similar to that of his team. He had gone to Butler University and played there, and since high school he had known he wanted to teach and coach. Growing up in so small a town, he had few other role models. When he first came to Milan, he made $4,000 a year coaching and teaching; one summer he augmented that by $1,000, working as a night guard in the Seagram building in Lawrenceburg. He was a serious, religious man; if he suggested on occasion that his players go to church on Sunday, he meant it. The only time any of his players ever saw him lose his temper was when one of them cursed during a baseball game. That was the unpardonable sin. He had been told by his own high school coach that Milan had plenty of talent, and he was quickly impressed by his team's ability. What struck him beyond their athletic skills, though, was their rare cohesiveness as a group. They were unusually close even for country boys. They seemed not so much teammates as brothers.

Wood immediately installed the "Hinkle system," developed by Tony Hinkle at Butler, a patterned, deliberate offense that suited the talents of these young, tough, disciplined players. The Hinkle system gave the team the ability to control the ball and thus the tempo of the game; it meant that a team of uniformly good shooters would always be able to get a good shot. This was critical, because playing against bigger, stronger players, they would almost surely be out-rebounded. In their junior year, wanting to slow down the pace of a game, Marvin Wood invented what he called his cat-and-mouse game (years later Dean Smith would name it the four-corner offense). Wood used it to bring other teams out of a zone; it fit his team perfectly.

Wood thought he was lucky to be coaching in an environment like this. He had almost no disciplinary problems. He set curfews during the season, 10:00 P.M. during the week, midnight on the weekends. On New Year's Eve he told them they could stay out until 1:00 A.M. He intended to check up on them. They had better, he added, set their watches to his. That night Bobby Plump and a friend went out on a double date, and on the way back to Plump's house the car broke down with a flat tire. Nevertheless, Plump and his girl made it back to his house by 12:55. They were sitting in the car, in front of the house, when a car pulled up. In it was Marvin Wood. Plump's watch showed 1:00. Wood's watch showed 1:05. Wood's watch won, and Plump did not dress for the next game. It all seemed, Plump thought thirty-two years later, much simpler then.

In their junior year, the dream began. When Milan went to the sectional tournament, a local GM dealer named Chris Volz had the entire team driven there in Chevrolets. He had them driven to the regionals in Pontiacs; to the semifinals in Buicks; and to the finals in Cadillacs. When they won the first game of the regional tournament, that was important, for a Milan team had never before won in the regionals. It made them the best Milan team of all time. That year they lost in the semifinal round of the final tournament to South Bend Central, 56–37. Bobby Plump had nineteen points. That evening South Bend won the state title. Wood was so depressed by the defeat that he thought of leaving coaching, going back to graduate school because he wasn't adequately prepared to coach his team. Instead he decided to stay on. The dream was in motion.

As their senior season unfolded, the whole state began to watch, then hope, then finally believe. The turnouts were so big that Milan's home games were moved to neighboring Versailles, where the gym could seat two thousand, twice as many as in Milan. Milan lost two games in the regular season. Everyone was confident now. Once again Volz supplied them with ascendingly expensive cars to drive to the tournaments. The critical game of the play-offs came in the regional final in Butler Fieldhouse against Crispus Attucks, an all-black school that had a very good team built around a young sophomore named Oscar Robertson.

Wood, watching the sheer power of Attucks and the innate grace and skill of Robertson, hoped that the experience of his own seniors would be enough. Robertson was simply so beautiful a player and so extraordinary an athlete that in a year it would be too late. Oscar as a junior would be too strong for these country boys. Yet Wood was intrigued by the confidence of his team; though other teams were reluctant to play Attucks—a certain apprehension about playing bigger, stronger blacks—his own squad had no such fears. If anything, he sensed, the Attucks players were a little nervous about playing these country boys about whom so much had been written. The Milan dressing room was right next to the drinking fountain in Butler Fieldhouse, and before the game, one by one, the Attucks players all came by for a drink of water, but mostly, Wood thought, to stare and try to figure out who these boys were and what the source of their magic was. Wood told his team to get ahead, try to get a ten-point lead in the second half and then sit on the ball. Milan was able to do exactly that, largely by some very good and very patient shooting.

As the game progressed, his team remained absolutely confident, and in the second half Attucks began to make mistakes under the pressure. Milan beat Attucks 65–52. (In that sense, Wood knew they were lucky in their timing. If these same teams met a year later, he was sure, there would be no doubt about the outcome.) Then Milan beat Terre Haute Gerstmeyer 60–48.

That brought them to the final against Muncie Central. Central was the traditional state basketball power in those days. Milan went ahead early and took a 15–7 lead. It was awesome, Wood thought, to be in a field house that held almost fifteen thousand people, all of them, it seemed, cheering for his team. At the first time-out, Gene White, giving away six inches at center but still the smartest high school player Wood had ever seen, came over to the huddle. He was sure he could handle Muncie's John Casterlow. "Coach," he asked, "what do you want me to do with him? I can move him anywhere you want. I can take him in, I can take him out, or I can put him in the bleachers." Confidence, Wood decided, was not going to be a problem that night.

Then Wood sent his team into his cat-and-mouse offense. Usually that was designed not so much to slow the game down as to control its tempo. This time it backfired. Muncie used the delay to creep back into the game and tie the score, but Milan still took a 23–17 half-time lead. In the second half, though, Milan went dry and did not score a field goal; at the end of the third quarter the score was tied at 26. Wood then decided to stop the flow of the game completely. He would hold the ball until the very end, and only then in the closing minutes would he put it back in play. In those closing minutes, he was sure Milan's experience and smarts would pay off. So at the beginning of the fourth quarter, his team now two points behind, Bobby Plump just stood at half court, holding the ball under one arm. He held it there for four minutes thirteen seconds. At one point in the middle of the stall Plump looked over at Wood. Wood was just looking down at his shoes. Then Milan put it in play, quickly tied the game at 28, and then again at 30. Then, with eighteen seconds left, Milan had the ball and a chance for the last shot. Marvin Wood called time out.

It became the most famous shot in the history of Indiana

basketball. There was no doubt who Milan wanted to take the last shot. It was Plump. He was their best player and particularly good under pressure. Plump, knowing that defenses were keying on him, would spend the early part of a game making sure that the other players got the ball and got it where they wanted it. Late in the game it was different. His quickness—that marvelous first step—put extra pressure on the defense. Gene White suggested that the other players clear out an area for Plump to drive in. Everyone else would move to one side. The ball would go to Plump. He would hold it until there were five or six seconds left, and then he would drive for the basket. Depending on how tightly he was covered, he would either pull up and take a jumper or go all the way to the basket. In a one-on-one situation he was very good at driving around people. (He had, he later reminisced, been doing it all his life at Pierceville. Nobody was quick enough to stop him there, so nobody was quick enough to stop him here.) That meant a defensive man had to give him room.

During the time out, Plump, sensing the crowd, and the noise and the tension, almost fifteen thousand people engulfed in their own madness, felt nervous for the first time. But the moment he stepped back on the court and the ball came to him, he felt oddly calm; all he had to do was play. Jimmy Barnes of Muncie Central was covering him, but Barnes had to play off him a bit because Plump was such a good foul shooter. With five seconds left, Plump started his drive, realized that Barnes was not going to let him go to the basket, pulled up, and with three seconds left took a fifteen-foot jumper. He knew instantly that the shot was true. The ball went in. Little Milan, with a total enrollment of 161, and only seventy-three boys in the entire school, had just lived the dream. People in Indiana had been waiting for it to happen for years, and they have been waiting for it to happen again ever since.

With that, the madness erupted. No one, as Wilt Chamberlain once noted, roots for Goliath. This was David's day. The parade route through Indianapolis was jammed. The crowd for the ceremonies back home in Milan was so great that the police and firemen from all the surrounding towns had to be summoned to help keep order. As many as thirty thousand people showed up. Some had to park nineteen miles away and walk to the town because the traffic jams were so great. For years to come, people would drive thirty, forty, and fifty miles out of their way to go through Milan, like pilgrims to Lourdes, to see if they could figure out what had occurred and why it had happened, and what had made this town different.

For the players, the season changed all of their lives. Where before very few people from Milan went on to college, the entire team now had a chance, and almost all of them went. As going to college, once unthinkable, became possible for them, so it became a possibility for other Milan kids as well. The team became famous, particularly Plump, who received letters addressed simply "Plump, Indiana." Plump went to Butler, where he had a very successful career, setting single-game and career scoring records before going on to play with the Phillips 66 Oilers of the National Industrial Basketball League.

Bobby Plump is forty-eight years old now, and it is thirty-one years since he took the ball with five seconds left and drove to the basket. But that season and that shot still mark him. It is a basic part of his identity. People still think of it (and where they were when he made it) when they see him. When his children, who are grown now, are in distant cities, someone will on occasion recognize the name and ask if they are by chance related to the boy who made the shot that won the state title for that little school back in Indiana. Thrust into the limelight, Plump learned over a long, painful period how to deal with it, how to give a short speech at a banquet. This most rural of boys who had always been so quiet, in part because he felt a little poorer than everyone else, grew in confidence; there was nothing they had, he gradually learned, that he did not have, and indeed he had something they did not have. Eventually he became a very successful insurance agent.

Over the years people have waited for it to happen again. It is harder now. The world has changed. The state has undergone a major reorganization and consolidation of its school districts (there was fierce opposition to the consolidation, not because it meant lesser education for the young people of Indiana but because it diluted precisely the kind of loyalties and identities that Milan represented). Some of the consolidated schools now have names like Southeast Central. The kids do not know one another as the kids in Milan once did; they are not as likely, in Marvin Wood's phrase, to be like brothers. The game has changed as well. The next year Oscar Robertson took his Attucks team to the championship. His team beat an all-black team from Gary. "Watch our colored boys beat the hell out of those Gary niggers," went the joke in white Indianapolis. Robertson's team repeated in 1956. Gradually, with the coming of teams like Attucks, the nature of the game had changed. The players were bigger, stronger, and faster, and they played above the rim. In the past, when the Milans of the world had conjured up big city schools, they had thought of schools with larger enrollments but the same kinds of kids. Now they had to envision bigger schools with bigger, stronger players.

It was harder now for the rural game to beat the city game. One moment brings it home: In the 1956 championship game, the second one for Robertson's team, Attucks played Lafayette Jefferson. Lafayette was a very good team of the old order, not unlike Milan; it played intelligent, controlled, careful basketball. Its players were good shooters. They shot their free throws underhand. In the championship game they did everything right. But it made no difference. Attucks was playing in the air. Blacks, according to myth then, were supposed to come apart under pressure, but Robertson played like a professional—cool, methodical, almost flawless. If he was double-teamed, he always found an open man. If he was played tightly on defense, he deftly faked and drove to the basket. All that raw talent at Attucks had suddenly been disciplined. It was like having an old man in a young body running a team. That night Robertson scored thirty-nine points. The old order had ended.

For Attucks, the hardest thing at first had been getting games. Until 1943, when the black schools were allowed into the Indiana High School Athletic Association, Attucks's teams could play only other black schools and had to go out of state to get enough games. Even when Attucks was finally a member of the association, the big powerhouse schools were wary of playing them, for there was nothing to be gained and a great deal to be lost. So in the beginning only smaller schools anxious to fill their gyms had been willing to schedule them. Nothing had been easy.

If Attucks played on the road, the team had a hard time finding places to eat. Attucks was so poor a school that it did not have a real gym; in desperation, it played most of its home games at Butler Fieldhouse. In those early days, as the team traveled through rural Indiana, the crowds were often hostile. The opposing players themselves were fairly well behaved; an odd kind of basketball etiquette raised sport above native prejudice. If anything, the bias showed more in the referees. It may not have been deliberate, but it was there. Close calls always went the other way, particularly if Attucks was ahead, which it usually was. Coach Ray Crowe told his players that the referees were worth ten points for the other teams, therefore they had to be that much more disciplined and had to work to get a sizable lead. Otherwise, the game would go the other way in the last few minutes. "If you have a big enough lead," he would tell them, "they'll leave you alone. Otherwise they'll referee the score and you won't win." He drilled them, as Branch Rickey had drilled Jackie Robinson, to be disciplined, not to respond to provocation, not to hear racial epithets, of which he thought there were surprisingly few. Talent was not a problem. All the Attucks players came from the "Dust Bowl," the playground nearby, where black kids played day and night, staying on the court only if they won. Years later, Robertson said that playing against white teams had not been particularly hard; what had been *hard* was making the Attucks team. Basketball was already a focal point of black talent, the one thing that all black kids wanted to do, and the competition within the school to make the team was fierce.

In a sense, Robertson thought, he was lucky in the way he grew up. His family was very stable. His father was a butcher. It was a disciplined life. The teachers at Attucks were first-rate. If anything, because there were so few outlets for educated middle-class blacks, they were overqualified. They were strong and sensitive men and women who in many ways could open doors for the children that the parents themselves could not. Crowe was shrewd and strong, Robertson thought. He emphasized to the players that in every game they would be on exhibit. At the same time he kept the dope dealers and the numbers men away from the school; his kids were going to have a chance to go to college if they could possibly make it. Some of them tended to slide away from classes; Crowe would have none of that. He was the home-room teacher for most of them, and he posted their grades so that everyone could see who was not working. He also allowed Robertson to grow to stardom without feeling too much pressure. Robertson himself was beginning to realize that, in some way he had never understood before, he was special at this sport. He was growing taller, from six two to six four, and he could do things that other players could not. His game was never fancy. In fact, some people complained that it was almost machinelike, as free of mistakes as it was of excess. It was as if Oscar had taken the game and reduced it to its fundamentals. Slowly that came through to the fans.

If any one player changed how basketball was perceived in Indiana, it was Oscar Robertson. Attucks's winning a title might have meant a lot of talented but faceless black kids, but Oscar somehow stood out; he was doing what they had always done and admired, and doing it better. It was not possible to love basketball and not appreciate him. Where there might have been deep resentment, there was finally acceptance and admiration, and there was acceptance because there was not the possibility of denial. The Indiana fans were hip and they could understand, long before he went on to excel in both college and the pros, Oscar's true greatness. When Attucks won their first championship, Robertson thought thirty years later, he had been too young to understand it. He had thought it was a game at first. Later he realized it was a piece of history. He remembered there was to be a parade through the downtown, and that thousands of people—black and white—turned out. The route was prescribed, and the officials had been very careful about seeing that it ended up in the northwest section of Indianapolis for the bonfire there; they did not want blacks getting out of control in other white sections of town.

There was one other upshot of the game. In the past, even though there were certain school-district lines that ran throughout the city, blacks, no matter where they lived, were allowed to go to Attucks. After that championship the various coaches had stopped the blacks in their areas from going to Attucks. Robertson, in more ways than he had realized, had helped integrate Indianapolis.

This season, though, for the first time in years, going into the regional finals there was the chance of another tiny rural school winning the championship. A small consolidated school named L&M, or officially Lyons and Marco, with a total enrollment of 132 students in the top four grades and seventy-two boys, fielded a very good team (not lightly put together, either—a good deal of political engineering went into it). Lyons, which is listed on the road map of Indiana (population: 782), is larger than Marco, which is not listed at all and now has a population of about three hundred.

On this night in December, Bobby Knight is driving down to Elnora to recruit Jeff Oliphant, a top player for the L&M team, which is coached by his father, Tom. Actually, the recruitment is more or less completed. Knight absolutely dominates this territory, and there are very few kids whom he wants who do not want to go to Indiana (he lost a young black center from an Indiana parochial school to Notre Dame a few years ago, in part because, as one friend said later, he failed to understand that in conflicts in modern America between church and state, state does not always win). They are playing at a neutral gym in Elnora, partially to accommodate the overflow crowd and partially because the L&M coach wants to get his team ready for bigger tournament games and hostile crowds; this gym is said to seat 4,200, while the L&M gym seats only 1,250. L&M is playing Terre Haute North, which in the glory days used to be known as Terre Haute Gerstmeyer.

Bobby is here scouting. His team is playing better, he has won a couple of close games, but it has been a hard season. He is exhausted from the Olympic Games, embittered by the recruiting violations he feels exist in the Big Ten, and his team is almost always less athletically skilled than its opponents. We enter at Elnora. He looks around the gym and nudges me. "Harley and Arley are here," he says. He is exultant. I have not seen him so pleased since he won the battle of restaurant prices several days ago. "Who are Arley and Harley?" I ask. He points to two middle-aged men sitting together on the other side of the court. He is delighted; Indiana basketball history is with us tonight, and he is about to give me a further indoctrination into schoolboy legends. Harley and Arley Andrews are identical twins, and in the early fifties, rural families being larger than most city ones, they played on the same Gerstmeyer team as their uncle Harold Andrews. The team was known, naturally enough, as "Harley, Arley, and Uncle Harold." In order to confuse referees further as to which Andrews had committed a foul, Howard Sharpe, their coach, made one wear "43" and the other "34." People claimed that at half time Sharpe would have them trade jerseys if one of them was in foul trouble. (Often they'd switch jerseys from game to game to confuse other teams' scouts as well.) If that worked for Sharpe most of the time, it went against him in the championship game in 1953. "They called a foul that Harley committed and marked it against Arley," says Bobby. "The coach protested, but they wouldn't change it. Arley was their best shooter, and he fouled out in the fourth quarter. Terre Haute lost." He looks at me with slight condescension because I need a fill-in on something so basic as this. "Everyone in Indiana knows that," he says. Someone adds that Harley and Arley turned fifty the day before. People in Indiana *know* things like this; they can mark their own ages and their own expanding waistlines by those of the Andrews twins.

The L&M team is deftly put together. Lyons, undergoing something of a revitalization, may now have as many as one thousand people, although it was down to five hundred fifteen years ago. It is hardly an affluent area; there was some marginal coal mining, some small farming, and a little bit of local commerce. Then Dr. Bill Powers, a hometown boy, and a few friends decided to start a clinic. Powers is what is called an activist in big cities, and a doer in small towns. Gradually the clinic has grown, and so has the town; the clinic has three doctors, two dentists, an optometrist, an audiologist, and several other professionals, plus a nursing staff. It serves not just the town but a region with a radius of fifty miles. In a way, its presence is like having a small industry in a town largely neglected by the industrial revolution. Because of the clinic, other stores opened.

Dr. Powers also cares about the identity of Lyons, and about basketball. In a town this size, he says, the priorities are different from those elsewhere. A crisis is someone getting sick with a lingering illness such as lung cancer; it is hard on the community, because everyone here knows everyone else. Powers played at

Lyons years ago, and though the teams were all right back then, they were nothing special. Powers was also the family doctor to both the Oliphant and the Patterson families. The Oliphant family is headed by Tom Oliphant, a Lyons boy who ended up coaching at nearby Worthington. Jeff, in the American tradition of coaches' sons, is a very good prospect, albeit most likely for the dread Worthington High. Meanwhile, Tony Patterson, also an excellent prospect, attended L&M. Patterson was as good a player as the town had boasted in years. Mrs. Oliphant, by even greater chance, worked as a receptionist at Powers's clinic. Gradually Powers began to talk up the idea that Tom might want to come over to coach at L&M and bring Jeff with him. Jeff could play for L&M in his junior and senior years. That meant the Oliphant boy could play with the Patterson boy. Jeff knew about Tony Patterson and Patterson knew of Jeff; the idea of playing together was a powerful magnet.

By coincidence, one of the nurses in Powers's clinic was on the Lyons school board and was amenable to a change in coaches; it was not hard to find others who were sympathetic to the idea, including Robert Patterson, Tony's father, who was also on the board. It was well within the established priority of small Indiana towns, where the requirements were first for a good doctor and second (though the order *could* be reversed) for a good high school basketball coach. Soon the deal was done; the old coach was let go, and Tom was hired to replace him. Someone said, however, that the Oliphants were having trouble finding a house in Lyons. "Hell, in that case we'll build them one," a local banker was reported to have said.

On this night it is like going back in time. Every seat in the Elnora gym is taken. Terre Haute is the much-feared big city to these fans. The crowd is certifiably rural. It is a surprisingly old crowd, not just high school kids. Terre Haute is bigger and faster. There are three black starters, and the center looks a good six feet nine. L&M is much shorter—Oliphant is six six and a half, Patterson six five and a half. But slowly L&M pulls away, more by not making mistakes than by anything else. Bobby is studying Oliphant, who moves nicely around the basket and always seems to be in position.

We leave early. Knight always leaves a game early, because

he wants to beat the traffic. He is pleased with what he's seen of Oliphant. Good passer, good hands, already well coached and disciplined, will fit nicely into the Indiana program. An agreement with both coach and son has already been worked out that will work to everyone's benefit: because IU is short of scholarships this year, Oliphant will come as a walk-on in his first year, probably red shirt, and then get a scholarship for four years. As a five-year student, he can pick up a master's degree if he so chooses.

"What do you project him as?" I asked Knight. "Small forward?"

But Knight insists he doesn't project such particulars. "I may be ten years behind the times," he says.

We drive through the night, a few friends of his, two assistant coaches, and two writers. They are talking basketball and I am thinking that with the exception of a rare team like L&M, Indiana high school basketball has changed because the state has changed. Rural communities were losing their identity anyway; small farmers were finally giving up and moving to the city, and as farms were being consolidated so were schools. Besides, the lives of the people who stayed behind have changed. They know what goes on not just in the next town but in Washington and in foreign countries. There are more stimuli now, more alternatives in life, more things to occupy their time. Even people in the smallest hamlets have color television sets, and that means that they are no longer alone, they are able to bring the world into their living rooms, whether it is news, sports, movies, or even wars.

High school basketball is simply less important. The state tournament still matters, but there is less magic to it. There are other distractions: one can watch the NFL and major-league baseball and the Olympics. There is a professional football team in Indianapolis. Mostly there is Bobby Knight's team in Bloomington, which is carried on a statewide network and has become the focal point of the fever. The state, because of television, has replaced the village as the operative community. The nature of the culture has not changed; the size of the community has. The new village is now the state of Indiana. Ohio State and Illinois have replaced the neighboring village as the community to war against. But sports here and elsewhere still mean as much, probably too much. It was, I thought, easy to measure the popularity of the sport in the old days as a safeguard against an unrelenting loneliness. Now it's different; people live in modern instant subdivisions and have neighbors only a few feet away, and they have their television sets connecting them to the world. In some ways they care as much or more about sports than ever. The hardest thing to measure here or anywhere else is the new loneliness.

███

Bearings

BLOOMINGTON, INDIANA

Population: 53,045
Bloomington was organized as a township in 1818; town plots were advertised in Ohio, Indiana, and Kentucky newspapers. The first land auction brought more than $14,000. Early storekeepers served whiskey free to their patrons.

Bloomington's first industry was salt, which was first removed from salt springs in the area in 1822. Indiana University was built in 1823.

Bloomington's citizens took their goods to market in Louisville, a five-day trip they called "going to the river."

In 1893 Indiana's first basketball game—and the first ever contested outside Massachusetts—was played above a tavern in Crawfordsville.

That decade's culinary craze was oyster stew.

Class warfare—between freshmen and sophomores at Indiana University—erupted in 1904. They roamed the streets armed with scissors to cut off the hair of the enemy.

Hoagy Carmichael wrote "Stardust" and "Georgia on My Mind" in a Bloomington restaurant, now a pizza parlor.

███

True Blue

Lynn Darling

In a softly falling snow Falco Paterra drives down to the gates of the National Works steel mill, the place that for thirty-four years defined his life. The mill is nearly closed now. There is nothing much to see except the maze of long, low buildings and rust-reddened smokestacks, no noise except the gossip and laughter of the security guards, but it remains an enormous presence, flanking the town of McKeesport for two miles along the Monongahela River.

It is still a little strange for him to see the mill this way, cold and quiet, strange to see the town this way. Downtown McKeesport is almost empty. The display windows of the big department stores are covered, giving the city a blind, groping quality. Deserted watchtowers look over the center of the town, where the railroad once ran, where the long trains of coal cars sometimes took half an hour to pass by. CLOSED UN   THER NO-TICE says the sign over the last movie theater.

LYNN DARLING was born in Pittsburgh, where her grandfather worked in the steel mills. She is a frequent contributor to *Esquire*.

Falco among the ruins: he is a working man, the son and the grandson of steelworkers, blue-collar all of his life. He is fifty-four years old, the father of three children, a square-built man with deep-set, dark-circled eyes and a voice that is perpetually hoarse, as if it had been worn away by the constant crash and roar of the mill. He wears a soft cloth cap over his head, partly because it is cold outside and partly because he is a little self-conscious about growing bald. Beneath his shirt he wears two medals: one of Saint Christopher, who protects the traveler, and the other of Saint Peter, "who was like me," he says, "weak and strong at the same time."

He is an ordinary man, leading an ordinary life, of the kind that usually become visible only when they crack, when anger or violence forces them open and the headlines examine the fragments for whatever meaning they can find. But Falco didn't crack. All his life he has done what has been expected of him and drawn his strength and his pride from the fact that he is the author of his family's fate. Doing right was the way he gained control of his life, in a world dominated by the arbitrary power of the mill.

But now there is nothing to do.

Now Falco's family is grown and the mill is closed and he has discovered that unemployment is a kind of exile from the rock on which he anchored himself. And yet he seems untouched by the bitterness and sense of betrayal that hang over much of McKeesport. "We're down, but we're not out," he likes to say to the wraithlike old men who were the local football heroes of his youth. The old men smile and nod their heads.

The mill was supposed to go on forever. That was part of the deal in the Monongahela Valley. And since the turn of the century, things stayed pretty much the same there as long as the steel was being made. It is a place of taverns and churches, of neat small homes on steep twisting streets that curve precipitously past the geography of rock and river. It is a place of hard work, saving grace, and cherished rituals, the kind of place where the commercials on late-night local television advertise sales on communion dresses.

But now the valley is dying, and the little towns that held the mills in their dependent embrace are dying, too. It was always a place of good times and bad times, but now the good times seem to be permanently gone. Now it's the hour for holding on to whatever's left, and what is left is family. It was the way the immigrants survived when they arrived here, and it is the way their descendants survive now. Family: it's what they preached in this valley. You've got nothing but your family.

Falco remembers so clearly what it was like when he was young, as if memory were a lighthouse calling him home. Years ago his world was round and whole, as smoothly perfect as an egg. He grew up in the Third Ward, hard by the river and the railroad tracks, where a train rushing by at night could shake a boy loose from his dreams. Everyone had pretty much the same then, which is to say, not much of anything, except the urge to have something better.

Like almost everyone in the valley, his neighbors came from someplace else. Falco's people, a family of black-haired, handsome men, came from Palena, Italy. The Paterra brothers all worked in the hot mill, and they all played football. Even Uncle Herb, who lost all his fingers in the mill, still found a way to catch the ball, to keep on playing. On Moran Field there was always the possibility of one clean moment—the bright arc of a ball, the anticipated play—that brought with it a giddy peace. Sports kept the community together; when you had nothing else, you could always play ball.

In the summer the old Third Ward gang, Flizzie and Clang and Bo and the rest, played street hockey and baseball and cooled off in the public pool. It was the season of national-day picnics and weddings. Every summer the Holy Family Polish Church held a carnival, and every summer Falco won a basket of fruit.

In winter the days were given over to the discipline of the nuns of St. Mary's German Catholic School, who kept the peace with wooden paddles and bamboo rattans. The priests were like God then: one of them called the boy Tony because, he said, there had never been a saint named Falco.

When Falco was in the ninth grade, his father got a better job in the mill and was working more steadily. They moved away from Railroad Street, up the hill to a dark-gray house on Jenny Lind Street. Falco's grandparents lived next door. There he danced with his aunts on the hard wood floor of the sun parlor and watched his grandfather make dark, sweet wine from the grapes he planted on the arbors in the back, and he grew up safe in a world that pointed him like an arrow to the mill.

"You wish it could be like that again," Falco says. "Things were a lot simpler then. You knew you could get a job. If you were willing to put up with the heat and the dirt, you could get a job anywhere."

He drives slowly through the old neighborhood, past empty lots and faded frame houses. He knows just about everyone he meets, the cop on the beat and the number baron's nephew, the pensioner heading home from 12:30 Mass. He still attends St. Mary's Church, but the stern-eyed nuns are gone now, and in their place is Father Tom Smith, who calls himself the Singing and Dancing Priest and forages for souls in the local supper clubs, wearing top hat and tails. Life is a gas, he sings, it's a ring-a-ding-ding.

There is talk that they'll tear the mills down and put up an industrial park, and then maybe the valley will live again. The politicians and the developers like to say that the area is changing its image, that a service-oriented high-tech economy will bring a new prosperity. The mill workers know what that means—they'll be flipping hamburgers instead of making steel. You can't stake a future on the minimum wage: the means to make it on their own will have gone for good.

Falco started in the mill when he was nineteen. He remembers the date: May 26, 1950. He was scared that first day, all that hot metal flying around and these guys getting so close to it he wondered how they didn't get burned. He began to see that working in a mill was like living in a foxhole. The pride came from knowing what to do in ridiculous, often dangerous situations. Once in a while, on the open hearth, there would be a wild heat, somebody was going to get burned up. You never knew.

It takes a man ten years just to learn his way around a steel mill. Falco started in the labor gang, digging ditches. He kept his mouth shut, did his job, lent a hand when he could. He worked the soaking pits, where a man walked knee-deep in water. He scaled away the crust that formed when the ingots were soaked, while the ash fell and the heat blazed. He stamped the steel and cut and hauled it. He learned the hot mill, from the catwalks to the pouring floor, the blast furnace, the open hearth, and learned how it all came together, the complicated alchemy that turned the red-orange of molten iron into cold, blue-gray steel.

Three years after he started in the mill, he married. Falco met Edna at a Sunday-afternoon football game when she was still in high school. She was standing on the sidelines, and he practically plowed into her on one play, covered with mud. The next time he saw her was at the Friday-night dance at St. Stephen's, where you could dance all evening for a dime. They danced to Sinatra singing "Five Minutes More," and after that no one else asked her to dance. He walked her home that night, but he waited two months before he kissed her.

Young men grow up fast in the valley. They marry girls they've known all their lives and have their children quickly. The talk, even when it is overheard in restaurants and shopping centers, is intensely intimate and interconnected, hungering for the latest dispatch on Jenny's other son, Karen's younger sister. So they raise their children and fly them like flags, a salute to their ability to make good.

Now some of the younger unemployed steelworkers are punch-drunk on their anger, having watched wives and children slip away like dust motes on the air. "Love goes out with the paycheck," they say between clenched teeth. But it was different for Falco and Edna.

They started out with nothing—rented rooms and borrowed furniture. A month after they were married, Falco was laid off. In the beginning that threat was always over their heads. He never knew how much he was going to work.

Edna was nineteen when she left her father's house for her husband's house. Two days after they were married, Falco went to work. It was a night shift, she remembers, because she had never in her life been alone at night.

"You're so stupid then," Edna says. "You don't think about being laid off, about not working. That was all I wanted out of life. Times were tough, but times are tougher now. We always figured things would keep getting better. We wanted to see our kids do better than we did, and if you have that to shoot at, you can make it."

There were years that ate all their savings, when they had to cash in an insurance policy in order to live, years when Falco's parents helped keep him afloat, but, he says, "She never made me feel bad about it."

"I always felt," Edna says, "that we were in it together." She is still a pretty woman, with dark eyes easily moved to laughter and to tears. There was a temper in her, too, in her younger days, she says; her husband's not so sure the past tense is appropriate.

"I have to give Edna 95 percent of the credit," he says.

"I knew how to save you money, didn't I?" she replies. "I knew how to stretch a penny. If I only had a dollar, I could still make supper on a dollar."

They had three children, two girls and then a boy, who grew up in the narrow two-story house with white aluminum siding they bought four years after they married, the house they live in still. They had wanted a brick home—there was more status to a brick home—but there was always something more important they needed the money for: the girls' weddings and their son's college education.

Falco didn't have much time with his children. He worked around the clock. Day shift followed night shift followed afternoon shift, a week of each. There was just enough time to get adjusted to one before it was time for the next. There was so much that he missed. Falco rarely saw his kids opening their presents on Christmas morning, and he never saw the way his daughters looked coming down the stairs in their prom dresses. His gift was the money he could bring them and the fierce watchfulness he cast over them.

Falco made the rules that kept them out of traffic when they were young and the harsher rules that protected them from even faster moves later on. His vigilance drove his daughters crazy.

That was how he kept them safe. Safe from the ways in which the world in the late seventies was changing—the drugs and the defiance and the fights between black and white. There in the little white house on the sloping hill, he surrounded them with his sense of right.

Janet and Linda followed their mother's lead and married young, to men who worked in the mill. For both of them, marriage wasn't a psychological sandbar on which to strand a life—it was a way to live. "I think my mom and dad are the reason why when I was nineteen I was ready to marry Mark," Linda says, "because they made it look so easy to run a family. I know they never had a lot of money to work with, the hard years that they had to put in, but we always ate, and when we needed clothes it was always, 'We'll get it.' They managed to make the money go."

Falco and Edna had made a promise to themselves: their children would not go through the uncertainty they had survived. But it didn't work out that way. Linda and Mark made a fast start, a baby and a two-story brick house within a year; but when Mark was laid off from the mill, the only work he could get was his current job, as a night watchman for the county.

It's been a little easier for Janet and Dan. Dan went back to college while he was still in the mill. Afterward, during one of the layoffs, he took a job with Equitable Life Assurance at less than half the pay. When the mill came back up for a while, Dan was tempted to return. It was Falco who told him to stay where he was.

Dan had a promotion recently, and the couple is looking for a bigger house. Edna teases them about leading the good life now. But Janet is still angry for her father.

"I'm bitter because he went to work every day and he didn't call in sick because it was Christmas. He gave it all. He sweated for the money to buy our dresses, he sweated for it all, and it wasn't a sacrifice, it was the right thing to do. He deserved more. It wasn't just a job to him, it was everything."

The last job Falco had in the mill was the one he liked the best. It was an office job, scheduler-expediter. He tracked the steel from beginning to end, saw it through its phases, scrounged and connived to get the heat up on time. In time he was talking to the bosses, telling them what to do when things weren't going right. Sometimes they'd even call him at home. It was a good job, it had prestige. He took pride when he heard the men say, "Falco's working tonight; we're gonna make money tonight."

It was steady work, and it paid well. By the time Jeff went to high school, Edna says, the other kids thought he was a rich man's son. They started saving for his college education when he

was still in grade school. He finished first in his class at McKeesport High School.

Last summer Jeff graduated from Carnegie-Mellon University and went to work in North Carolina for IBM, making nearly
as much money at the beginning of his career as his father did
at the end of his. Are things different for his son? "Yes," says his
father softly. Will they change him? "I hope not," he says, but
in the end Falco must know it's a gamble.

Each generation is stepping up and stepping away. Falco Paterra
wanted his son to go to college. Paul Paterra, Falco's father,
wanted his sons to stay on the right side of God and the law.
"They stayed out of trouble, that was the main thing," he says.

Paul Paterra is old now, pale and bent by recent heart attacks, and his gaunt frame bears only mute testimony to the
power and strength that still fire the imagination of his son. He
started in the mill when he was fourteen and retired ten years ago,
when he was sixty-five. The old man still remembers how his
childhood ended, how he finished the eighth grade in the morning and went to work that afternoon, walking past the pool and
into the hot mill, where grown men fainted from the heat. "You
learn to live tough," he says of that time.

It's hard now for the father to see his son tossed out of work
at such an early age. "He don't let on how he's doing. So many
times, we try to give him something, and he says, 'No, Mama, I
don't need it.' Oh, he's proud, I told her, he's too proud. I try to
give him money or something, we pretend it's a gift, but he's too
proud to take anything from us. He's smart though, he keeps
himself occupied."

Falco carried his responsibilities in the mill with pride, but
he had no illusions about his importance. The mill had a way of
reminding him just where he fit in. One day he found a dead man
there. It was the man who always gave him the hot-metal tonnage
reports. He found him slumped over his desk.

He ran out to call someone, but the only one around was
Yuno, the dwarf from the janitorial crew, who said, "What's the
matter, what's the matter with Tom?"

"Don't go in there, Yuno," Falco said. He told him Tom was
dead.

Yuno went running by Falco, screaming like a banshee.

Falco called the guards, and when they came he helped them to carry Tom out and put him in an ambulance.

As he was walking back through the mill, one of the observers, Ross Azzarello, walked by and said, "Hey, Falco, what are you doing there?" and Falco said, "Keep quiet, Ross, I think old Tom is dead." And just then, as they were standing there, the whistle blew loud and long and sharp, and that meant "Give us an ingot now, we're ready to roll it."

Falco said, "Look at that, Ross, here's this guy dead here, and we ain't even shut the mill down, we're still rolling ingots, nobody even cares that he's dead. They hauled that guy out and they never lost a minute. To them he's nothing."

"When me and you go, Falco, it's going to be the same," Ross said. "They ain't gonna care about us."

But it wasn't quite the same when Falco went. The end came slowly, with a series of signs that something was wrong. Work that was normally done in their end was taken someplace else. A machine would break down, and instead of repairing it, they'd steal a part from another place in the mill, cannibalizing the machinery.

Falco started running in the hours after his shift was finished —it was a way to release the dread. He didn't want the family to know, didn't want his wife to worry; Jeff was still in school.

But it came finally, the last day the rolling mills ran. It was in March 1982. Falco was the last man out. Before he left he had to tally everything up, do the inventory, finalize all the records. He stayed a couple of hours, had a last look around, then walked out of the mill alone. He took the bag that held his clothes and work shoes, but he left his helmet inside. He figured he was still coming back.

"In the back of my mind, I always had hopes that the fact that we were so skillful down there would convince the company to keep the work here," he says. "I couldn't see them being dumb enough to let the work go elsewhere, where it wouldn't be handled the right way, like we could handle it in this plant. I didn't know that there wasn't going to be the orders to bring here. Or anywhere."

He went to the unemployment office to collect the benefits that were due him, but he couldn't stand it, the way the men standing in line tried to hide from one another. He found out that with his seniority he could go back into the mill if he were willing to work on the janitorial crew. It was the bottom rung of the ladder, but it was work. He called his daughters to make sure they wouldn't be embarrassed; they told him they would be proud.

It was torture going in there in the mornings, he remembers. He'd walk into the offices of the managers who used to consult him, and they'd look up and smile and say, "Well, if it isn't the expert from the lower end," just as they always had, only this time all he had to say in return was, "Where's your toilet at?"

They wouldn't believe it at first, the smiling young men who had come to him for help. But he showed them his bucket and his mop, and they showed him where the washroom was.

Even that job came to an end after a few months. Last year Falco got the letter telling him to come in and sign up for his pension, and whatever lingering hope there was finally had to be put to rest.

It was over. He had watched his world slide slowly away, but through it all he kept to his code. He worked hard, he provided for his family, and against forces larger than himself he made them safe. In the end he forged a kind of heroism in the promises that he kept.

But now that Falco is retired, the days stretch long and empty at times, and he and Edna are careful to stay out of each other's way. In the spring and summer he coaches high school baseball, in the fall he referees high school football, and in the long winter months he runs. Every Tuesday Edna volunteers down at the Allegheny County home for senior citizens; on Fridays she brings them Holy Communion.

The future now is narrow. The modest expectations of a trip to Italy, a newer house, have been replaced by the fear that the new brick senior-citizens' apartment building will be their final home. But the deepest regret is for their grandchildren. "I would have liked to have been around so that if they needed money for college, I could have helped them," Falco says. "I'm still hoping I can do it somehow." He is still a young man, too young to have nothing to do, but too old to be hired for a new job, he has discovered. Yet he still goes through the classifieds, looking for something to fill up the days. "I'm still not used to it," he says. "Every day, you have to think about what you're going to do."

Jeffrey Paterra drives down the broad boulevards of Charlotte, North Carolina, in a brand-new car, dark-haired, intently serious, and very young. His voice is already swept clean of a Pittsburgh accent, meeting the discreet demands of his corporate culture. Still, there are echoes of his father in the large, dark eyes, in the quiet guard he has set on his privacy.

He lives alone in an apartment overlooking the tennis courts in a stucco townhouse complex with other young singles he rarely sees. At night he watches MTV or listens to Bruce Springsteen or the Who, cooks his dinner, and goes to bed on time, for it does neither him nor IBM any good if he doesn't get his rest.

He works on flextime in an office building of white stone and smoked glass, and he talks proudly of how well Big Blue takes care of its employees. He is a mechanical engineer, but his work is confidential, something to do with the development of a new printer.

He chose IBM after interviews with thirty other companies. He flirted with the automakers, but the environment reminded him too much of the steel industry: the sheet-metal siding on the big plants, the union influence, the history of layoffs.

He talks about the mobility he will have, the places he wants to go. No, there is nothing about McKeesport he will miss, except for his family. He had known almost from the beginning that his life was going to be different from Falco's. He knew he would get a job that was more secure than his father's, a decent, respectable job. "I don't think that working in the mill was not respectable," he says. "I think it is, but I think a lot of people have a misconception about the kinds of people that work there."

He remembers watching a football game last year, the Bears against the 49ers. The announcers were talking about Mike Ditka. They talked about how, as a player, he'd been nicknamed Iron Mike, how he came from the valley, that his father was a steelworker. And, they said, he played like it.

"And I wanted to say, 'How does the son of a lawyer play football?' " he remembers. " 'Does he go for his books and say *whereas* and *therefore?*' I don't know. So what were they trying to imply, that he would bite, scratch, and kick? . . . I didn't like that at all, really. Because it meant that he had different values, would approach anything in life differently than the son of a lawyer or a doctor or anything else."

He talks to his parents every week. "A lot of things happened to our family," he says, "and a lot of people may consider them harsh, but they never seemed bad, because we knew that the family was there, and that held everything together. There was nothing to worry about, because we always had each other. That sounds like something out of one of those TV shows, but it's really true."

One summer, between semesters at Carnegie-Mellon, Jeff worked in the steel mill. He learned some lessons there. "Your father is your father," he says, "and you may not analyze him the way you might someone else, maybe because you don't feel like you're entitled to. When I was in the mill I could see that a lot of people there may have been wishing they were doing something else, but that wasn't the way their life worked out. But they knew they couldn't just quit and go to college and get a degree, that was not realistic, so they just . . . put up with it. They were doing it because they had responsibilities, they had a family and they had to provide for them. I thought that was really admirable. You could see it in their faces almost, that some of them didn't want to be there and yet they were, every day, they were there."

At the end of the summer the company offered the college boys permanent jobs. Jeff asked his father what he thought of his going into the mill.

Falco said he'd shoot him first.

Bearings

PITTSBURGH, PENNSYLVANIA

Population: 415,000

In 1753 twenty-one-year-old British army major George Washington passed the future site of Pittsburgh and pronounced it "extremely well situated for a fort." Fort Prince George was built in 1754 and was immediately captured by the French.

In 1786 Hugh Brackenridge wrote of Pittsburgh, "This town in future time will be a place of great manufactory. Indeed, the greatest on the continent, or perhaps in the world."

Charles Dickens visited Pittsburgh in 1842 and commented, "It certainly has a great quantity of smoke hanging over it." In a more eloquent moment he termed the city "hell with the lid off."

The city's first antismoke ordinance was proposed in 1804; the first one was implemented in 1946. Until the ordinance was put into effect, Pittsburgh was often so dark that the streetlights had to be lit during the day.

Today one steelmaker operates within the city limits.

Pittsburgh lost twenty-four thousand manufacturing jobs between 1970 and 1980, yet 50 percent of the city's residents have lived here for twenty years or more. In the same period the total employment grew by 10 percent.

The city's largest employer is the University of Pittsburgh.

For years the city's unofficial motto was "A smoky Pittsburgh is a healthy Pittsburgh." It has been known as Steel City, The Smoky City, and The City of Champions, but Pittsburgh-born quarterback Dan Marino calls it "a beer-and-a-shot town."

PART 3

AMBITION AND CONTINUING PROSPERITY

LAFAYETTE, LOUISIANA
Striking It Rich

MIAMI, FLORIDA
Assimilation

NEW YORK, NEW YORK
Elegance and Propriety

DALLAS, TEXAS
Giantism

WESTWOOD, CALIFORNIA
Youthfulness

ABOARD THE EASTERN SHUTTLE
Power

Mr. Jimmie
Hits Pay Dirt

John Ed Bradley

Some writer from an uppity home-living magazine once described Mr. Jimmie Owen's house off Bayou Parkway as a "marble mansion" and wrote that the old man had been worth $30 million at the peak of his career in the early 1960s—all of it achieved with no better than a sixth-grade education; the story also said Mr. Jimmie had served as a doughboy in World War I. The old man himself, feeling mildly wounded by this misrepresentation, went about town addressing the magazine's mistakes: he'd attended Southern Methodist University in Dallas and had served only as a go-nowhere pilot in the Army Air Corps, based at Benbrook Field in Texas. When asked about the magazine piece, Mr. Jimmie would clutch the neck of his aluminum walking cane to stress the extent of his indifference and say, "just as long's they spell my name right. . . . " His wife, Corita, wearing a funny face of aggravation, was always one step behind him, saying, "And our house is certainly no mansion."

JOHN ED BRADLEY grew up near the oil fields in Acadiana and attended Louisiana State University.

Old man Jimmie could have passed for the fellow who sold five-cycle washing machines at the Montgomery Ward, but that wasn't his game. He liked to wake up every morning and put on a freshly cleaned coat and tie, even when he had no plans to leave the house. He had a big, strong voice and wore black horn-rimmed glasses. He wore tweed and polyester in a world that called for khaki and denim, and his shoes always looked newly polished or bought. His face was ancient and round—a handsome "Moon Pie face," I liked to call it—with no hard angles to hold the light. And he was probably the only fellow in south Louisiana who could quote Shakespeare and chew tobacco at the same time.

One day last winter Mr. Jimmie took Corita to the Petroleum Club for lunch and met up with Alfred Lamson, a highly successful explorationist from my hometown who had also been wrongly depicted in the magazine story. Lamson was sitting at a big round table, eating candied yams, black-bean soup, and a fried veal cutlet. Mr. Jimmie said, "You say you never wrote Cajun songs in your life, and they said you did. I guess they blundered on you too, didn't they, Al?"

"I guess they most certainly did, Mr. Jimmie," Alfred Lamson said, taking a sip of tea. "I guess they got us both pretty good."

"Just as long's they spell my name right," Mr. Jimmie said.

And Corita whispered behind him, "I hope you know that we never for a day lived in a marble mansion."

Early last December I went back home to Opelousas, Louisiana, a town of about twenty thousand people that sits like a little blemish on the upper lip of Acadiana, and drove down roads I had not traveled in what seemed like a decade but was probably half that. Everything about the place seemed to have shifted in my absence, picking up a thing or two as it did so, embracing more of what was than what is. It appeared to have turned full circle and returned to the country of my growing up, as wide and empty as some childish dream of heaven, and I imagined myself no longer alone but a passenger in a car filled with many people:

We had been on our way to see the oil well on my grandfather's property, and Po Po was driving and singing Cajun ballads that made his voice crack and roll at all the sad parts. I felt, as did the rest of my family in the car, that simply by visiting the

well I would somehow be made different, changed in the way the
Queen of Angels priest said money always changes people. They
were going to strike it rich at Po Po's place and make up for his
one terrific failure at using the business of oil to draw the curtain
on his unexcellent past. A few years before, he had tried to get
a patent on a contraption that one of his drinking buddies had
invented, one that was supposed to filter and cleanse oil on boats
that serviced the galaxy of rigs in the Gulf of Mexico. He had lost
more than $20,000 in the deal, which my father had called lame-
brained, and turned to drinking rotgut varnish at the Plantation
Lounge in town and killing good time on those stupid Yambilee
tours organized by the sponsors of the yam festival.

But now he was stepping quickly across a cattle guard and
through a field of new potatoes, getting closer and closer to the
great derrick strung up with lights like white fire. He had turned
suddenly and was saying something I could not hear for the noise
of steel slapping steel and the earth rumbling, but he looked
happy and satisfied, as though he'd had his fill or was about to.
His tie flapped on the breeze, and his arms were outstretched
before him, with half-moons of perspiration under each sleeve. He
was reaching to grasp something he would never know in his life,
never know because the land turned out to be dry. There was no
oil, and the rig came down with his dream of being forever rich.

That all came back to me last time I was home. And now
I was going through it all again: the farm reports on KSLO, the
way Po Po could never remember the words to "Jole Blon," and
the smell of Early Times and smoke, *his* smell. It was no good,
looking that far back, knowing how he died, how he lived, and
wondering, What was it you were saying to me, old man? And
why does it matter now?

I knew old man Jimmie Owen's house long before I knew him,
knew it from my days living just twenty miles down the road and
driving by his place on empty Saturday nights. We'd do this
sometimes after watching dirty movies at the drive-in picture
show off Johnston Street in Lafayette or after getting thrown out
of Mother's Mantle or the Keg Lounge for lack of proper identification. We'd sit staring at the great house or at the other enormous homes on Bayou Parkway, just staring at them without

saying a word, until somebody needed the bathroom and stepped outside. There was always a pint bottle of Boone's Farm Apple Wine to share and get happy on, and a ten-cent cigar somebody stole from Mr. John Marino's grocery in Opelousas.

I always thought the most impressive feature of the house was a matching pair of concrete balls on the brick pilings out front, issuing a declarative statement of wealth and class. Every few minutes we'd spot shadows floating like moths across the front picture windows, but never did a body emerge to verify the images of human perfection we held in mind. A long driveway ran up to the kitchen window on one side and disappeared behind a neat privet hedge that stood about waist-high. The house was built on the bank of the Vermilion River, with floors of Alabama marble an inch thick and brick from an old Baton Rouge warehouse that had been cannonaded by Union gunboats moving up the Mississippi. There was a door in front that never opened, and only once or twice did a car back down the drive.

None of us really knew Mr. Jimmie then, but I did know he was legendary, a wildcatter from Texas who came to south Louisiana after World War II looking for oil in the fields of Acadiana, and finding it. You saw his picture in the newspaper every so often: Mr. Jimmie giving money to a hospital or a college, or posing in a fancy Mardi Gras gown. He was a do-gooder, a fifty-year Mason with a record of clean and gracious living. He drove an Olds Ninety-Eight with power everything, and Ronald Reagan had once come by his house for a dinner party, years before he was elected President. Mr. Jimmie and Corita sent out Christmas cards showing a big cake of ice in the shape of a Republican elephant melting on the cinder-block wall that ran down the property line.

Early on, I knew that Dan and Timmy and I would never wind up slaving in the Louisiana oil fields, working seven days on a rig in the Gulf and then coming home for seven more. Most every rig hand I knew back then chased tail as if with the last breath he owned, although I later knew men who understood and dealt with the awful compromises that kind of life demanded. You could always find a cadre of drunken roughnecks playing dominoes at Black Tom's place off Main Street or feeding the last of their pay into the Donkey Kong and Space Invaders machines

at the Phil-A-Sack off Union Street in Opelousas. Sometimes
they'd cross the tracks and go down the Lewisburg road to Jean's
Lounge, where they'd park their big-wheeled pickups on the
bleached-shell lot and wait for the motel doors to open, for the
painted ladies to let them in.

My cousin Jody, who came to know the mental poverty of
offshore-oil-field work shortly after he dropped out of school, told
me once, "I never really found a single day of fun doing that shit."
But after his first six months on a production rig he bought a
Mercedes 240-D dressed in a rich-bronze coat and drove it all over
Opelousas, with the crud of monkey grease under his nails. He'd
go to the Delta Lounge on Saturday nights and listen to Uncle
Harold play chanky-chank and train songs, and walk around telling pretty women, "Make it go away, baby. Just make it go away."
Jody hated the work offshore and later quit to get on with Schlum-
berger, a well-logging company that serviced mostly land rigs. A
few years ago when the oil industry fell into a depression, Jody got
laid off and made do painting houses and barns until the work
picked up again. "Back to jail," he said. "One more life in the
freeze-frame."

He left his back door open for Mo Mo Euna to come by once
a week to wash and iron his party shirts and make up his bed.
There was always a note for his grandmother on the icebox door,
saying, "Gone to Cindy's." "Gone to Peggy's." "Gone to
Susan's." "Gone to work."

But some people I knew liked the work or liked what it gave
them. Billy Joe Hensley flies helicopters for Mama Mobil down
in Morgan City and lives in Centerville with his wife, Sue, and
son, Trey. They own a two-bedroom trailer anchored on the back
lot of Shirley's Mobile Park, just across the state road from Hana-
griff's Garage. It hugs a sugarcane field that runs clear to the
interstate, plenty room for his big dog, Leftover, to hide its bones.
Billy Joe is a family man all the way, with high-minded plans of
quitting his seven-and-seven labor and using the money he's saved
to go to law school. He once told a technical-writing class at the
University of Southwestern Louisiana, "You know I am an idealis-
tic person. Well, this bidness has been good to me and my wife
and boy. But it's not the almighty end. I'll just do it till I get a
big belly full and feel it's time to push on."

And my old friend Donnie Carlin still likes it, and makes a pretty good living selling pump jacks and running the company his old man started in 1964. We all thought Donnie would never grow up, just rely on the family business to set him free. Then Muff Carlin took sick with lung cancer and died, and my mother and I stood in the December cold waiting for the hearse to make the big iron gates. We were at a memorial ground in Lafayette, and Donnie came out of a white four-door sedan with his little sister clutching his arm. That was the last time I'd seen him, the day they buried his father.

"Thanks for coming to help us bury Daddy," he told me, three years later. I told him, "Anytime, man. You know that."

Now he's got a baby and one on the way and lives in a pretty place just down the road from Mr. Jimmie Owen, whose own wealth and good glory helped fashion our private visions of the future. It was the dream of being rich and famous and a living legend that brought us to park before Mr. Jimmie's great house on those Saturday nights long ago, there in the shadow of a wildcatter with money and oil rigs and pretty granddaughters who dressed nice and went to the girls' school, Grand Coteau. We were just boys looking to grow up, hicks from out of town. You had to know us, stopping at a topless bar off Highway 167, out near Evangeline Downs, where so many nighthawks went to clear their heads and play bourrée and toss coins at the naked ladies. You had to know Timmy, who drank near-beer and bought quarter condoms from the vending machines over the toilet, then gave those balloons life with tap water and threw them at stop signs. "I hate to stop," he'd say, loving a bottle. "And I always will."

And Dan, who wanted to be a priest and save souls. Once he asked a girl what her thing cost, and why so damned much. Dan went to a Connecticut seminary for a semester, then moved back home to Opelousas, found work digging up abstracts for oil companies and breeding Alaskan malamutes. And way back, after they put a rig on a stretch of ground near his daddy's farm, we'd drive there every other afternoon after gym class and listen to the lightning rods of steel pound the big earth. It was gorgeous and perfectly obscene, but the oil was someplace else. They never hit the black stuff out there. They probably never will.

Jimmie Owen grew up in Waco, Texas, and as a child knew the wounds of poverty and exile and the hurt and shame of an orphaned heart. He had always meant to accumulate as much wealth as he possibly could, and he wanted a family to enjoy it. His mother had died just two years after his birth, and then when Jimmie was five his father died of influenza. That was in 1903. Rather than move into the Methodist orphan home, he lived with an aunt and uncle in downtown Waco. Even now, at eighty-eight, with a wife and a son and a daughter and seven grown grandchildren and eight little great-grandchildren, he still thinks of himself as an orphan and owns the same lonesome and irrepressible dream of family that haunted him as a boy.

Days of quiet at home, he likes to remember his older brother, Marshall, who married a woman he met on vacation. Marshall's wife was a Catholic, raised by nuns in a St. Louis convent, and she wore a black rosary around her neck, with the crucifix tucked into her bosom. Marshall had bought Jimmie a bicycle and an air gun with the money he made working as a stenographer and bookkeeper, and Jimmie loved him dearly. They used to play ball on the front lawn and sit on the porch steps watching the trolley cars bump and groan down Fifth Street.

Marshall's wife wore strong perfume and what looked like a mortician's mask of makeup, and she wanted to play dominoes after Sunday dinner. Jimmie later regretted not coming right out and telling her, "Good Christians do not play games on Sunday, not as long as Aunt Laura is alive."

Even Marshall could see that she didn't belong, and he soon set about leaving. He said, "Goodbye, Jay," and embraced Jimmie near the street curb. Then he led his wife down the sidewalk and into the night. Mr. Jimmie never saw his brother again, or his brother's wife, but he has known many Catholics. "The state is full of 'em," he told me and chuckled.

Most of the Cajun people in south Louisiana were Roman Catholics, although the oil boom attracted scores of Protestant preachers who had seduced members of the community with desperate cries for rebirth. After British rule forced the Cajuns from the colony of Acadia in Nova Scotia in the 1700s, they populated what are now the twenty-two parishes of Acadiana. These rich lowlands produced crops of sugarcane, cotton, soybeans, and sweet potatoes. But in 1901 a rice farmer named Jules Clement discovered bubbling black sludge in his fields, and a different kind of crop was born, one that would produce twelve billion barrels of oil and 102 trillion cubic feet of natural gas, enough to keep New York City in the glow until 2484.

Jimmie Owen had never known his grandfather, he told me one day several months ago. We were on our way to Don's Restaurant for a bowl of shrimp-and-oyster gumbo and a bloody mary. It was noon or a little after, and Mr. Jimmie was pointing out the office buildings that lined the busy blacktop streets of the Lafayette Oil Center, which serves as the hub for the parish of 150,000, and making a big fuss over all the little shops built on land that had once been a nursery and a soybean field. There was a five-and-dime, a flower shop, a shoe store, an A&P, and a complex of simple-looking offices. This was his little corner of the world, he was saying, "with the greatest concentration of oil and gas men this side of Dallas, Texas. Houston, too."

We were in front of the Hamilton Medical Center when Mr. Jimmie figured he'd put on his brakes and stop the car in the middle of the road. He rubbed his stubby little hands together and checked his look in the rearview, saw the black-rimmed glasses clouded over with a filmlike dew, the white hair parted over the left ear and drawn straight back with a wide-tooth comb. There was a kid on a big black Harley sitting on Mr. Jimmie's back bumper, but I don't think Mr. Jimmie noticed him. The boy was flashing his lights on and off and punching his bug horn and shooting everybody the bird.

"I've always been a grandpa man," Mr. Jimmie said and let his chin turn weak and trembly. "Always, my whole life. Ever since I can remember."

"I never really was," I said, knowing he wasn't paying much mind to me or the traffic pileup he'd created on Coolidge Street. "Me and my grandfather, we'd been different places. I could never understand why he did the things he did."

"Well, I always was a grandpa man," Mr. Jimmie said. "And I always will be, I suppose. But I never even knew my grandpa. He died fighting Yankees in the Civil War shortly after being wounded at the Battle of Mansfield. I spent a good part of my adult life looking for his bones. Looking, looking everywhere."

I asked him if he ever found his grandfather, and I knew the answer as soon as he stepped off the brake and started the car down the road again. "I always did have a nose for discovery," he said, more than a little proud. "Oil or otherwise."

For most of my years back home I'd heard that Jimmie Owen had discovered more oil in Louisiana than seemed rightly human. He had come to the region of Acadiana like so many wildcatters who figured luck and location would be on their side and that acquiring a good lease and boring a hole in the earth was less a high roll than a harmless shell game between God and man. Jimmie Owen had drilled over eight hundred wells during his career as a wildcatter, and discovered forty-eight oil fields. He had engineered reserves of about two trillion cubic feet of natural gas and forty-five million barrels of oil and condensate. "I was always looking for something," I heard him say, "whether it be oil or Grandpa."

Mr. Jimmie's legend grew out of his unwillingness to surrender his dream of being the greatest oilman ever to live and work in Louisiana. Back in 1964 he sold out his business to the General American Oil Company of Texas for more than $15 million. After taxes and filling the wide-open palms of the people he owed, he had about $8 million in CDs, and everybody was counting on a big retirement party, complete with a multitiered cake and a brass band and booze bar, with all the help going, "Yessir, Mr. Jimmie done good. Done got rich for hisself."

But the old man wouldn't quit. He took Corita to a Rotary International Convention in Tokyo, then took her back home to the new house he'd built on Bayou Parkway. His son, James Jr., himself a big-time oilman, told Mr. Jimmie to buy a fancy shotgun and a set of golf clubs and to start throwing spare change at the stock market. There were all kinds of ways to blow time and money. James Jr. also wanted his old man to lay low and enjoy what everybody was calling "the best years of your life" and "the kind of peace you deserve."

Jimmie Owen wouldn't listen. He liked wildcatting, knew nothing better, and told you so with a defiant huff. It really wasn't sad at all, seeing his ambition outdo his common sense. He was only doing what he figured he was meant to do. He took his money and put it right back into the ground, digging, digging, digging, hoping to find a spit of that sweet amber blood of locomotion.

You had to know him in his moment of discovery, of triumph, to understand what drove him back to the earth, and deep into it, drilling to distances of a quarter mile and more. It was like coring a giant apple with a kitchen tool and pulling up the middle to see what the seeds looked like. Sometimes the seeds came out in dense chunks of brown sugary sand, and all the hands would stand around in their soiled blue denim and khaki suits, with their aluminum hard hats pushed back just enough to reveal an expression of profound disbelief.

"Oh, good Jesus," Mr. Jimmie would offer under his breath. "Oh, beautiful, beautiful Lord." There would be the fatigue that mounts short moments before certain victory, and the chief tool pusher would drag a corrugated tin sheet up to the derrick floor.

You'd see parked out on the board road leading up to the great steel skeleton an Olds Ninety-Eight with one door cocked open and some church choir blowing baby Jesus out of the dash and into the outlying bean fields and the deep, fertile womb of the rig. That would be Mr. Jimmie Owen's car, idling in neutral with the emergency brake on. You'd see somebody grab his crotch as if he suddenly couldn't hold himself, not for another minute, as if the excitement of the find had undone the natural cork in his bladder. And then Mr. Jimmie, without doubt the luckiest man in the state of Louisiana, would say something to break the quiet. He'd say, "How's your wife, Rip?" And the old tool pusher, stuffing his hands in his pockets and rocking back on his heels, would say, "She's fine, Mr. Jimmie. How's Miss Corita?" And Jimmie Owen would say, "She's fine, Rip. I thank you and will tell her you asked."

Then a minute wouldn't have gone by before old Rip was looking into the core barrel and asking Mr. Jimmie to come stick his hand in there. It was like christening a new ocean liner with a bottle of champagne and a prayer, Mr. Jimmie's taking a rich, crystalline wedge of pay and throwing it on the tin sheet. A run of honey-gold fluid would ease down the fine line of corrugation and pool at your feet on the wrought-iron floor. You'd give an obligatory shout of congratulations, or whistle your relief, maybe even throw a hard hat into the field. It was "all nice and humbling," everyone would be heard to say later. But nobody on the face of the earth ever felt better with oil on his shoes than Mr. Jimmie Owen.

All the time I had known his story, or heard tell of it, I had admired the old man for his courage and for knowing that you don't get enough of a good thing. By 1972 he had driven one too many steel Pixie straws into fallow ground, sucked out too much dry air, and went bust. On his seventy-fourth birthday, when he might have been shooting ducks out of a reed blind or playing bumper pool at the municipal country club, Mr. Jimmie declared bankruptcy and vowed to start all over again, all in the course of one hour. They repossessed his Ninety-Eight, backed it right out of the garage and down the drive onto the parkway, sped off without a goodbye honk of the horn. They took most everything of value he owned but the house, "and only because I didn't own it," he was saying one morning over coffee and fritters. "I'd had my attorney draw up an irrevocable deed back when it was first built, in '62, and I signed it over to Corita. I wanted to be sure there would always be a place to come to, should I lose my wallet down the road.

"Will Hall, the lawyer who handled the deal, told me, "The house is all hers, Jimmie. The only way you'll get it back is if she threatens your life before witnesses. And then you can only sue for half of it.""

Mr. Jimmie hit it good on three wells after the disaster in '72, but a dry hole and a blowout that cost him $6.5 million put him in bankruptcy court again. That was in 1982, and now Jimmie Owen has resurrected himself for one last play at glory. He has generated the support of several local investors who plan to help him drill two wells on his Cameron Parish lease that, if his geological report is accurate, will produce $25,000 a day. "All I can do is hope," he said. "All anybody who goes out looking like I do, drilling my holes . . . all anybody can do is hope."

"I just hate this business," Corita was saying, washing down plates in the kitchen sink. "Jimmie sits over there in the living room, talking to all those people on the phone. It's a big game to him, and it's fun. All he wants is to strike it rich again, but I just hate this business. I hate it with a passion. I should have asked him to take us back to Texas, where we came from, long ago."

They would never go back, I knew. I should have told her that you can never go back, no matter how old you are. Mr. Jimmie said he wanted to be buried in Lafayette, where the oil ran true and where he had family and a name that would endure. He was a man of history, one who struck as big and hard as a refiner's fire. All his days standing on derrick floors and he still was not accustomed to being called a wildcatter. It sounded, as he said, "somewhat undignified to my ear," even knowing that he was nothing more, nothing less, and that being one would always keep him hungry to live. He had told me with much sadness, "I have so much left to do. If only for time . . ."

And I had said, unthinking, and maybe unfeeling, "If only for a lot of things."

"Always been a grandpa man," he said again, days after our gumbo lunch at Don's. "Always felt I had to find his grave, and knew I would. Wildcatting is thinking you can find anything, you know, even when you're only out looking for yourself."

Mr. Jimmie asked me to feel the worn and silky-smooth pages of a book entitled *The Geography of the United States*, written by a Massachusetts Congregationalist preacher and published in 1833. It was the only possession of Grandpa's that Jimmie had ever been able to acquire. There was not a single map in the entire text of some one thousand pages, he told me, but deep in the body of the book there was a page with an elaborate script that warned:

> Steal not this book, my friend,
> Lest the gallows be your end,
> Signed,
> B. D. Owen. April 4, Sabbath

Grandpa B. D. Owen had planted cotton and taught school in Natchitoches Parish before his conscience demanded he join the Confederate Army and do battle with the Union boys. He had owned a generous run of farmland near Middle Creek and was buried at the base of a big cedar tree. That information came from an uncle, and there were few other clues as to where Grandpa was buried, save the pounding in Mr. Jimmie's chest every time he traveled the red sandy roads of the Kisatchie National Forest in central Louisiana.

It was raining that day in 1964 when he and Corita set out to find B. D. Owen's grave. All the back roads had turned into ribbons of miserable red slop. Mr. Jimmie had found that most tips took him from hope to frustration and back again. But he had learned to enjoy a solemn kinship with the dead and relished the clean rush he felt when walking over ground populated with the long departed. "You'd be surprised how pretty a graveyard can be," he said. "I should know, I've seen so many . . . looking for Grandpa."

They were following a tip from a cousin in Baton Rouge, an attorney who called one day and said the grave was in the old Hawkins Cemetery, but that was all he knew. Another lead came days later and brought them closer still: there was a Civil War graveyard somewhere southwest of Bellwood, deep in the nether reaches of an evergreen forest. "But there ain't no point," the informant said. "Those graves, they've all been robbed."

The road Mr. Jimmie chose to turn off onto was white and sandy, partially covered with broken boughs from pine trees, and marked with a fresh set of tire treads. It climbed a pair of small rounded hills and confronted, as if by accident, a one-lane bridge that crossed a fat bend in Middle Creek. He stopped the car at the foot of the bridge and saw, up ahead in the road, a truck with a steady column of exhaust lifting from its tail end. Two men stepped from the cab and relieved themselves in the brush cover on the side of the road, in plain view of Corita and Mr. Jimmie, who grinned at their immodesty and said, "Well, at least they aren't moonshiners. They look all right."

Corita said, "Maybe."

Jimmie drove slowly up the hill, planning to shoot past the men if either looked like trouble. This was redneck country, and a different set of rules applied. He made a crack in his window and called out to the driver, who was wearing tattered work clothes covered with mud and grease, "You know where the old Hawkins Cemetery is?"

The man, Mr. Jimmie told me, looked sorely like a newly escaped convict from the Angola Penitentiary, or, worse, a grave robber. He leaned forward, peering through the wet pane of glass, and said, "You're Mr. Jimmie Owen, ain't you? I used to drive a truck for you. Out in the oil field."

The improbability of such a reunion drew Mr. Jimmie out of his car and into the rain that had begun to fall in a slow, steady drizzle to get a better look at the man. They shook hands, then Mr. Jimmie retrieved a cigar from his coat pocket and gave it to his benefactor. "That old cemetery is down back aways," the man said, pointing at a copse of pine and cedar. "But you won't find nothing. Robbers picked it clean."

Knowing that country, I can picture the gray, bristling steam and how it sat like bursts of gossamer on the forest floor. Mr. Jimmie said the whole of the sky seemed to be spun around the rain-darkened trunks of the trees. He backed down the road in low gear, exhilarated. How, he asked me some twenty years later, had he ever made out the tombstone set strong in the obscuring shadows? And how had he ever found the strength to walk unaided through the terrific underbrush and stand before the heavy sandstone slab enveloped in ground ivy and honeysuckle?

He had been wearing trifocals and could not read the letters carved into the weathered face of the gravestone, but here, looming before him like a great red angel of uncertain wing, stood the stump of a big cedar tree . . . *Grandpa.* He removed his glasses and wiped the rain from his eyes, then dropped to his knees and ran his fingers over the lettering, over the words that sang and danced in his mind like a palisade of fabulous light:

B. D. OWEN
39 YEARS OLD
JUNE 19, 1864

There were many reasons why Mr. Jimmie, weeks after the discovery, contracted a funeral director to disinter his grandfather's remains, but the one that best applied often came in a strained whisper. Seismographic crews had periodically shot off explosives near the old cemetery, and loggers and moonshiners had violated the sanctity of the land. Mr. Jimmie, who knew the loneliness of an orphaned heart, wanted to move the bones to a family plot at the permanent-care cemetery in Bellwood.

So they came with shovels and picks and a pine box, and he stood at some distance and watched in silence as the gravediggers thrust their tools into the earth. They worked through a hammock weave of cedar roots still clutching the rich loam, down to nine feet and more, before uncovering a skeleton dressed in the eroded fabric of war.

Mr. Jimmie, who had not objected when Corita refused to get out of the car and join him at the grave site, asked his wife if she might like to have a closer look. She refused, and he said, "You're just superstitious." She replied, "I'm not superstitious, old man. I just think it's horrible."

He further outraged Corita by taking pictures of the skeleton with a Polaroid and saving the knots of cedar roots the funeral director had set aside. The wood was clean and delicate and looked like the cruciform fingers of a very old man. As a joke, and because he was proud, Mr. Jimmie displayed the collection of photographs and roots at a family get-together the next summer, and everyone but Corita gave it a happy chuckle. "But that had nothing to do with being superstitious," she said.

In his old age, Mr. Jimmie had come to know the cuts of cedar as "Grandpa's roots," and he gave them a special place on the mantle over the living-room fireplace. "Have you seen Grandpa's roots?" he asked me that day last December, and he rose with great effort from his easy chair. "They are really something to see."

I watched him cross the room and stand before the emboldening light of a pine-knot fire. The light had crossed a valley of a thousand years, and he saw it bright and pure and primordial, as those before him had once seen it. And as I saw it. There was a fractured heave of memory moving through his body, and it seemed as if something of tremendous power and portent had awakened within him and started on its way into the night. There were tears in his eyes as he lifted high the gnarled bones of Grandpa's tree in a triumphant act of expiation.

"I'm not crying," he said and looked my way. "I'm just thinking."

Bearings

LAFAYETTE, LOUISIANA

Population: 94,600
*Lafayette's original inhabitants were the Attakapas
Indians, who were famous for eating their prisoners of
war.*

*The first white inhabitants of Lafayette were
Acadians, the French settlers from Normandy who had
been banished from Nova Scotia in 1755. Driven out of
New Orleans in 1765, they migrated across the
Atchafalaya swamp to what is now Lafayette. It took a
week to cross the swamp by boat.*

Cajun *is a corruption of "Acadian." In the
twenty-two parishes that comprise Acadiana, the native
language of almost half the population is a French dialect
originally spoken in Normandy. Lafayette is the capital of
Acadiana.*

*Before the oil boom began in 1970, Lafayette's
population was some seventy thousand. Between 1980 and
1983 it was the eighth-fastest-growing city in the country.*

The New York Times *estimated that one in fifteen
Lafayette families has assets of $1 million or more. In
1981 it ranked ninth in the value of retail sales per
household.*

*Lafayette is said to have the largest ski club in the
country.*

Melting-Pot High

John Rothchild

In a single summer the Mariel boatlift delivered a mass of newcomers to Miami's shores equal to nearly one third of the city's entire population. Haitians still wade in from scuttled and unseaworthy vessels. Colombians fly in, Nicaraguans drive in via Mexico to escape their left-wing government. Two decades ago there were Cuban airlifts, and a decade before that the Bronx and Chicago carlifts brought a steady supply of Yankees escaping cold weather.

Over the past thirty years Miami has absorbed more immigrants per capita than any other American city. Miami is two hundred years of New England compressed into fifty: people hardly settle down long enough to learn about mildew and hurricanes before they are thought of as forefathers by more recent arrivals, who themselves are rendered obsolete in a boatlift or two. Huge incursions make foreigners of the erstwhile natives. Erst-

JOHN ROTHCHILD lives in Miami Beach. His Florida history, *Up for Grabs* (Viking), was published in 1985.

while natives either migrate up to Fort Lauderdale or stay and speculate: When will all these outsiders ever fit in?

Just off Flagler Street and a few blocks from downtown sits the oldest high school in the city, Miami Senior High School. An ornate structure built in the old Spanish style, Miami High looks as though it were destined for Spanish occupation: less a public school than an old San Juan hotel or a cloister from the Christianized Moors. It has archways as deep as tunnels, corridors of brown Cuban tile as wide as skating rinks, restful little indoor patios with potted palms, a big bust of the great Cuban poet José Martí, and lately a student body that can recognize him.

The students break for lunch across Colombia Park, Burger King to the right of them and the Cafeteria Mirita, with its *medianoche* sandwiches and *pastelitos*, to the left: 90 percent of them Hispanic; 6 percent black; the previous Miami establishment winnowed to 4 percent "other"—yesterday's gringo ruling class officially dismissed as non-Hispanic white.

Gringo alumni can trace their influence back as far as Prohibition, when the new Miami High School opened its doors to the children of immigrants arriving on Henry Flagler's trainlifts from Georgia or North Carolina. Miami was still *Miamuh.* The school nickname, Stingaree, was the likely local pronunciation of *stingray;* the yearbooks were edited by the Prossers, Kents, Wrights, and Lassiters of this world. William Jennings Bryan, the silver-tongued lot salesman in Coral Gables, was their favorite guest speaker. Did they foresee the inevitable even then? In the school's debating club the most popular topic in the early 1920s was: "Resolved that all immigration should be prohibited for the present."

The occasional Cuban student complemented the Miami High architecture: Bebe Rebozo, for instance, and Desi Arnaz. The Arnaz family had fled to Miami after the fall of Cuban president Gerardo Machado in the 1930s. There weren't enough Cubans at Miami High to be thought of categorically, and perhaps that was a key to their acceptance. For thirty years in the city's Anglolithic Era the blacks were corralled into two tight little ghettos and attended separate schools, and the anti-Semitic hoteliers working for developer Carl Fisher on Miami Beach looked

out for "Jewish noses." Miami High had its Courtesy Week, its
Father and Son Banquets, and the only real threats to cultural
stability were the incoming Yankees.

What divided Stingarees then was North versus South, although in those days there was no official recognition of it—
registrars didn't have categories like non-Confederate white. Billie Wills, one of those unforgettable teachers who make high
schools worthwhile, got a job in the Miami High Spanish department in 1957, when it was still Yankee, not Spanish accents that
disturbed the locals. She remembers the lunchroom, generally the
place where such differences sort themselves out: "Southerners
wouldn't sit with northern people. I was of Greek descent, but it
wasn't fashionable to advertise it. One of our history teachers
wouldn't sit near me because one of my cake recipes called for
alcohol."

More important than any of this was Stingaree pride. By the
1940s Miami High had produced Florida senator George Smath-
ers, tennis star Gardnar Mulloy, Phil Graham of *The Washington
Post*, Arnold Tucker of the Army backfield, judges and legislators
too numerous to mention, regional and national football cham-
pionships, and Veronica Lake. More crucial in that era than any
Civil War was the annual game with rival Edison High School
(Edison never won). High school spirit turns out to be one of the
hidden safeguards of democracy, uniting the upcoming generations around arbitrary distinctions like Stings versus Red Raiders,
as opposed to something serious.

The 1950s brought thousands of easterners, many of them
Jewish, to the Miami area. The Jews had broken out of their
vacationers' ghetto on South Beach; hoteliers in other sections
repealed their anti-Semitic prohibitions. There were more Jewish
lawyers, doctors, entrepreneurs throughout the region, and
enough Jewish students at Miami High to raise the question: But
will these outsiders ever fit in?

Across from Miami High was Shirley's, a hamburger place
known as the Christian hangout. The Mason-Dixon line in the
school cafeteria gave way to more up-to-date distinctions as Christians on both sides of the southern question closed ranks. Old
grads from this period can't wait to ask: "Have you heard about
'Little Jerusalem'?" Little Jerusalem was the school's east court-

yard, informally adopted as the spot where Jews would naturally want to congregate.

School social clubs, sponsored by local civic organizations, continued to pick their little magnolia blossoms right out of the classrooms. For decades this was Miami's way of reinforcing the caste system of society at large against the threat of too much commingling in the schools. If you ever doubted where you really belonged, the social clubs inevitably sorted it all out. To be tapped for Little Women or Honoria was one thing; to be Jewish was another. Jewish students countered by joining the more liberal-minded social clubs: Anchor and the Junior Debs.

More important than any of this was being a Stingaree. From the yearbooks, you can almost write a Law of Inevitable Acceptance: Goldfarbs and Leibowitzes first appearing as mere faces, then as honored scholars; as pep boosters; as academic-club members; as occasional Honorias or Little Women; and at last as homecoming royalty—the relentless straight line of Miami High goyishe kings and queens broken by Joan Ackerman in 1963.

About the time of this Judaic ascension to royalty, Batista fell, and suddenly Little Jerusalem ceased to exist at all. The Cuban Revolution indirectly wiped it out. Suddenly there was a Judeo-Yankee-southern establishment, as opposed to the Cubans who were installed on the fourth floor of the high school.

Billie Wills's students finally had somebody Spanish to talk to, and so, as the teacher remembers it, "the interest in Spanish was beginning to drop." There were the Prossers and Wrights of this world, not to mention the Goldfarbs and Leibowitzes, abandoning the Spanish Club for the French club, Entre Nous, hoping to put distance between themselves and the living Hispanics, who wore strange blazers with the names of their prep schools back in Havana.

Miami as a whole was going through it, measuring its limited compassion for victims of communism against its skepticism of Caribbean intruders. Many of the first Cubans were sons and daughters of professors, government officials, and industrialists. They distinguished themselves in the Miami High classrooms as the Jews once had. Taking weekend rifle practice with paramilitary units in the Everglades added to their dramatic appeal.

Still, to be Little Women or Honorias was not to be Cuban.

A separate but equal Pan American Club was devised in 1963 by Diego Garcia, a teacher with Spanish parents. Billie Wills, who had stopped teaching languages altogether since the exodus to French, devoted herself to the challenge of Cuban adjustment as the school's activities director.

Wills remembers the Cubans coming off the fourth floor to read speeches and leave flowers at the statue of José Martí, their national hero, who previously was just a bust on the lawn. Martí was donated to Miami High after the school's Million Dollar Band took a trip to Havana in the 1940s, back when our interest in Latin America was not so reciprocal.

"I felt for those kids," Wills says. "One time they staged a big Cuban party, or *cumparsa*. Their mothers made all the costumes. Incredible costumes. Cubans from all over the country, dignitaries, politicians, came to see the show. They wanted to prove how great they were, and they did."

By the time Miami High was integrated in 1970, the blacks had to wonder if they weren't being bused into Caracas or Santiago. In 1971 there were Bill Capps and Nancy Arnold, token gringos in the homecoming court; on the first pages of that year's yearbook are six Alvarezes and six Acostas. History and science were being taught through bilingual instruction for students with language difficulties. The Prossers and Wrights of this world were vanishing toward the 4-percent level of the present. Administrator Pete Nelson walks through the wide corridors today and jokes, "I'd be hard pressed to show you one."

Billie Wills, who began her career teaching Spanish to the English, has switched to teaching English to the Spanish. Diego Garcia, the former Spanish teacher and founder of the Pan American Club, is the current Miami High principal. Spanish is the language of the hallways; English is the language of the classroom. Non-Hispanic blacks are frightfully outnumbered and practice *-ar, -er,* and *-ir* verbs in the hope of landing local counter jobs.

Billie Wills had the challenge of helping the immigrants from the 1980 Mariel boatlift, along with the Nicaraguans, to adjust. Some were named Fidelito and Raulito, raised on communism, speaking in strange and disturbing phrases foreign to normal Miami-domestic Spanish. Wills remembers the first

Marielito year as follows: "They came in droves. You'd say, 'Sit down,' and they'd say, '*¿Qué?*' This was America, Land of Freedom. Freedom meant you didn't have to sit down. Some stood on chairs during classes. The toughest ones dropped out."

You can see it in the yearbooks of the early 1980s. Marielitos appearing first as photos, then as class officers, and finally in 1984 there is a Marielito student-government president. No king or queen yet, but it is inevitable.

In 1984 a video class is making a tape about fatal mistakes in syntax that result from too-literal translations between English and Spanish: little skits in which a lady unwittingly announces she is pregnant *(embarazada)* when she means she is embarrassed, or in which a man says he is *intoxicado* meaning "drunk," when *intoxicado* really means "poisoned." Billie Wills is teaching the class; the students are mostly from Mariel. She asks whether their Cuban relatives will be coming if they get the chance, and all but one raises his hand.

Miami High is the essence of Miami's present and perpetual condition: the outsiders taking over, the erstwhile natives estranged.

And yet, is there not something reassuringly familiar here? The second floor is called the Marielito floor; more seasoned immigrants occupy the third and the first. The important distinctions are early Cuban versus late Cuban, Nicaraguan versus Colombian. The Cuban establishment wonders of these late arrivals: Will they ever fit in?

More important than any of this is Stingaree pride. The 1983 Miami High yearbook speculates:

"Where else but at Miami High School would the 89.2 percent Hispanic population, a minority, be a majority to the 10 percent Caucasians who in time learned to eat pastelitos and say 'ah, chico' like most of the crowd?

". . . But as he became part of the institution, he learned that before he was a Cuban, black, or white, he was a Stingaree, and that was all that really mattered."

Bearings

MIAMI, FLORIDA

Population: 350,000

The future of modern Miami was secured when, during the great freeze of 1894 and 1895, Miami widow Julia Tuttle sent a fresh orange blossom north to Henry Flagler in St. Augustine. In 1896 Flagler built a railroad to Miami; in the same year he built the Royal Palm, Miami's first hotel.

Many of the islands in Biscayne Bay, as well as much of Miami Beach, are man-made. The city's highest point is a bump in a park created by the burial of surplus construction machinery.

Before 1960 Miami was 90-percent Anglo. Today the figure is 19 percent. Fifty-three percent of its residents are foreign-born; 52.1 percent of those over eighteen speak English poorly or not at all. A common joke among white Miamians is, "Will the last American to leave the city please lower the flag?"

A Miami real estate developer dubbed the city's oversize cockroaches "palmetto bugs."

In 1981 Miami's drug trade was estimated at $10 billion. In that year the Miami Beach branch of the Federal Reserve had more money on hand at the end of each day than all other Federal Reserve branches combined.

Miami Beach is the only city in the country with a kosher inspector on its payroll.

Proper Places

Tom Wolfe

The San Francisco matron who decides it's time to graduate from Merla Zellerbach's column in the *Chronicle* to the partypicture pages of *W* . . . the Hong Kong currency arbitrager who wants his daughter to become princess of a world bigger than Kowloon . . . the Australian who inherits a business from his daddy and wants to prove he's not merely a rich booby of the outback. . . . the Argentinean who wants to get out of the pampas before his capital is shrunk to nothing by inflation . . . the Baltimore real estate developer who makes his first $10 million (the new boundary line, replacing the old "millionaire") only to discover that no one in *tout le monde* knows who he is . . . plus the usual crowd of French rag-trade counts, Italian liquid-as-set refugees, British publishers, Cincinnati lavatory-puck manufacturers yearning to be known as industrialists, and young Dallas and Houston second

TOM WOLFE, a native of Richmond, Virginia, is a longtime resident and observer of New York's East Side. Each spring he hosts a party for friends from Virginia who are now living in Manhattan.

wives (of the old boys) who want to meet some people they've read about for a change at parties—in short, the international tribe of those who want to be *where things are happening*—today, in the last quarter of the twentieth century, they head not to Paris or London but to New York. And the whole glorious mob is desperate to live in what are known as the Good Buildings.

The obsession is not confined to people from out of town, however. By no means. The heaving financial markets of the late 1970s and early 1980s have produced, in New York itself, a new swarm of investment bankers, portfolio managers, bond traders, bullion brokers, and short-sellers who make money and spend money at a rate that would have made a Gatsby blink. As far as they are concerned, the 1980s are the 1920s all over again, a state of mind rendered yet more carefree by the fact that none of them is old enough to remember the 1920s. They are busy buying up the very same twenty- and thirty-room summer places in Southampton and East Hampton that were built in the 1920s and abandoned in the 1950s as white elephants. Servants' wings? Why not? (We have the servants.) Tennis courts? You bet. Magicians, acrobats, and carnival rides, complete with carnival workers, brought in for children's birthday parties? You got it. (A thriving little service industry.) And in Manhattan . . . they want the same Good Buildings.

These so-called Good Buildings are forty-two cooperative apartment houses built more than half a century ago. Thirty-seven of them are located in a small wedge of Manhattan's Upper East Side known as the Triangle. The rest are along the East River. No map of the Good Buildings or the Triangle has ever been published, and yet today that very map circulates throughout the world like Romany, the unwritten international language of the gypsies. For fifty years New York has been the only city in America where apartments, not houses, are the customary homes of those who want to be in Society. Today the rush to New York has turned that custom into a baying mania.

The prices of apartments in the Good Buildings have gone up in a trajectory that seems to have no ceiling. They have quadrupled since 1980. In 1980 apartments at 550 Park Avenue were for sale for $750,000. Today, an apartment on the fourteenth floor at 550 Park Avenue is on the market for $4 million and will fetch close to that. Prices have *doubled* in many cases in the past twenty-four months. Forty-two apartment buildings is a large number, and they contain about five hundred apartments in all. But at any given moment no more than twenty-five are likely to be on the market—and our panting mob is so huge!

At this writing, twenty-two Good Apartments are up for sale. The average asking price is almost exactly $4 million, with the lowest, at $2 million, at 50 East Seventy-seventh Street, and the highest, at about $6 million each, at 820 Fifth Avenue and 998 Fifth Avenue. Two million is regarded as a bargain in this market. The apartment at 50 East Seventy-seventh faces north; moreover, it doesn't have the north-and-west corner exposure at Madison Avenue and Seventy-seventh Street since the corner space is taken up by the upper half of the living room of the apartment down below, which has a twenty-foot-high ceiling. In contrast, the apartment at 820 Fifth Avenue occupies the entire fifth floor of the building, giving it four exposures, as well as eighteen rooms, and it looks over Fifth Avenue and into the trees of Central Park. Into but not above the trees. Above would be better, for one of the cries of the moment is: "I want to be on Fifth Avenue above the tree line!" Nevertheless, the apartment at 820 Fifth is in the $6-million class. The building has a limestone facade, which is good, because another cry is: "Limestone—not brick!" Worshipers of Plutus (the god of riches) regard brick facades as a bit common, even though quite a few Good Buildings, such as 635 Park Avenue, are brick.

Here is an example of how fast the prices are going up. At 1 Beekman Place, on the East River, there are three two-story apartments on the market at $4 million each. One of them belonged to Huntington Hartford for about thirty years. But the Good Buildings are organized like clubs, and in 1982 the board of directors of 1 Beekman Place took the extraordinary step of voting Hartford out of the building after some so-called unacceptable incidents. Hartford sold the apartment in 1984 for $1.5 million. It's once again on the market, now at $4 million. An offer of $3.5 million has been turned down.

Two blocks up the river is 435 East Fifty-second Street, which is known as River House, the only Good Building with a name and not merely an address, and the only one even remotely

familiar to the public generally. This is due not to the name or
any architectural distinction but to the boat tours. The guides
who give the spiels over a microphone on the twelve-dollar voyage
around Manhattan point out River House as they head up the
East River because Henry Kissinger lives there and Gloria Van-
derbilt was refused admission, resulting in a much-publicized legal
battle. They don't mention the Good Building about thirty blocks
upriver that let her in, even though the boat sails right by.

Today at River House there's an apartment on the twelfth
floor for sale for $3.4 million, a three-story maisonette (an apart-
ment with a front door opening out onto the sidewalk) for $3.75
million, and a two-story apartment on the twenty-fourth and
twenty-fifth floors for $5.3 million. This last belongs to John
Gutfreund, head of Salomon Brothers, the investment house.
Gutfreund and his wife, Susan, are departing after a dispute with
their upstairs (penthouse) neighbors, who filed a $35.5-million
lawsuit after the Gutfreunds had a twenty-foot-plus Christmas
tree hoisted up via a block-and-tackle rig on their penthouse roof.

The Gutfreunds have bought another two-story apartment
at another Good Building, 834 Fifth Avenue, for about $6 mil-
lion, from Jaquine Lachman, erstwhile fourth wife of Charles
Lachman, Charles Revson's silent partner in the Revlon cosmet-
ics company, who died in 1978. The apartment has a two-story
entry gallery the size of the Central Park South lobby of the Plaza
Hotel, a curved staircase worthy of the Paris Opera, and twenty-
odd rooms. The master bedroom suites overlook the Central Park
Zoo. In the easy-come, easy-go days prior to 1980, residents were
known to move out of 834 Fifth because the barking of the seals
annoyed them. Since 1980 people have not treated the place so
cavalierly. John DeLorean bought an apartment at 834 Fifth a
few years before The Troubles, and he has hung on to it. Good
thinking, as it turns out. It is now worth at least $5 million.

Meantime, Jaquine Lachman, now remarried, has moved
into an apartment at yet another Good Building, 1 Sutton Place
South, five blocks upriver from River House. The price was $3
million, which already looks like a good buy. The only apartment
currently on the market at 1 Sutton Place South is listed at $4
million.

All forty-two Good Buildings are among several hundred

cooperative buildings built in New York from 1910 to about 1932, at a time when developers still had to convince people it was as elegant and respectable to live in an apartment as in a private house. One-floor apartments—that is, apartments whose bedrooms were on the same floor as the living room—were known as French flats, French as in *risqué*. The solution was to create apartment buildings that were, in effect, made up of containerized houses. The apartments were built with everything a New York mansion had: entry galleries, reception halls, guest salons, libraries, servants' wings with bedrooms as well as common rooms ("servants' halls"), enormous kitchens with butler's pantries, main and servants' staircases to an upper floor, parqueted floors, hardwood doors two to three inches thick, walls a foot thick, exterior walls thick as a fort's, fireplaces, fireplaces, fireplaces, even though the buildings were centrally heated, twelve- to twenty-foot ceilings, living rooms forty feet long or more (960 Fifth Avenue), and dining rooms only a little smaller. Containerized mansions! You just happened to reach your front door via elevator rather than from the sidewalk. Your elevator vestibule led to only one door—yours—or at most yours and one other, as at 812 Park Avenue.

The New York real estate market collapsed during the Depression, and the containerized mansions were never built again, and perhaps never will be. What the developers now present as "luxury" apartments—the various Towers, such as the Olympic, the Trump, the 500 Park, with their eight- to nine-foot ceilings, their "living/dining areas," their stand-up kitchens—strike today's strivers as a bit Low-Rent. It's the low ceilings that they notice first. Someone moves into an apartment on the fifteenth floor of a new building on Park Avenue and is happy enough until he realizes his living room is dead level with the tenth floor of the Good Building across the street.

What drives people wild, at bottom, is the simple fact that *le monde* is sheerly divided into Good Buildings and those that, for whatever reason, are not Good. It may have nothing to do with space, construction, or grandeur. After all, if sheer visible grandeur is the measure, there are no buildings on the Good list that can compare with 1 West Seventy-second Street, known as the Dakota, and few that can compare with 322 East Fifty-seventh

Street. But neither is Good; the Dakota, because it is on the West
Side of Manhattan and therefore is neither in the Triangle nor
on the East River and because it admits celebrities, even *popular
music* celebrities, such as John Lennon. Number 322 East Fifty-
seventh Street has living rooms thirty by thirty feet with twenty-
foot ceilings and Rue de Rivoli–style casement windows, but it is
too egalitarian in its admissions procedures, even though these are
not exactly what you would call plebiscites. The term Good Building was originally uttered sotto voce. Before the First World War
it was code for "restricted to Protestants of northern European
stock"; therefore, no Irish, Jews, or Others. Blacks and Asians
were so far out of the question, they weren't even included in the
code. In the case of blacks, that remains pretty much the situation
today.

Nevertheless, the implications of "Good" have changed
vastly. A few buildings still try to maintain a predominantly Protestant cast, and the buildings on Park Avenue above Seventy-
ninth Street are still sometimes referred to, with a snigger, as the
Irish Gold Coast. But being Irish has long since ceased to be an
impediment for those dying to get into Good Buildings, and the
vast majority are open to Jews and, for that matter, Chinese,
Japanese, Lebanese, Greeks, Italians, Iranians (so long as they are
of the shah's stripe), Filipinos, Latin Americans, and indeed, most
comers except for American and African blacks and Indians from
India, who have a rough time with co-op boards. Non-Lebanese
Arabs have a difficult but not impossible time. Not many try; they
prefer Los Angeles. (As for American Indians, the question has
apparently never arisen.)

Today Good certainly doesn't mean democratic, but it does
pertain to attributes that are at least more broadly available than
Protestant grandparents: namely, decorous demeanor, dignified
behavior, business and social connections, and sheer wealth. In
short, bourgeois respectability. The co-op boards want quiet, con-
servatively dressed families, although not with too many children.
Children tie up the elevators and make noise in the lobby. Young
unmarried apartment owners are not desirable, no matter what
their backgrounds. Provided they are not young, homosexuals
with top-drawer social connections and flawless deportment may
manage to get by. Most boards are leery of celebrities, and celebri-

ties from the worlds of popular music, sports, the movies, television, and show business generally are less desirable by far than homosexuals. The exceptions are old Protestant movie stars, who ascend to a curious sort of royal status once they have retired, and TV news broadcasters, who are okay, although none save the occasional network anchorman are likely to meet the financial requirements.

The boards raise and lower their financial requirements, as well as their social requirements, with the temperature of the market, and today, as we have seen, the market is very hot. The first requirement is that the buyer be able to pay for the apartment in cash. Which is to say, he cannot use his apartment as collateral for a mortgage. The second, in many buildings, is that he not be dependent on his job or profession to pay for his monthly maintenance fees and keep up appearances. The maintenance fees range from about $1,750 a month for smaller apartments (three bedrooms, plus two maid's rooms) on lower floors to more than $10,000 a month for a two-story apartment at 834 Fifth Avenue. That may sound like a terrific amount, but it is about a third of what you would pay to rent comparable space if you could find it, which, in fact, you couldn't. Many of the Good Buildings require complete net-worth statements from prospective buyers. Since this is an application not for a loan but for an apartment, there is no penalty for perjury, and as a result there ensues a fair amount of what might be called . . . lying. The prospects and their families are also expected to drop by the building for "cocktails," which is an inspection of dress and deportment. Prospects are also required to swear that they will reside in the apartment on a full-time basis.

The stiffest known financial requirements are at a Good Building on Park Avenue in the seventies, where the board asks that a purchaser of an apartment demonstrate a net worth of at least $30 million. The interesting thing is that to the eager aspirants this does not seem like an unreasonable condition, not even to those who can't come close to meeting it. After all, you have to have assets of $10 million just to be what a millionaire was fifty years ago. Another building, on upper Fifth Avenue, requires the purchaser to demonstrate a net worth ten times greater than the purchase price of the apartment. With apartments there going for

$2 million, this makes it one of the hardest tickets in the Triangle. But that is only money; it is not regarded as a Good Building. (Just not the right club.)

The ticklish business of steering people up to the doors of the clubs is mainly in the hands of about twenty real estate brokers who specialize in the top end of the market. Some of them can recite the name and approximate age of every owner of every apartment, floor by floor, in every Good Building. They are expected to have finesse in screening applicants to avoid not merely wasted time but also the terrible business of rejections. Today, the brokers are beginning to take on a certain cachet of their own. Not to mention wealth—the conventional 6-percent fee in the sale of the typical $4-million Good apartment comes to $240,000.

At Le Cirque, a restaurant famous for its fashionable turnout at lunch, there was recently the following lineup at the tables along a banquette under the front window: At one end Richard Nixon was having lunch with Adnan Khashoggi. Jerome Zipkin, a man well known for the many well-known people who know him well, was having lunch with Yasmin Khan, daughter of Aly Khan. Just down the way was Eleanor Lambert, a public-relations woman who is impresario of the Best Dressed List. At the far end was a real estate broker named Alice Mason. Two men entered the restaurant. They paused. One surveyed the banquette, starting at the far end and panning slowly until he reached Adnan Khashoggi, one of the most spectacular of the Arab financiers who began to rock the world's economy in the 1970s, and Richard Nixon, twice elected President, architect of the Reopening of China to the West, central figure of the most enormous political scandal in the history of the United States, and he turned to his companion and said in a low voice: "Look, there's Alice Mason."

Bearings

UPPER EAST SIDE

As early as 1757 a Manhattan woman complained, "One might as well be out of the world as out of the mode."

In the 1790s a well-dressed gentleman was got up in a style known as the Macaroni, with a short waistcoat, an enormous wig, a small cocked hat, and a switch with tassels.

In the 1850s Reverend Isaac Brown, the official arbiter of New York society, said, "I cannot undertake to control society above Fiftieth Street." Another man told the builder of two apartment houses on Fifty-sixth Street, "Gentlemen will never consent to live on mere shelves under a common roof."

About one third of the working authors in the U.S. live in greater New York, and more than one hundred thousand working artists.

Six million pounds of paper are used to print the Sunday New York Times. The city's sanitation department picks up thirty-four million pounds of trash a day.

Mark Twain called New York "a splendid desert—a domed and steepled solitude, where a stranger is lonely in the midst of a million of his race." H. G. Wells said it is "full of the sense of spending from an inexhaustible supply." An English journalist said it resembles "a magic cauldron. Those who are cast into it are born again."

The congressional district of which the Upper East Side is a part has long been known as the Silk Stocking District.

A Few Words with the Biggest Man in Dallas

Bob Greene

I f the new model for American life involves scaling down—miniaturizing, trimming, cutting back—then Dallas flies in the face of everything that is currently thought to be wise. To drive around Dallas is to see a city seemingly in an endless frenzy of building and expansion, often on the hugest of scales.

The cliché in Dallas—repeated so often that it no longer brings a grin—is that the official municipal bird is the construction crane. Believe it: Dallas continues to sprout new buildings almost faster than anyone can keep track.

In Dallas the businessman—the builder, the developer—is a genuine hero. Dozens of people in Dallas are known as high-powered real estate and construction barons, and they rank lofty in the social hierarchy because they know how to turn money, cement, steel, and glass into brawny and imposing new towers. There is talk about who among these builders is more important

BOB GREENE, who grew up in Columbus, Ohio, is a contributing editor of *Esquire* magazine. *Cheeseburgers*, a collection of his essays, was published in 1985 by Atheneum.

than other builders; the bigger you are in the land development game, the larger you loom in the esteem of official Dallas.

So names are bandied about; one year one man may be on a roll, the next year another man may have moved above him. It all makes for interesting and intriguing gossip, but everyone is always aware of one thing: builders may rise and builders may fall, fortunes may be won and fortunes may be lost, but there is one builder in Dallas who stands so far above the rest as to be virtually unreachable by the remainder of the world, and that man is Trammell Crow.

Trammell Crow, seventy, is the founder of the Trammell Crow Company, which is the largest landlord in America. *Texas Monthly* magazine, in attempting to sum up the extent of Trammell Crow's holdings, finally put it this way: "How big is Trammell Crow's empire? Unimaginably big."

You can see it in Dallas itself; there is a portion of Stemmons Freeway that contains so many gigantic Trammell Crow projects that it more resembles some ludicrous, futuristic exhibit at Disney World than a real American city: the Homefurnishings Mart, the Trade Mart, the Apparel Mart, the World Trade Center, the Infomart, Market Hall, the Loews Anatole Hotel. If that was all that Trammell Crow had built, it would be astonishing enough.

It's just a fraction—just a local Texas fraction. The Trammell Crow Company has more than $6 billion in total assets; it owns and manages more than 175 million square feet of commercial property, not just in Dallas but in eighty-nine other cities. There are fifty-five fully staffed Trammell Crow offices in the United States and four outside the United States; last year the company had more than $2 billion in new construction starts. This year another $2 billion in construction starts is anticipated. Trammell Crow himself personally owns between 15 percent and 50 percent of every building ever built by the Trammel Crow Company. His personal wealth has been estimated at in excess of $500 million.

I met Trammell Crow on the thirty-fifth floor of his company's new Dallas skyscraper, LTV Center. Something curious immediately became apparent: he does not have a private office.

Rather, he sits out in a bullpen area, surrounded by secretaries and other employees. If you were somehow to walk in and not know where you were, you might assume that the old fellow at the desk over by the wall was a long-tenured bookkeeper, still working away, in the midst of younger folks in a hurry to move past him on their way up through the corporation.

I sat with him, and we looked out the windows; there, far below, was the Dallas that he had done so much to form. I asked him what he thought about as he looked at that.

"I remember in this city, about twenty years ago, we had a business leader by the name of Thornton," he said. "Bob Thornton. One of the things he was concerned about was whether Dallas might grow too much and become too congested."

Crow looked out the windows some more. "I happen to like congestion," he said. "What we need is more congestion."

As we talked, all of the other people in the area could hear what was being said. Crow didn't seem to mind this a bit. With his thin smile and constant squint, he bore a certain resemblance to another prominent Dallas resident: Dallas Cowboys football coach Tom Landry.

Crow explained that he had started his empire by building warehouses after the end of World War II. He talked in pleasant, conversational tones, with the deadpan self-confidence that must come when your company is worth six billion.

"Most developers want to do things that are a credit to themselves and to their cities," he said. "Many can't always do that, because they are faced with constraints of finance. Fortunately, our company does not face those constraints. Fortunately, we are in a position to do whatever we want to do."

I told Crow that I was a person who can't even keep his checkbook straight. In the business environment of the eighties, when the concept of an entrepreneurial visionary often revolves around something like opening a chain of franchised chocolate-chip-cookie stands in shopping malls, I was curious about what drove a man like him. There seemed to be so many smaller ways to make a lot of money. Why does a man build buildings?

"That's probably more of a question than you think it is," he said. "In my case, first it was a case of needing to accomplish some success for success' own sake. I had the need to earn a living. So I started building.

"Now let's jump over all that time from then to now. Right

now I don't need to do anything I don't want to do. So why do I keep doing it? It's not to make more money, I'll tell you that."

"Then why are you still at it?" I said.

"To feel more . . ." He hesitated, then started over. "To feel like a more important player in the game. To be, or to have been, somebody. To be in that game. I will tell you this: I will work till that last day."

"What last day?" I said.

"Some night I'll go home and I'll pass away," he said. "But I will have spent the whole day that day in the office. Damn right."

I asked him why, with all he had accomplished, he still participated in such a high-risk business. He cut me off in midquestion.

"There's as much risk in doing nothing as in doing something," he said. "The risk is that if I stopped doing this, I would cease to be me. If I had nothing to eat for two weeks, then there would be nothing more important to me than a dinner on the table. But that's not where I am."

I asked him if he ever worried over the multimillion-dollar decisions he had to make.

"No, it's been a long time since I've done that," he said. "When we first started I would worry—but after we reached a certain level of success, I ceased being apprehensive. I came to trust my own judgments. I would think about something, and I would decide, 'This is not a risk. This will work.'

"What I'm trying to tell you is that if I did nothing, I would turn into a nothing. 'The king is in his countinghouse, counting all his money. The maid is in the garden, eating bread and honey.' That's nothing, to live that way. Nothing. If I were somehow to be forced out of the game, I think I would have to buy my way back in."

I talked about all of the best-selling books about management skills that have sprung up lately, and all of the high-tuition business schools. I asked Crow—he has no college degree—how he had learned to manage people.

"I started an organization that was just me," he said. "Then there were two people. Then there were five people. Then there were twenty people. Then there were fifty people. No one ever taught me. There was never a time when it occurred to me that I couldn't manage people."

I began to ask a question in which, again, I used the word *visionary*. He shook his head vigorously.

"That's not a word you ought to use," he said. "I wouldn't use the word *visionary* or *vision*. Just say *idea*. The heart of any business's success or nonsuccess rests on how good the ideas are. You know the old line 'The play's the thing'? In business the idea is the thing. Don't make it any more complicated than that. If your ideas are worthy, you will succeed."

"Does being a gambler have anything to do with it?" I said.

"Oh, I suppose that I'm a little bit of a gambler," he said. "I'm willing to get out there on that thin ice where some other people won't go. But it comes back to the ideas. I think I'm willing to back my ideas more than most people are."

I asked him whether, at this point, any thing he did could still be considered a gamble.

"I have done things that would conceivably lose money," he said. "But I haven't done anything that would hurt me financially. Nor will I. The circumstances of our company are such that the failure of a project would not be a disaster."

I said that must be an awfully good feeling.

"It is," he said. "But you don't think about it. You take it for granted."

I asked him if when he walked into buildings constructed and managed by other developers, he was overly critical of the way they did things, as opposed to the way he might do things.

"I look at everything I can see, and a lot of times I get awful jealous," he said. "And then I go home and I do those things. In some cases I might not like something that I see, and I might say to myself, 'This is not something that we need to be doing right now.' But most of the time when I look at other buildings and projects, I'm looking with an eye toward trying to learn something."

"There's still something in this business for you to learn?" I said.

"I know about half of it now," he said.

I asked him how he felt people thought about him.

"Depends on who they are," he said. "If they grew up with

me, they probably look at me and think, 'How in the hell . . .?'
If I owe them money, they probably hope that I keep going. If
they're one of my partners, they probably put their arm around
me. The man on the street? He probably thinks average of me—
maybe a little above average."

"What did you mean when you said that the people who
grew up with you might look at you and go, 'How in the hell
. . .?' " I said.

"Well, the people you went to high school with . . . I mean,
who do you think would ever have believed that Ronald Reagan
would grow up to be President when he was in high school?" he
said. "Everything's developed right for me. I was born in a city
that allowed this to happen. I benefited genetically from my
parents. It all adds up."

I asked him whether a man like himself—a man who, starting with nothing, had built up personal wealth almost beyond
comprehension—looked with contempt on people who weren't
able to do that. Whether there was a sense of "I did it—why can't
they?"

"No," he said. "I don't have contempt for anybody except
for people who are bad."

"Bad?" I said.

"People who just don't live right," he said. "And even them,
I wouldn't say it was contempt I have for them. It's more pathos.
I try to spend no time on negatives. Negatives and the past are
two things I don't have much time for.

"I don't have much time in general. I'm as busy as anybody
I know. My mind is always on a specific piece of business. You
know how it is—your mind is rolling, rolling, rolling. It's life. It's
nature."

I said that as I had been waiting for him in the thirty-fifth-
floor reception area I had been sitting with three young businessmen who were waiting for some other Trammell Crow Company
executives. I was of the same generation as the three businessmen
—we were people who had been part of a college generation that,
fifteen or twenty years ago, had had a lot of sneering, negative
feelings for the business world. Now the three of them were
sitting there in their blue suits—and when Trammell Crow, in
shirt sleeves, had come out to greet me and to lead me back to
his desk, I had looked in the eyes of those three young business-

men. Seeing Crow standing before them in person had seemed to affect them the same way that seeing Mick Jagger prancing onto a stage might once have done.

"I think that attitude in the 1960s was as unfair as it could be," he said. "I know what the image back then was—that businessmen were callous, uncaring, only profit-oriented, the public be damned. Now what you're saying is that the image has changed.

"Well, that's all that has changed—the image. The businessmen haven't changed. The majority of people I know in business are hardworking, well-meaning, generous human beings. It wasn't business that was wrong back then. It was the image makers who were erroneous."

He presented those thoughts as simple facts. I asked him if he had any self-doubts at all.

"I'm not a person who has been blessed with self-doubts," he said. "I'm not troubled with what you might call self-doubts.

"When I make a decision, it's made. Frequently you'll keep something in your mind for months. Like a cow chews its cud. You'll keep bringing it back up. But then when the decision is made, that's it. I've never been troubled with waking up at night wondering whether I've made the right decision. I've never stopped a project once I've started it.

"In our business, it's not like mathematics, where one answer is correct and every other answer is incorrect. You just make the best decision you can, and hope that it works out the best it can. There's no magic. Like I told you, it's just a certain assurance based on a belief in my judgments."

I asked him what went through his mind when he looked at all of his buildings.

"Hell, I've never seen most of the Trammell Crow buildings," he said.

"You haven't seen them?" I said.

"I'd say that more than half of the Trammell Crow buildings that have been built in the last ten years I've never seen," he said.

"Why?" I said.

"There's only twenty-four hours in a day," he said. "Seven days in a week. That's that. The buildings are out there somewhere, but I don't know."

"Do you know how many buildings you own?" I said.

"I have no idea," he said. "Thousands."

"And you haven't even seen most of them?" I said.

"That's right," he said.

"That's pretty weird," I said.

"Why do you say it's weird?" he said.

"To own all of those buildings and never to have set eyes on them," I said.

"It doesn't strike me as weird," he said. "I couldn't do it. It couldn't be done."

I said that I had to ask him about the bullpen arrangement. In a world where so many executives measure their status by the size and location of their offices, why did he not have an office? Was it the ultimate expression of self-assuredness—he was so big that he didn't need any office at all? Or was it something else?

"I don't know," he said. "I've never had a private office in my life. I like it this way."

"But what if you want privacy?" I said.

"I don't want privacy," he said.

"But what if you get a phone call that you want to be private?" I said.

"Like what?" he said.

"Well, like when your wife called," I said. During our conversation his wife had phoned him. He had taken the call, had held a brief discussion with her, and had then returned to our talk.

"I don't need to talk to her in private," he said. "Look, I don't even have a locked desk. There's no lock on it. If people want to know what's in my desk, they're welcome to look. The way I figure it, the more they know, the better.

"I tell my assistants that if a letter to me is marked 'Personal,' open that letter first. I have no such thing as private mail. And as far as a private office goes, I'm certainly not going to start now."

We were looking out the windows at Dallas again, and suddenly, for the second time during our conversation, he started talking about dying.

"Look," he said, "you're just a guy. I'm just a guy. You're going to die. I'm going to die. We're all just kind of moving through here.

"For me, it could be tomorrow. It could be twenty-five years from now. If you ask me, most likely it'll be in twenty-five years. I'm in great shape. But it could be at any time."

I asked him if looking out at all of the buildings was what had made him start thinking about his own mortality. Did the buildings represent the legacy he would leave behind?

"I don't know," he said. "Who built the great buildings of the past? Do you know? I don't. Probably only the family of the builder knows. My name isn't on my buildings. Maybe they're monuments, but the public will never know it."

"Then what's the point of being a builder?" I said.

He looked at me with an intensity that seemed to be greater than anything he had shown all afternoon.

"I don't know anything that could be better than to be a builder," he said. "When you're a builder, you've done something. When you're a builder, you've caused something to happen. Damn right."

Bearings

DALLAS, TEXAS

Population: 938,250
John Neely Bryan first settled Dallas in 1841, building his cabin almost precisely on the spot where President Kennedy was to be assassinated. Bryan thought the site on the Trinity River would be the northwestern terminus of Gulf of Mexico navigation. Two boats made it up the river in the next hundred years.

In his time Bryan lured prospective settlers with free whiskey and sold most of his 580 acres for $7,000. Today a square foot of his holding goes for as much as $300–$350.

In 1983 Dallas builders put up nineteen thousand single-family homes; one hundred companies a month relocated to the city; and the city's matrons threw some 120 charity balls at one hundred dollars or more a plate.

In the same year Dallas car dealers sold one Mercedes every three hours.

In the last five years the city has spent $133 million on the construction of facilities for the arts.

A luxury box at Texas Stadium sold this year for $1.5 million.

Dallas is known to some as the Can-Do City and to others as The City That Works, although Houston businessman Lan Bentsen says that Dallas residents "have no sense of humor." The city's divorce and teen pregnancy rates are among the highest in the nation.

Dallas residents have been heard to say that the TV series bearing their city's name more accurately reflects the values of Houston.

■■■■■■

Tinsel Teens

Charlie Haas

S ome of us, years after graduating from college, still love
college towns. We hit these little European pockets of
America and feel right at home, happy to see an entire local
economy running on strong coffee, imported cigarettes, and used
books. The Vivaldi and chess in the bus-your-own coffeehouses,
the day packs and bicycles aren't clichés to us, they're fraternal
high signs. Some of us like these places so much that we graduate
and never move away; others collect new college towns all our
lives, always looking for these funky holdouts against a landscape
that lights up, beeps, and buzzes.

Westwood Village is *nothing* like that. Westwood Village,
which adjoins UCLA but looks like MTV, is a kids' chic business
district so marvelously slick that you can enter it at twilight and
glide all evening along the goofily curved and angled streets,
feeling no friction and seeing, in a few blocks, the diet of hipness
that will be fed to kids in slower regions for the next five years,
after clearance from Westwood's spotless test boutiques.

CHARLIE HAAS currently lives in the relatively untrendy city of Oakland.

If the currencies of past youth scenes were cultural ideas and political positions, the currency of Westwood is currency, and plenty of it: this is the Greenwich Village of moneyed leisure, the Left Bank of beautiful-brute hype. You can rummage in college towns for wisdom, but you go to Westwood for cleverness—clever clothes on clever bodies, droll food at arch tables. Westwood is your college town as remade by Hollywood. On weekend nights it is hardly a college town at all. On those nights Westwood is teen heaven.

Westwood doesn't attract teenagers with bitchin' surf, straight drag strips, hot dance floors, or anything so prosaically teen. If you ask a fifteen-year-old girl in state-of-the-art *haute* -tramp exposed-midriff fashion and a two-hour eye-makeup job what she likes about Westwood and close your eyes as she answers, you can imagine that you're hearing an upper-middle-class, upper-middle-aged lady describe a favored destination in Europe: "Yes, well, there are a lot of nice *shops*, you know, the *gift* shops and so on, and there are, *ah*, some nice *restaurants*, and of course it's nice to, oh, go to a restaurant and then, say, a movie. . . ."

On a Saturday afternoon the kids start drifting in from all over the city to kick things off with some serious clothes shopping. Boys who can name you every designer in their outfit, from Generra all-cotton jacket down, are heard to swear undying love for the shoes at Leather Bound. The Limited Express, with technopop on the PA, offers Day-Glo sweat-fleece cardigans and other punch-line looks; a few doors down, at the other Limited store, the emphasis is on foreign designs—Forenza, Kenzo. But what is key for the Westwood girl of the moment—even more key than Esprit—is Guess?, a line of sportswear heavy on soft-shaped whites, pastels, and denims. "They'll buy anything Guess?—the *label* sells," says a seventeen-year-old salesgirl at MGA. "They spend a lot of money, but then, *clothes* are a lot of money now." The biggest hit garment with the girls is a hugely oversize white jacket with overlapping seams, a jacket so shapeless and enveloping that its wearers look like sculptures waiting to be unveiled at adulthood.

In the meantime, there is Westwood, high school polite society. The Village is easily walked across, but a pedicab service has sprung up, with all the "drivers" in black bow ties and some in formal dress. For those over twenty-one there are bars with alcohol, and they too are models of decorum: upstairs at T. J. Honeycutt's, clean-cut young people dance under a mirror ball to recorded pop you can talk over. At Baxter's downstairs bar, where the cocktail waitresses wear tiny sport shorts and satin team jackets, amiable chatter drowns out the rock videos on the multiple monitors, and a banner says WEDNESDAY NIGHT IS DYNASTY NIGHT —CHAMPAGNE 25¢, 9 P.M. There are video games in Westwood, but they are massed in one arcade, just as junk-jewelry vendors are confined to one courtyard, instead of lining several sleazy blocks as they do near UC Berkeley. If down these clean streets a man must go, he can do so for hours without being asked for spare change. There is a sprinkling of kids in the spirit-of-1976 punk look; an ambling few of them say that their idea of a hot time in Westwood, like anyone else's, is dinner and a movie—though, as hard-core anarchists, they make a point of copping meals and admissions from friends with jobs on the inside.

In the restaurants, fifteen-year-old diners place polite orders with sixteen-year-old waitresses, but a full-course meal is not the only option: in Westwood, not even the junk food is junk. There are bulging falafels at Me & Me; Louisiana hot links at The Wurst; a clean, well-lit building housing an international arcade of GYRO SOUVLAKI TANDOORI CURRY KEBAB. There is Fatburger, "the last great hamburger stand," where the king chili-cheese-egg burger is so wetly unmanageable that watching someone eat one is an invasion of privacy. You can buy Bordeaux-chocolate-flavored popcorn in a gourmet popcorn store, order Heath Bar chips chopped into your raspberry custard ice cream with rum-soaked raisins poured on top at an icecream place, eat New York-style pizza in a storefront decorated as a New York subway station. When a new method is discovered for achieving treats, the technology is rushed instantly to Westwood, the Silicon Valley of silly delight.

When a new movie is released, same deal: to go to a picture here is to go to a *show,* to glide under the neon-crammed marquee of a heroic old theater, up to a cashier's cage where computers monitor ticket sales, past the studios' proudest die-cut star-photo stand-ups, across the lush undergrowth pictured on the old-fashioned lobby carpet, to projection and sound of a quality that has become rare.

But as sound-stage spectacles, movies in Westwood have to compete with the stores. In the Nike sports-fashion store on Westwood Boulevard a giant fire-red 3-D plastic Nike swoosh logo hangs from the ceiling, its point sticking through the plate-glass window and out over the street, with faked burn damage in the masonry overhead. *Aahs!* a store that sells the same Jetson-family T-shirts, naughty greeting cards, and candy-colored planning diaries as half a dozen other Westwood stores yet achieves distinction through sheer size, limits the number of customers, so kids line up on the sidewalk, patient victims of Saturday Night Browsing Fever. In one T-shirt store the salesgirl says that a shirt with a plain pink pig on it is her biggest seller ("I think because people consider themselves pigs"); at another, Lacoste-type knit shirts with pairs of screwing alligators are moving fast. At a third, the I FUCK ON THE FIRST DATE T-SHIRT is big, as are some devoted to Westwood's true compulsion: WHEN THE GOING GETS TOUGH, THE TOUGH GO SHOPPING, and I CAN'T BE OVERDRAWN, I STILL HAVE SOME CHECKS. But all of these, sweetly, are outsold by FEED THE WORLD and WAR IS STUPID.

By 10:00 P.M. the sidewalks are packed with kids from all over the city, and the streets are filled with slow-cruising cars, kids striking up acquaintances in shouts, visiting one another in grid-locked Z's and Baja trucks. Even in Westwood, a fifteen-year-old's sophistication runs only so deep, and some of the kids are like farmers come to town: "Look at *that!* Look at *her!* Hey!" They are boisterous, but in a mild, vacationing way—Westwood is a place where people who live four freeway exits away become resort tourists in their own city. There are a lot of couples but also a lot of same-sex pairs and packs, and no urgent mating frenzy: a pack of boys sweeps up to a pack of girls on a corner, collects phone numbers, and breezes on. The kids are genuinely happy, which makes sense: sure, they live in the shadow of the nuclear bomb, but they also stand within walking distance of *two* all-night Fatburgers.

As it gets late a mass of kids crowd onto the wedge of sidewalk in front of Glendale Federal Savings and Loan (it takes real style to look cool in front of posters about interest rates). A couple of LAPD cops keep an eye on the crowd and hand out a few traffic tickets. "Westwood is orderly," one of them says, "because we keep it orderly. We have eight officers on foot patrol here on weekend nights, two during the week. Occasionally there will be trouble—a knife fight or something—because they're coming from all over now."

His fellow officer is letting a young woman talk him into signing a piece of paper that says she got thirty-two people to sing "Row, Row, Row Your Boat." "It's for Lifespring," she says. "That's a self-awareness organization, but I'm not allowed to talk about it." Meanwhile six Asian teenage girls wearing Oreo-cookie costumes "as part of our Hell Week" for a sorority march through the crowd, followed by six Asian teenage boys who exchange graphic fantasies regarding the girls. Pledge a sorority, pledge a self-awareness scheme: one-stop shopping.

The cop's words aside, the Westwood kids look more inclined to diet than riot. Adults who work in Westwood almost invariably describe weekend nights there as "a zoo." This is accurate, but perhaps in more ways than the speakers intend: Westwood is a place where kid wildness is neatly restrained, where the central pleasure is to check one another out like little loaned pandas. (Youth wants to know: Is your Guess? as good as mine?) The kids in front of Glendale Federal mill around just as they do at school recess, but this is gourmet recess, the all-city walking-around finals.

The conventional jive about L.A. is that the neighborhoods are insular, that ethnic and racial groups don't mix, and that nobody walks. The Westwood kids, ignoring all that, have fashioned an integrated promenade that makes the adult visitors envious. Westwood is slick, but it is not a mall or an amusement park, not forged or run by a single intelligence. Instead, it's an actual urban neighborhood, with at least some randomness; if you've been growing up in Woodland Hills, this alone can seem a dizzying freedom. And Westwood actually invites kids, offers them a physical place to match their moment. Everyone is welcome—be a punk if you want, that's fine, punks add color, but be a *designer* punk, all right? Because this is not the Beach, not the Valley; tonight we are playing the Palace, the Carson show, of being a kid. A little élan; we are walking in *Westwood,* and what we do and wear here this Saturday night they will be doing and wearing six months from now in New York, two years from now in Cleveland, ten years from now at nostalgia-themed charity balls.

And on Sunday morning there is a ton of litter on the sidewalk in front of Glendale Federal. All of it in the trash baskets.

Bearings

WESTWOOD, CALIFORNIA

Population: 35,543
In 1919 department-store magnate Arthur Letts bought 3,296 acres of lima-bean fields for $2 million and entrusted them to his son-in-law Harold Janss for development. Janss conceived Westwood as a "Mediterranean shopping village" and billed it as "America's most unique shopping center." The village was opened in 1929.

In the five blocks that comprise Westwood there are eleven first-run movie theaters—the highest concentration in the world—eighty-four restaurants, and, at recent count, six cookie stores. On a recent evening fifty people waited in line at Mrs. Fields.

Westwood has no hardware stores, supermarkets, or laundromats—they were forced out by high rents—and there are no massage parlors, bowling alleys, or adult movie theaters, which are prohibited by zoning laws.

The village contains the three busiest intersections in Los Angeles, one of which handles 108,000 vehicles a day.

The mean value of a Westwood home is $250,000.

Westwood has been described as a giant movie theater surrounded by a giant concession stand. Merchant Jerry Oster calls it "the only place in L.A. where you can see people from the neck down."

The High
and the Mighty Crowd

Peter Davis

I'd never spend time so fruitlessly myself, but a friend of mine has recently made a number of journeys along the air corridor between New York and Washington. He admits he did not have any appointments in either of the cities and was riding up and down for no purpose more noble than mere observation. My friend's objective was to do research for a thesis he planned to entitle "An Ethnographic Comparison of Status Acquisition in the Eastern United States and Western Africa," his theory being that he was studying two societies of hunters who, regardless of their actual needs, were in a constant state of wanting. Alas, my friend's stomach for this undertaking proved stronger than his mind.

His principal means of locomotion was the Eastern Air-Shuttle. He had begun not with the Shuttle itself but with the notion of talking to alumni of Ivy League colleges between the

PETER DAVIS is a contributing editor of *Esquire* who lives in New York City. He has been traveling on the Eastern Air-Shuttle since its inception in 1961.

tenth and twenty-fifth reunions of their graduating classes. The idea was to catch them *after* their occupational patterns had become clear but *before* they became chairmen of their companies, changed careers, ran for the Senate, committed leveraged buyout on the floor of the Stock Exchange, or found their third wives. He was expecting to leave for Botswana when he finished his domestic research. Diligently, my friend set about tracking down the Ivy grads.

To his astonishment, none of them ever seemed to be in the offices they had listed in their alumni directories. "Mr. Brown caught the 8:00 and will be with the Air Force procurement board all day at the Pentagon," a secretary in New York would tell my friend. Mr. Green was not at his Washington law office because he had hopped the 7:00 to advise a New York corporate client on the tax implications of a proposed merger. Mr. Black of Wall Street had taken the 9:00 to see Mr. White of the Treasury, but they weren't in Mr. White's office either, because they had both gone up to the Hill to testify before Congressman Gray's Subcommittee on Greed. As for Mr. Silver and Mr. Gold, the former planned to stay overnight at the Princeton Club on Forty-third Street and would try to be back *down* in the morning, while the latter would be staying at the Hay-Adams in Lafayette Square and might not be back *up* until Thursday night.

My friend, as a result, began taking the Shuttle himself just to see what was going on. He would haul his books on tribal customs along with him, still hoping to decamp for Africa before long, and he would look up and down the aisles for Mr. Green or Mr. White or whomever. He always saw someone he knew but never found anyone he was looking for. Back and forth he flew, up and down the Shuttleway between the capitals of finance and politics. He grew dizzy, but it wasn't air sickness.

The outcome is obvious enough. My friend was forced to abandon his ethnographic project when he contracted a severe depression. His doctor not only grounded him but claimed that he was in danger of irreversible brain damage due to constant buffeting by status symbols.

My friend's gone south now, gone south permanently, where he claims to be the youngest year-round resident of Dunedin, Florida. In the end, his distraction led him to rip out a page from his African research and affix it defiantly to the top of these Shuttle notes:

> By the age of thirty a man enters the most productive period of his hunting career, which is likely to extend for at least fifteen years. During this time, he will walk between 1,200 and 2,100 miles a year in the pursuit of the fifty-five species of mammals, birds, reptiles, and insects considered edible. He will use various methods to capture animals living above and below the ground, including knocking them down with sticks, snaring them, chasing them with or without dogs, and hunting them in the classic style with poisoned arrows and spears. Relying on his own and other people's knowledge of environmental conditions, he will decide in which direction the hunters should go on a particular day.

It may not matter that the excerpt was from a study of the !Kung, a tribe in West Africa, by Marjorie Shostak. Signs of my friend's derangement are prompt, unavoidable. They recede at times, always to return.

Hello, my life, old pal, what's the Shuttle scuttle?

Measure your jobs, kids, wives, anxiety attacks in Shuttle spoonfuls.

You've ridden Shuttle shotgun since the Sixties. Did you lose that first chance at a vice-presidency because you couldn't think what to say to old H. G. as he sat next to you and blinded you with his emerald cuff links in '67? You had been wanted and found trying. Shuttle-upmanship.

Classmate, we said we'd keep in touch for sure when we met here in the first Shuttle and New Frontier year of '61, each of us newly wed, and what happened that we never did? Money talks, but all it ever says is goodbye.

So H. G. passed you over, but a kid was on the way and opportunity beckoned again and was answered when you won the race to the SEC and Amalgamated lost, and they made you V.P. in '73, though no longer the youngest.

Hello, Hickey-Freeman, what suits you?

Seven-fifteen A.M. at LaGuardia for the 8:00 Shuttle, first section. It fills up early with early birds. The power Shuttle.

Assistants and managers take the 7:00; CEOs and senators take the 9:00 or the 10:00, but in a sense they aren't even flying, because they have already got where they're going. The action is on the first section of the 8:00, the flight for the man in motion. Coming of age in the wanting class.

We are looking here at predominantly white males, packed in with Styrofoam coffee cups, breathing the ink of the *Times, Post, Journal,* and *USA Today.* For the discriminating traveler who demands more than Styrofoam, Au Bon Pain, the French bakery in the boarding area, offers croissant aux épinards, pain au chocolat, Perrier, and Orangina. All aboard the subway-in-the-sky cattle car, but they are prize Guernseys and Charolais, every one of them.

The power Shuttle: so much ambition packed into so small a space, asphyxiating and exhilarating. One is not usually asleep in a Shuttle seat but not fully awake either. There is a state of semialertness, as in waking, but of semidreamlikeness, as in sleep. England and France have their political and financial power in their capitals. We don't, so we have to have the Shuttle. Power becalmed, strapped to its seat back in the upright position, tray table folded into the seat back in front of it, but power nonetheless. Power bubbles up through the headlines the passengers shroud themselves in. REAGAN VOWS FIGHT FOR MX IN CONGRESS, EXHORTS GOLDWATER. DIVIDEND IS SAFE, AT&T SAYS.

I said, Hello, Hickey-Freeman, what suits you this morning?

Hey there, Stetson, where you heading? Don't you high-hat me.

Well, hi, Rolex, who are you watching today?

"The International Monetary Fund, actually."

And, actually, how do you clock them, Rolex?

"At a high rate, thanks."

Good, good, that's a start. May I know your name, then? "Get lost."

"I'd like to ask you to give us your attention while we review safety features with you. Will you please take a moment to familiarize yourself . . ." Minimal nonsense between passengers and flight attendants—stewardesses, as the pre-1970 M.B.A. generation still calls them. The attendants like the Shuttle; they can grow their nails long since they don't have to serve food, and they're home every night. They run their pushcart up and down the aisles twenty thousand feet above the ground to collect fares, and that's about it. Fifty-five minutes, over and out.

BANK OFFICERS SMUGGLED POT . . . and MARR-YIN' LIZ HAS A NEW FIANCÉ, *USA Today* proclaims saucily.

IRAN IS ADAMANT ON THE HIJACKERS and RE-LIEF OFFICIAL ACCUSES ETHIOPIA OF "BITING THE HAND" THAT FEEDS IT, cautions the *Times*.

Come on, says the *Times*, get serious. F.A.A. INSPEC-TIONS CURB 16 AIRLINES. Though Eastern is not involved, this is surely of interest to Shuttle passengers; who knows where they have to fly next? But *USA Today* peddles no gloom, prefers to see the same glass much more than half full—AIRLINE SAFETY: 95% PASS.

Blue-and-white-striped shirt in a window seat, strangling respectably in foulard tie, cuff links of onyx and gold, black shoes, but they're loafers with tassels—he's big enough to permit himself a whisper of flair, if only on his lower terminals. Go back again to the tie: chalk-white circles on a field of investment-banker blue silk crepe de chine. The point is inside the white circles, from each of which gleams the bloodshot eye that never blinks. Try to look away from that red dot in a meeting at the FDA, FTC, State, Commerce, Agriculture, or Justice. Onyx and gold, too, there's class for you.

The pilot apologizes for a slight ground delay. No one seems impatient. It's not as though the World Bank will come to an end if someone walks into a 10:00 meeting at five past. "Ladies and gentlemen, I'm happy to report we're now at the head of the line and will be departing momentarily." The Piaget in the next seat says 8:02, but maybe he trains it to run five minutes fast, as so many of them do, in which case we're still just before the hour, like the first section is supposed to be, ladies and gentlemen. Ladies? Who's he talking to, his own flight attendants? On this chockablock first section of the 8:00, with almost 170 seats filled, I have been able to head-count ninety-two passengers. This is an equal-opportunity narrative, composed without regard for race, creed, color, gender, or country of national origin, but so far we are looking at seventy-seven white males, six white females, four black males, one black female, and four Japanese males. "Why exactly many savages have made it a rule to refrain from women in time of war," Sir James Frazer tells us in *The Golden Bough*, "we cannot say for certain, but we may conjecture that their motive was a superstitious fear lest, on the principles of sympathetic magic, close contact with women should infect them with feminine weakness and cowardice."

In the air, no one gazes out the windows; almost everyone has made this trip too many times before. Shuttlers look at the reports they are set to deliver, charts they were supposed to learn last night before they got too sleepy. The onyx-and-gold cuff links on the blue-and-white-striped shirt are turning pages in a leather-bound notebook marked LEHMAN BROTHERS on the outside. A historical artifact, since Lehman was lately swallowed by Shearson/American Express.

An attractive woman in a yellow cashmere sweater sporting a Bonwit's circle pin worries that the flight attendant will keep her Visa card and is afraid she hasn't signed the receipt. "You signed it before you boarded," the flight attendant tells her with a smile, returning her card and passing along to more frequent travelers. The woman in cashmere is not dressed for business and is going to Washington only to visit relatives, a typical passenger on any other flight, an almost ostracized outsider on an early-morning Shuttle.

Two other women sit next to each other, dressed properly for Shuttledom. One, the only black woman aboard, wears her Chester Barrie London W1 midnight-blue blazer over her open-neck sky-blue silk blouse and the single strand of milky pearls. She is going to argue about software with the General Services Administration, which supplies government agencies with most of the equipment they use. Her accidental companion—that is, they do not know each other but they may have chosen proximity to create a defensive perimeter—is negotiating a contract with the Navy for her electronics company on Long Island. She sets off her blond hair with a gray suit over a powder-blue rayon blouse and a gold chain necklace. Her level, she says, is middle management, and, like the black woman, she declines to share her name. "In my business, you can only lose when the press identifies you." She comes down once a month and does not feel strange as one of the very few women on board. "It used to be worse. You are surrounded, and yet I hardly notice anymore. How would you feel on a plane with ninety or 150 women?"

The man with the onyx-and-gold cuff links on the striped shirt has a finely woven gray herringbone for his outer wrapping. The chart he studies inside his Lehman Brothers notebook is titled "The EuroDollar Floating Rate Notes." Intent as he is upon the task of preparing himself, he is unfailingly polite when interrupted. It cannot come as a total shock that he is an investment banker on his way to the World Bank. He still has his youth and a measure of vulnerability about him, burdens he bears respectfully. "I'll be advising the Bank today, if I can. Nothing all that out of the ordinary."

How many of you will be there?

"Possibly half a dozen of us. We'll spend the morning discussing how the Bank can best position itself to borrow in the international capital markets."

How much will it be needing to borrow?

"I'd rather not say. It depends."

Depends on what?

"Interest rates. What the debtor nations are in need of at any given time and what the capital markets have available."

Well, is it in the hundreds of millions?

"At least. *Uh*, if you'll excuse me, I really have to get ready . . ."

Sure, sure, in a moment. Do you mind if I ask your name?

"I'm afraid I do. *Uh*, thank you."

Thank *you*. But we're still trapped six inches apart.

Bolting at last into the aisle, I search for other industrial and corporate folkways. Here is a computer programmer Shuttling to set up new hardware in his company's exclusive government marketing center. Over there are two IBMers commuting to rent more space in the capital for their company. A salesman from Champion International is going down to investigate complaints by the Federal Emergency Management Agency. In the afternoon he will call on Contel, the information-satellite transmission company. "You go to see what the other guy *really* thinks, which you can't quite do on the phone."

"Some aspects of the elaboration theory of instruction facilitate learner control over content, while others impede it," a developmental psychologist reads as he prepares for a meeting at the *National Geographic* division that produces videodisks for classroom use. "FCC Declaratory Ruling in the Interconnection of Carriers," runs the heading for a sprightly subparagraph being studied by a NYNEX lawyer who works with the Washington legal community as well as with the FCC. The breakup of AT&T is the still point between the B.C. and the A.D. of the communications world. "People think the telephone industry is susceptible to more market competition than really exists," he says. "It's a natural monopoly. Since divestiture, we have begun to adjust from a regulated monopoly to a competitive marketplace, but you'll see in a few years . . . MCI, GTE, Sprint, ITT, and a few others will survive; the hundreds of small carriers won't make it."

Down the aisle, phrases float over the jet hum like clouds above a still lake.

". . . never even alleged to be liable . . ."

". . . the kinda schedule I'm on, we're lucky . . ."

". . . absolutely nonnegotiable bottom line . . ."

". . . if we screw three times a month, no-frills at that, like this plane . . ."

". . . whatever we have to do to get it, we have to do it fast . . ."

But most people are reading the newspapers that connect them to one another, that do not so much define as reflect their interests. Why do I think this? Because there is a quality to the reading that gives it the force of ritual; it is being done less for revelation than for confirmation. People nod as they pore over the familiar liturgies. New information fits into old patterns, arguments will be butressed, future conversation levers will be forged, then the rest of the story is skipped. Eyes glaze, attention clicks off and on.

The discriminating passenger eventually finds himself riveted to *The Wall Street Journal*'s shorts. These, on the evidence, predict many of the Shuttlers' own aims and fears. "The SEC accused a former McGraw-Hill executive of insider trading in Monchik-Weber stock." "SmithKline Beckman pleaded guilty to charges of failing to quickly report side effects of an anti-hypertension drug since linked to at least twenty-five deaths." "Peat Marwick Mitchell was sued for more than $130 million by the FDIC on charges that it had failed to conduct a proper audit of Penn Square Bank." "Coca-Cola hopes to inject fresh life into its soft-drink sales abroad." A few pages on, the *Journal* is addressing deficits and the contention between financial and political power. CURBING THE PENTAGON—CUTTING THE BUDGET, PART IV, AN EDITORIAL SERIES. REGAN SAYS ADMINISTRATION IS WEIGHING PROPOSAL TO PLACE SOME CONTROLS ON FED. SEC CENSURES E.F. HUTTON OVER FUNDS' USE. Ads for Tiffany, Mellon Bank, Taittinger, Ameritec, Sea Island, Chase, ITT, Dialog Information Services, Bulgari, Gates Learjet, Wang, Barbados, Tourneau, and Drexel Burnham leave little doubt as to the wants of the wanting class.

Any Shuttler can see what a proud time it is for capital, what a miserable moment the other side is having. "Life is getting rough these days for the world's Marxists. Marxist regimes everywhere have those continuing, niggling problems with breadlines," the *Journal* announces in an editorial. "More telling, Marxist governments just don't work very well. North Korea sputters while South Korea soars. Vietnam stagnates while Thailand spurts. East Germans watch West German TV and sometimes go over the Wall; no one goes in the other direction."

Travelers along this two-hundred-mile umbilical cord between the centers of capital and governance know what they are going for. They may be immobilized in their seats, like babies impatient to be born. They may display aspects of themselves only wives are normally close enough to them to know about—a shawl of dandruff, a whistling snore. But they know their purpose as well as their direction. They are not the chosen but the choosing people. These Shuttlers and their fixed goals are reminders that American businessmen, perhaps alone among us, know what they want. Their bottom line *is* the bottom line. Lincoln told us labor was prior to capital, but we do not believe him. Capital and profits are still sacramental to us.

Isn't the lesson of these catnapping Shuttlers, for whom ambition has been elevated to theology, that the ignored history of America is a business history? "Yea I say that any honest laborious man may in a shorte time become riche in this Country," cried Peter Arundle of Virginia in 1622, giving early voice to the continental ideology. This may be why businessmen are so much more potent than others in determining our national myths. A politician, athlete, cowboy, movie star, or even a journalist—frequent Shuttlers all—may become a kind of hero, but he always wears a mask. Ripped off, the mask reveals him to be a business success, a man who markets his ideals, his scoops, his brand of justice more adroitly and convincingly than his competitors do. Anyone who does not "in a shorte time become riche" has only himself to blame. Knowing what they want, American businessmen strive to get it, while the rest of us make laws to keep them from getting too much of it.

At the heart of the Shuttle condition is the businessman's knowledge of what he is here for. The chronicles of earlier civilizations revolved around wars, famines, and migrations; our own are punctuated by the rise and fall of mercantile, industrial, and financial dynasties. These are where a regularly denied essence of America asserts itself. For in any business the rights of property precede the rights of men and women, the U.S. Constitution notwithstanding. It is in a political sense alone that we can claim democracy. We are asked periodically to approve or disapprove of our governors, but we are never asked whether a business enterprise is serving our needs. Hierarchic ideas, repressed officially in the organs and rhetoric of the state, surge forward in the economic expressions of our selves known as businesses.

The prevailing complaint now is that the government interferes with the individual baronies, duchies, and monarchies of commerce and industry. Yet how much impact on the habit of financial kingship has regulatory government managed to have? Would anyone claim that Henry II of Ford was less a king than his grandfather, Henry I? Chairman Rand V. Araskog of ITT may be less famous than Andrew Carnegie was, but is he less powerful? Doesn't the crowned head of a multinational conglomerate achieve at least a trade-off with the industrial titans of the past, his power less autocratic but measurably more far-flung? In absolute terms, he must delegate more decisions, listen to more stockholders, and worry more about the SEC, but in relative terms his sway is over vastly more wealth and territory. When we rejected monarchy as our political model, we enshrined it in our economic lives, putting it at the heart of our daily quest for food, clothing, shelter, and control over the lives of others. "The people who own the country ought to govern it," said John Jay, our first Foreign Secretary and first Chief Justice of the Supreme Court. The tone was set.

"Have a successful day in Washington." We're on the ground, and she does not say "Have a nice day," or "Enjoy your stay," or even "It's been a pleasure serving you." She knows what you're here for. The final count: 169 passengers, 154 white males.

The flight attendants, having brought their cargo to its destination if not its destiny, often take time for breakfast before they turn around and work the 10:00 back. "Outside the Shuttle corridor," Gloria Ryland says, "people are warmer and kinder. Here it's always push and rush. I like it because it gets me home at night, but passengers on the other runs are more laid-back, pleasanter, and calmer. Here they're hyper." She is a light-skinned black woman who has spent nine years on the Shuttle. "In the early seventies you might get one black on a Shuttle in two days. Now you see maybe half a dozen on a crowded flight. A few more women will ride than used to. There's some change, but it's not going as fast as people think."

"Look at the ones who carry luggage," says Patricia Polhill, who has been Shuttling for three years. "They're spear carriers. The heads of companies carry nothing, like Reagan going to his helicopter. The power brokers have the thinnest briefcases. If they're schlepping a garment bag and a lot of carry-on stuff, they're footmen. Either they don't like their jobs or they haven't made it yet and they're not taking much care to cover that up. If I want to meet someone, I'll look for a man with a thin attaché case and a Patek Philippe or a Rolex on his wrist." She is smiling and enjoying herself, as she does in flight, but the other flight attendants nod when she talks about who carries and wears which marks of his station. "You used to be able to tell by the gold credit cards, but gold isn't enough anymore. Now some of them have platinum. Platinum is power, baby."

"Never again!" Sally Miller shakes her long blond hair as she remembers the one date she had with a passenger. "Four years on the Shuttle, I go out with one guy I meet on a flight, just one, and he turns out to be a rape artist. Never again." Later, she laughingly refers to herself and her companions as Shuttle Princesses and admits she has broken down and accepted a date with a passenger who sells stereo systems to hotel lounges. It is not clear if Patricia Polhill would approve of a stereo salesman, or what color his credit card may turn out to be, but Sally Miller is going to give it another try.

Celebrities enliven the day for all Shuttle attendants. Name-dropping is not a tactic, just a game. "We saw Taylor all the time when she was married to Senator Warner." "David Brinkley." "Joe Theismann." "Don't forget his girlfriend, Cathy Lee Crosby." "Sonny Jurgensen." "Javits used to live on the Shuttle." "Kennedy still does." "All the Kennedys." "One of the girls married a Secret Service agent she met on a flight. He's not famous himself, but he took care of people who were." "Moynihan and Cranston." "Moshe Dayan." "I. M. Pei—they say he made the first sketch for the East Wing on the back of his Shuttle boarding pass." "Paul Newman, but we treat everyone the same, the Shuttle's a great leveler." "Except for Jeane Kirkpatrick. She sends people ahead to save a whole row for her, then she comes on all haughty." "Elliot Richardson's a nice guy; he's held a lot of higher offices than she has." "Geraldine was on last week; do you think she'll run for the Senate?" "Bill Bradley yesterday." "Tony Randall." "Warren Beatty." "Roberta Flack." "Senator D'Amato." "Justice Powell." "You can always tell when Congress is in session and the Supreme Court is sitting. We're full." "Bishop Tutu made my day." "Irma Bombeck made mine." "Dr. Ruth Westheimer, the tiny sexologist." "Warner Wolf lives on the Shuttle." "Ed Koch." "How's he doing?" "David Hartman." "Alexander Haig." "Lots of soap stars." "Pat Neal." "Dan Rather." "The same faces all the time, moving up a notch. Barbara Walters brings her P.A. and you think, Gee, that's democracy, but then you think, No, it isn't, it's only the top end of the system, because that little toady may become Barbara's producer in five years; they're on exactly the same track, and most people I know are nowhere near it." "Jesse Helms." "Jesse Jackson."

Sometimes the flight attendants will do as many as three round trips a day, but sometimes after three one-ways—La-

Guardia to National to LaGuardia to National—they can dead-head back to New York on the 2:00 and have the rest of the day to themselves. "The Shuttle is a great relief," Patricia Polhill says. "You don't deal with being away, you don't deal with meals, and you don't deal with the passengers, because they're only with you an hour. You see the same commuters every week. A black woman like me is a double minority, and you learn to observe the "in" crowd. The pecking order puts the white male first, and that's who rides the Shuttle. Within their own group they have another stratification separating spear carrier from chief. The women and the blacks have the rights, but we don't have the money to penetrate into that club the white males control. Look at what we generally call the animal kingdom and you'll see the same thing going on there. Who's who in the zoo."

A black man in a brown suit and a white man in a blue suit scurry for an 11:00 to LaGuardia. Excuse me, may I ask why you're going up to New York?

They both answer at once, on top of each other. "We're with the government."

What branch might that be?

"Treasury."

They move toward the gate, though the plane is not yet boarding. I still don't get it. They have loosened ties and are built like linebackers.

You're going up to discuss finance then, with someone on Wall Street?

"Not at all."

Just going to see your friendly banker, ha ha?

"Not hardly."

May I ask what you gentlemen will be doing in New York today?

"Can't deal with that, fella. We're T-men." They scuttle off. Did they learn their lines from Saturday-morning cartoons? As Treasury agents, they could be with the Secret Service, or the IRS, or they could be tracking down drug peddlers, the illegal export of U.S. technology, a counterfeit ring, or bomb threats.

A PR man and a West Coast computer executive are going up to see someone at RCA to get a project financed that could "revolutionize communications." Rendering conversation obsolete, perhaps. One of them carries a book called *Overcoming Indecisiveness—The Eight Stages of Effective Decision-Making.*

A television producer is shuttling to CBS News to get his documentary on the fortieth anniversary of the A-bomb under way lest, in the year of fortieth anniversaries, the most significant birthday of all, the one that designed the decades ahead of it, be forgot.

A Puerto Rican courier for Goldman Sachs slips onto the 2:00 just before the gate closes. He was hustled down on the 7:00 A.M. to file a new issue with the SEC, instructed to make a pickup at the IMF before racing back. A $300 messenger service, but waiting for the mails is no way to beat the competition, who are using Shuttle runners themselves.

By 3:15 the waiting lounge for the first section of the 4:00 is filling up. The 4:00 and the 5:00 are the power Shuttles back to LaGuardia. Returnees are in the majority in their Hart Schaffner & Marx, Hickey-Freeman, and Brooks Brothers traditionals, but now there is a sprinkling of Washington's elite going up for a Big Apple evening and not about to be out-individualized. Taking calculated risks, it seems, but not really, not when they begin to mingle. Just calculated, then. Giorgio Armani, meet Ralph Lauren. Gianfranco Ferré, of course you know Perry Ellis and Christian Dior. Oh, it's you again, Versace, what are you saying to Piatelli?

"They're ready to do business, Larry. It went real well, real well. I'm going to need more documents, but so far so good. I think we have them by the short ones. Did you hear about your bonus? Neither have I. No, I don't want to talk to him, I'll see him in the morning. Thanks, Larry."

Interim reports back to home offices are made in the phone booths off the waiting lounge. It is the only time emotion is expressed. A curly-headed young man twists a paper clip open and shut while he accounts for himself to his boss. "Same to you, sir. More brass than I ever saw, even in the service. My only problem when we started was I didn't know whether to salute, ha ha, or shake hands with them. But it went like you said, sir. We cleaned their clocks. Do you want me to call again when we get to LaGuardia, just in case you might need me tonight?"

"The order got cut, but no one's telling me how much. Lou and Dick might have helped; I probably should have brought them. I may come in late tomorrow. I'll call you. Get Leslie down here; they beat my ass."

"I need to meet the twenty-four-dozen price, which isn't bad. He'll try to hit us up for a discount, and we may have to give a bit. It could build substantially. The old son of a bitch remembered my father. Keep your fingers crossed. This baby can build. Yeah, small world."

Paranoia is crowding me now, I'll admit that. I keep imagining all the passengers are carrying copies of *People Management*. It is no help to remember what Ruth Benedict found on the island of Dobu: "They are the feared and distrusted savages of the islands surrounding them. The Dobuans amply deserve the character they are given by their neighbors. They are lawless and treacherous. Every man's hand is against every other man." The living pity. Come off it, these are a bunch of nice guys. But nice guys finish last, and these guys are all fighting for the pennant. I am starting to unravel.

Here's a nice guy. Maybe he can help calibrate the quest for power. He's asleep, asleep in his seat on the 4:00 back to La-Guardia. White shirt with initialed French cuffs and gold cuff links. Gray suit with blue pinstripes, brown tie decorated with blue circles, inside of which are yellow dots. Gray hair, too.

A few minutes before, filing onto the plane, I was squeezed between two Secret Service agents, bulges in their Jaeger plaids hitting me fore and aft. As the passengers snaked along from the boarding gate toward the seats, some of them joked, their long workday over, but this was no conga line. Most were silent. No sign or signal disclosed whether the day was ending in triumph or ignominy. You find seats as you would at the theater, and everyone stares forward in the same direction as if for a show. The show never begins.

The man next to me in the gray suit, with the gray hair, is now awake. He is a lawyer who has spent part of the day at the Patent Office arguing an appeal over a cold-cut slicing machine on behalf of its manufacturer. "Basically, a patent is an exception to our antimonopoly laws," he explains.

"What I try to do is get as broad a monopoly as possible for my client. The rest of the day I was asking the Customs Office to stop the smuggling of housewares that compete with another client's products in violation of the Tariff Act. If you can get the government to do the enforcement for you, it's a lot cheaper than suing the foreign competitor. Both Patents and Customs restrict competition; you try to give yourself an open field to run in."

I try to calculate the cumulative annual income on this plane. Surely my mind is decaying rapidly now. What's $170,000 times 170 passengers? Or is that too simple, too low? March to the tune of herringbone and flannel, worsted and screen check and sharkskin.

But soft, who goes there on the other side of the aisle, one row ahead, three seats over? Tall, authoritative, commanding. Unmistakably Paul Volcker. He can make sense of the Shuttle if anyone can.

"Please stay in your seat, sir. We'll be landing shortly, and the seat-belt sign is on."

No, dammit, I've got to see the chairman of the Fed. He unites the two, political and financial power. He understands all this. Just give me five minutes.

"Sir, I said *stay in your seat.* I don't want to have to call for assistance."

"Better do what she says, buddy. Didn't you see the plane's swarming with agents?" Two seats away, J. Press in green twill, paisley tie.

No, I mean, maybe I saw a couple when we boarded.

J. Press gets confidential. "Old Paul's up there by himself, probably figuring out what to do about interest rates now that he's licked inflation. But way up beyond him, in the very front, there's all those guys wearing the badge with a star on it and the small flesh-colored earphones with the tiny cords like the old-fashioned hearing aids. Must be eight or ten of them, though I think some are off duty."

Who are they with, if not Volcker?

"Maureen. Isn't that a kick? Paul Volcker saved the country and no one protects him, but the President's daughter, *huh,* probably going up to see a musical and she gets a squadron of armed guards."

All right, Maureen then. She can tell me what's going on, the link between money and government, God and man, truth and consequences. My hinges are coming off, that's clear. But wait, if it's Maureen, couldn't she make just one call . . .?

No, look, sticking out of the seat pocket next to Volcker. That magazine in front of him, right on the cover. "SUCCESS!" it shouts. "IT IS THE RELIGION OF THE EIGHTIES." Save us. Okay, boss, if that's your decision. *Et tu,* Paul? Then fall, Caesars Palace! I don't know how much more of this I can *taaaaaaaaaa*

aaaaaaaake him away! said the flight attendant to the two passengers on either side of my friend as soon as they landed at La-Guardia. His notes, of course, break off at that point, so we never get to experience the Shuttler's homecoming as he saw it. He was claiming outlandishly to have known Maureen Reagan in an earlier incarnation, and he muttered that she should somehow "reorder the proto-social priorities," as one of the men helping him off explained to me later. Fortunately, Ms. Reagan was far enough in front of him so that she never knew a passenger was disintegrating on her flight, and the Secret Service men were not needed. My friend then asked to see Frank Borman, the yuppie legend who went from pilot to astronaut to chairman of Eastern Airlines; he was going to implore Borman to cancel the Shuttle service and support a Constitutional amendment that would establish a unified political and financial capital at a single New York–Washington midpoint 22.5 miles northeast of Wilmington, Delaware.

The poor man was put in Payne Whitney Psychiatric for a couple of weeks until we could arrange the spot for him down in Dunedin. How he ruined his promise should be a caution to all of us. What a shame he was unable to keep himself aloof from what he observed. A doctor or lawyer like that would not last a week. At the end my friend was simply not playing with a full deck.

He still isn't. Oh, he's better; he never goes near a Hilton down there, and he tries not to eat in any place that takes credit cards. But he still has his fixation on primitive cultures. The other day I got a strange piece of mail. My friend had apparently eaten in one of those fast-food spots that has paper place mats to entertain customers with a quiz for the ninety seconds between the moment you decide on fried clams and when the rubbery husks are deposited in front of you. He had folded up the place mat and stuck it in an envelope. On the front of the mat half the questions were about U.S. Presidents and the other half about NFL quarterbacks. I didn't get it until I turned the place mat over. On its reverse side he quoted a passage from his reading about the !Kung. It's too bad he can't get those tough and gritty little dudes out of his head, because now, of course, he'll never get to see them.

"!Kung men vary widely in their skill at hunting," my friend copied out in penmanship that has still not retrieved the poise we used to admire. "Self-deprecation and understatedness are rigorously required of the hunter after a successful hunt. This modesty is in evidence from the moment he enters his village to relay his news. Walking silently, he sits down by a fire—his own or someone else's. He greets people and waits. When they ask, he says, 'No, I didn't see anything today. At least, nothing worth talking about.' The others, well versed in the rules, press for details: 'That nothing you saw . . . did you get close enough to strike it?' Thus the conversation slowly reveals that an eland, gemsbok, or even a giraffe has been shot. Excitement ripples through the camp as the news spreads."

Bearings

THE EASTERN SHUTTLE

In the late eighteenth century, carriage travel on the Eastern Seaboard averaged seven miles an hour. In 1826 Josiah Quincy made the trip from New York to Washington in a carriage "capable of holding some sixteen passengers with decent comfort to themselves, but actually encumbered with some dozen more." His trip took four days.

In 1812 Oliver Evans said, "The time will come

when people will travel in stages moved by steam engines, from one city to another, almost as fast as birds fly, fifteen or twenty miles an hour. A carriage will set out from Washington in the morning, the passengers will breakfast in Baltimore . . . and sup in New York the same day."

A passenger on a train from New York to Washington in the 1850s had to change trains twice. The trip cost $8.60.

The Eastern Air-Shuttle was inaugurated on April 30, 1961. An Eastern executive said, "The number of people who say they were on Rickenbacker's raft in the Pacific or who were supposed to have been Frank Borman's roommates at West Point is exceeded only by those who claim to have thought up the Shuttle." Eastern president Eddie Rickenbacker called it "a damned bus service."

The Shuttle has come close to being discontinued three times, twice because it was losing money and once during the oil crisis of '74 and '75.

A Shuttle flight will take off even if only one passenger is aboard, a situation that has occurred five times.

━━━━━━

PART 4

INDIVIDUALITY
AND
RECKLESS
IMAGINATION

SAN FRANCISCO, CALIFORNIA
Tolerance

MONTICELLO, NEW YORK
Jewish Humor

TUCSON, ARIZONA
Activism and Devotion

NORFOLK, NEBRASKA
Magnificent Obsession

Officer Hicks, Gay Cop

Joe Kane

The Potrero is among the toughest of San Francisco's nine police districts. Within its boundaries lie almost half the city's public-housing projects, its most economically depressed neighborhoods, and its largest concentration of poor blacks, who find themselves in bitter competition with the growing number of Samoans, Laotians, and Vietnamese in the area. The Potrero is not necessarily more violent than other parts of the city, but its violence is unique. "In Potrero, you don't just get shot," is how one cop put it. "You get your head erased with a twelve-gauge shotgun."

In short, it's no choice assignment. It is a hard, dangerous, unglamorous place stuck on a mostly forgotten edge of the city. It is where J. D. Hicks has worked for four of the five years he has been on the force, and it has left its mark on him: under his right eye is a deep, permanent knife scar; for the past month he's limped from a fractured kneecap.

JOE KANE, who has lived in northern California most of his life, wrote "On the Edge," a San Francisco success story, in the February 1985 *Esquire*.

By any measure, J. D. Hicks is a good cop. In his five years he's earned some thirty-five captain's commendations for outstanding police work. In his first three years he won three Medals of Valor for bravery, the highest honor the city of San Francisco can bestow on an officer of the law. In 1984 the International Footprint Association gave him its National Heroism Award, one of the most prestigious awards a United States policeman can receive. He is the only San Francisco cop ever to win it.

But J. D. Hicks is more than just a good cop. He's a good homosexual cop, and therein lies a distinction far more subtle than anything you might find in Joseph Wambaugh.

It's another brutal winter day in San Francisco—70 degrees, blue skies—and the first thing Hicks does is drive Car 61 four blocks to a delicatessen. Coffee. Three old people sit near a window, taking the sun, and Hicks stops to chat. "You write down that J. D. is the nicest officer in the neighborhood," one of them tells me. I say I will think about it.

Hicks has to make a phone call, and I get my first chance to talk to Hicks's partner, Matt Krimsky, alone. Krimsky is Hicks's antithesis: where Hicks is cool, Krimsky is driven, a hothead: where Hicks is inclined to enforce the spirit of the law, Krimsky does things by the book. Hicks is slim and fair. Krimsky burly and dark; Krimsky is straight. He and Hicks have been partners just over a year.

"I'll say this about my partner," Krimsky tells me. "It's what I'd say about any cop: I don't care who they go to bed with, I don't care where they go to church. All I care about is, can they do the job? When my life is on the line, can they cut it?" Krimsky pauses to light a cigarette. "And I'll say this too: J. D. Hicks is the best cop I've ever worked with."

Yet there's no doubt that when Krimsky fantasized as a kid about being a cop, a gay partner was not part of the plan. Granted, there have been homosexuals in law enforcement as long as there's been law enforcement, but not until the 1980s in San Francisco had there been openly gay cops in the U.S., gays who were encouraged by the powers that be to join the municipal police department specifically because they were gay. On the one hand, that's what you'd expect; after all, this is San Francisco we're talking about.

On the other hand, there was a day not too long ago when Dan White, San-Francisco-born-and-bred ex-cop, walked into the city offices and shot the mayor and the city's first gay supervisor in cold blood. A local jury gave White seven years, eight months; he got off in five. A good chunk of the police force wore FREE DAN WHITE T-shirts. San Francisco might have been the most enlightened city in America, but America was still America, and a cop was still a cop.

It was just two weeks after the Dan White shootings that J. D. Hicks moved to San Francisco. He was thirty-three, old enough to have been through some changes. He had been raised on a ranch in Louisiana and grew up loving baseball and basketball and the outdoors. He got married when he was eighteen, had a son, became a paramedic. But five years into the marriage, things began to change.

"An old childhood buddy got killed in Vietnam, and that triggered it," he says. "It was the kind of emotional jarring that makes you confront things at a gut level. I knew I wasn't happy with who or where I was. Finally, I had to accept that I was gay, and deal with things from there."

He split up with his wife on good terms, moved to Texas, and soon began a long-term relationship with a male lover. Texas was hardly fertile ground for a gay relationship, however, and Hicks paid a visit to San Francisco. It was as if he were visiting another planet.

"At first I was shocked," he says. "Here were men walking arm in arm on the street, men kissing other men. It was wide open, crazy. I loved it." Soon thereafter, Hicks and his companion moved to San Francisco. Hicks took a temporary job managing a delivery service, and then one afternoon, reading the classifieds, he ran across an ad placed by a civilian group encouraging gays to apply for the police force. "It sounded interesting," he says, "so I went for it."

Hicks and three other gays were accepted into a police-academy class of forty cadets. Now in the 1,987-man San Francisco Police Department an estimated 150 officers are homosexual.

The Potrero is Hicks's regular beat. It is a tense assignment, eight hours of constant watchfulness interrupted by family fights, drunk drivers, and medical emergencies. Real action—such as the time Hicks broke into a burning warehouse and saved the lives of seven people trapped on the third and fourth floors, thereby earning his first Medal of Valor—is rare; indeed, Hicks was off-duty for that one.

But there's no telling. On its first stop of the day Car 61 pulls over a driver with an unsafely loaded car. "All yours, Matthew," Hicks says, but his generosity is superfluous. Krimsky is already out of the car, ticket book in hand. "Easy now," Hicks says under his breath and turns to me. "Matt'll ticket him for everything from no registration to his bald tires," he says. "That's not my style. In a neighborhood like this, I find that compassion often works better than a ticket."

I ask whether that derives from empathy—the oppressed helping the oppressed—but Hicks insists it doesn't, that it's simply a pragmatic concern. As if in confirmation, a young black man driving a low-slung Riviera glides by and gives Hicks the high sign. "Like that guy," he says. "I pulled him over last week for hot rodding. Chewed him out good but didn't give him a ticket. Now he's on my side."

It's also part of a code Hicks has worked out for himself, a code that bit by bit I'll begin to pick up. One tenet of that code is a sense of place; as far as Hicks is concerned, he's ready to spend the rest of his career in the Potrero. "A lot of guys get bored, so they change stations every few years," he says. He lights the first of some two dozen Winstons he'll smoke during his shift. "But it seems to me that if you know you're gonna be in a place day after day, year after year, you're gonna be a lot more careful about how you treat people. You'll be dealin' with 'em again."

Hicks is smiling, but his eyes are trained on the car in front of him and on his partner. "There are good people here," he says, "but there are some real badasses, too."

Hicks found himself alone one night in a situation not unlike this. When he approached the car, the driver jumped out and pulled a knife. Hicks would have been within his rights to shoot, but he didn't. Instead, he grabbed the knife by the only part of it available to him—the blade—wrestled the man to the ground, fought off his attempts to get Hicks's gun, and finally subdued him. Hick's assailant went to jail with his body physically intact; Hicks got a sliced-up hand, the scar under his right eye, and another Medal of Valor for his restraint.

Krimsky returns, delivers a *"Nyuck, nyuck, nyuck"* in his best Curly Joe style, and has no sooner settled into his seat than a call comes over the radio. Hicks guns the beat-up Chrysler down Third Street, the Potrero's main drag. "Man down in the street," says Krimsky. "Could be a fight, could be a junkie."

On a sunny back alley they find two black men, one young and agitated, the other middle-aged and sitting with his back propped up against the fence, staring off into infinity.

"My man just went down," the younger man says. The two cops hurry over. Each spent several years as a paramedic before joining the police force. Now they question the older man and make a quick diagnosis: heart attack. "He's had a history of heart problems," Hicks says as he hustles to call the fire department's medical team. "He has a prescription for nitro, but he ran out of money last week and couldn't buy any more."

The fire department truck arrives within a minute and a half, and while Krimsky helps load the patient for a trip to the hospital Hicks checks in with the station, then leans up against the patrol car and lights another Winston. A black kid who looks about ten years old wheels up on his bike.

"Hey, J. D.," he says. "He drunk?"

"Nah. Heart attack."

The kid looks at the man, then at Hicks. "Too much that smokin'."

"You're right."

The kid looks at me. "You doin' paragraphs for teacher?"

"Sort of."

He looks back to Hicks. "You guys gotta lotta undercover on Third Street today."

I'm amazed; Hicks just laughs and says, "They always know." Bored, the kid leaves, but not without first discussing various aspects of the universe with Hicks and wishing him a warm goodbye. "Kids want to like you," Hicks says. "Sometimes I'll give 'em fifty cents to watch my car when I'm away from it —that's cheaper than coming back and finding the tires slashed.

And you'll find that when you're on a chase, one of those kids'll tell you 'He went that way' or 'He threw the purse in those bushes.' "

But I sense something more. Hicks's attitude toward the boy was almost paternal, and I remember that Hicks has a son of his own.

"How old's your kid?" I ask.

"Twenty."

"What's he up to?"

Hicks takes a long drag off his Winston, exhales, grins, and says, "He wants to move to San Francisco and be a cop."

Shortly after he joined the force, Hicks split up with the man he'd been involved with for nine years; the primary cause of the split, he says, was the unexpected stress of his new job. He lives alone now, in a Twin Peaks apartment with a splendid view of the city, and finds his social circle increasingly confined to cops, both straight and gay, which he says is just fine with him.

"When you're a cop, you tend to have mostly cops for friends," says Hicks. "Your other friends drop away. I mean, who wants to invite a cop to a party? What am I going to do when they bring out the drugs?" At Thanksgiving and Christmas he and Krimsky set up a kitchen at the station and cooked a big meal for the cops who had to work. "Most of 'em don't really have any family in the city anyway," says Hicks. "The station's their home."

Within his "family," Hicks comes in for an inordinate amount of praise. "He is someone I'd trust my life to," says his platoon commander, Lieutenant Greg Corrales. Coming from Corrales, that's no small praise. A macho Chicano and former Marine with fifteen and a half years on the force, Corrales is known, as he puts it, as "*the* oppressor of gays in San Francisco." Indeed, he's voluntarily "doing time" in the Potrero—Siberia, as it's known within the force—for allegedly harassing gays while running the street enforcement section of the city's narcotics squad.

"Hicks is open about his homosexuality, but he doesn't flaunt it, and that makes a lot of difference," says Corrales. "In all honesty, if he were flagrant about it—you know, if he wore

leather to work and talked with a lisp—he'd have a lot of trouble.
That kind of stuff embarrasses a partner and makes it hard to get
the job done."

In 1979, in response to a suit filed in federal court, the SFPD
increased its hiring and promotion of women and minorities—a
policy Corrales, himself a member of an "oppressed" minority,
chafes under. "It's a crutch for people not really qualified to be
cops," he says. In 1982 the Board of Supervisors issued its own
minority-hiring resolution, one product of which was a gay outreach and recruiting program, the only one of its kind in the
nation. "The gays have been accepted far better than I would
have thought," says Corrales. "Cops are realists, and you'd have
to be a mental dwarf not to realize what's going on in San Francisco. There's going to be gays on the force, so the question
becomes, Where do we go from here? What kind of job can they
do?"

Directorship of the gay outreach program went to Paul Seidler, a San Francisco native with eighteen years on the force, ten
of them openly as a homosexual. Seidler's view of the integration
of homosexuals into the police force is, as he says, "not quite so
hunky-dory as some other people's."

In fact, Seidler himself spent about seven months fighting
a case that he views as gay harassment by the department. At San
Francisco's Gay Freedom Day parade last year, Seidler was filmed
in uniform kissing another man. The shot ran on the evening
news, and the next day a retired police lieutenant filed a formal
complaint, claiming that Seidler's smooch was conduct unbecoming a police officer. Seidler's defense: given the city's law against
discrimination on the basis of sexual orientation, straight cops
photographed in uniform kissing women on New Year's Eve had
likewise transgressed, if indeed his action was a transgression. The
police chief eventually decided that it was, but no action was
taken against Seidler.

"J. D. Hicks is the kind of cop who makes other gay cops
proud," says Seidler. "He makes them say, 'Look, this is how good
we can be.' But J. D. is not what you'd call outspoken. People who
are aren't always treated so well."

One example Seidler points to is a guy we'll call Len
Thomas, who failed to pass the police-academy tests in 1982, and

who asked that his name be withheld because he is afraid of further trouble. Thomas charged that he'd been discriminated against because of his homosexuality, and under oath, the commanding officers admitted they'd lowered his grade for exactly that reason.

Thomas became a cop, but his career so far has been one of constant harassment. Recently, on patrol alone, Thomas raced to answer an assault-with-a-deadly-weapon call. Caught in a tough spot, he radioed for a backup but found his radio was being jammed anonymously by one of his fellow cops. It was a potentially deadly trick, and one pulled on him more than once.

"Thomas came in with a reputation as an asshole after the academy, and he's paying the price for it," says one gay cop, who also asked that his name not be used. "He's not the type to go along with locker-room jokes and that kind of thing. Cops don't like people who don't fit in."

J. D. Hicks and other gay officers like him find themselves walking a strangely perilous tightrope. On one end sits the old guard of the San Francisco Police Department—what one gay cop called "the Irish alcoholic brain-dead"—into whose strict and unwritten fraternal code Hicks must work his life as a gay man.

But on the other end, surprisingly enough, is the San Francisco gay community, which is at least partially responsible for Hicks's job as a cop. One reason Hicks chose to stay in the Potrero, he says, is that it's "the least gay district in the city. It doesn't have gay communities, like the Castro or Polk Street. When you work among gays, situations polarize very quickly. Either you back them unconditionally or they brand you a turncoat, 'one of those.' I didn't want to go through that."

In addition to the ordinary pressures of being a police officer, there is this balancing act. Hicks's style is low-key and accommodating: At one point in the evening, I will watch him and his partner haul a young, violent, very drunk Latin man into one of the station's two holding cells to dry out. They will remove his jewelry and his belt—a standard safety precaution—the drunk will struggle, and his pants will drop down around his knees, unveiling a spectacular set of white silk undershorts.

Four cops nearby will gurgle with laughter. "Keep Hicks away!" one of them will yell. Hicks will react the way another cop would if, say, he were being kidded about his bald head or big nose: no big deal.

Now, as he loads a shotgun into his patrol car and prepares to head back out on his rounds, he underscores what that means. "I am not a gay cop, and I am not a politician," he says. "I am a cop, period."

Car 61 takes a dinner break, and shortly after that the Potrero begins to heat up. The workweek is over, people have been in the bars awhile, and the district's surly underside is beginning to rumble. Within the space of a couple of hours Car 61 picks up three violent drunks and mediates two family fights—husbands beating wives, parents beating kids.

"Family fights are always a wild card," says Hicks. A month earlier Hicks had responded to such a call and found upon his arrival a scene that his commanding officer, in writing up yet another commendation for him, would describe as "pandemonium right out of Milton's *Paradise Lost*": a hysterical witness; a wife who spoke no English, with injuries to her head, chest, and stomach; a husband bleeding heavily from stab wounds to his neck.

Hicks and the two cops with him saved the husband's life, then booked him and the witness, who, as it turned out, had come upon the husband beating the wife and gone after him with a knife.

"Just a little family dispute," says Hicks.

Tonight, shortly after 9:00, comes an assault-with-a-deadly-weapon call from the Sunnydale projects, probably the most hard-core area of San Francisco. By the time Car 61 arrives, four other squad cars are there and a grumbling crowd of some seventy-five blacks and Samoans has gathered. A cold night fog has rolled in, and in the misty, abstract glare of a single streetlight an old Chevy Impala sits with its windows caved in and two little kids crying in the backseat.

Nearby, two frenzied women scream and hurl curses at each other. It takes two cops on each to restrain them. As is often the case, the degree of violence has little relation to what precipitated it—this time one of the women had lightly rear-ended the other's car. But within minutes the whole desperate frustration of life in the projects had bubbled up, and one had gone after the other with a tire iron.

With the arrival of yet another police car, the crowd grows more agitated. Several people hold barely concealed rocks and bottles. A few cops are visibly nervous; the crowd begins to make noise, and I heard one of them yell, "Sissy!"

I look to see how J. D. Hicks reacts. And as I do, Hicks is striding out of the glare, guiding one of the women gently toward Car 61, talking to her in careful, even tones, even as she is shrieking, "MOTHAFUCKINGUGLYBLACKBITCH," with tears cascading down her cheeks. Here is Hicks opening the back door of Car 61, saying, "We'll get this straightened out and get you home just as soon as we can, ma'am," gently helping her in, a slight grin never leaving his face; and then she sits, just silently sobbing in the backseat, as Car 61 glides out of the projects and down Third Street safely toward home.

Ten-thirty. Almost quitting time, almost time for Hicks to head home and, as he does most nights, watch a movie on cable TV, and maybe do a little packing for the weekend, when he'll load up his four-wheel-drive pickup and head for a friend's cabin north of the city.

Krimsky is in the station house doing paper work; I'm riding shotgun in Car 61. It has been a draining night, yet Hicks is alert, his ears following two different police radios, his eyes scanning the warehouses below Third Street. It is no idle exercise. Two years ago, in this same area, Hicks had driven past a parked car, noticed what seemed to be excess moisture on the windshield, stopped, found the car running, broke into it, and hauled out a man and two kids almost dead from carbon monoxide poisoning. He gave them mouth-to-mouth, all three lived, and he wound up with another commendation.

Tonight, however, the warehouse district is empty—except, that is, for two elderly little women hobbling down a back street. Car 61 is no more than fifty yards past them when a call comes over the radio: two elderly, senile women walked out of their rest home late in the afternoon and haven't been seen since.

Hicks looks at me. I look at Hicks. Hicks throws Car 61 into reverse.

He stops next to the two women and gets out. "Excuse me, ladies," he says. "Do you know where you are?" The two tiny women look at Hicks, look at each other in silent, cosmic consultation, then say, at once, "Why, no."

Hicks helps them down off the sidewalk—"Hold on like you were giving me a big hug"—and eases them into the patrol car. Their hands are like ice; another hour and they'd have been in serious trouble.

Hicks drives them home, a good four miles away, and when he arrives a huge woman rushes out, crying for all she's worth. "Oh, my poor, precious babies, where did you go?" she says and gives Hicks a big hug. The two old ladies wander into their rooms, chattering away as if nothing at all had happened.

Back in the car, Hicks is grinning ear to ear. "That makes my night," he says. "Family fights, drunks—something like this just erases all that. I'll go home feeling like I've done a good job."

A close friend of mine growing up had an uncle named Mike. Uncle Mike had been a beat cop in the Potrero, where he kept the peace—and if he broke a few bones doing it, well, so be it.

Uncle Mike knew about those who, in the words of Christopher Durang's Sister Mary Ignatius, "did that thing that makes Jesus puke." "Cupcakes," he called them. "We hauled those cupcakes downtown and cured 'em." If he was feeling particularly animated—well soaked in his regimen of Budweiser and Paddy's—he'd cock an eyebrow and deliver, in a basso profundo grunt, his ultimate condemnation: "El Strange-o."

As Hicks and I head for the station I wonder what Uncle Mike would say if he were here right now. I know what I would tell Uncle Mike. I would borrow a line from Allen Ginsberg. I would say J. D. Hicks has put "his queer shoulder to the wheel." And I, for one, am damn grateful that he has.

Bearings

SAN FRANCISCO, CALIFORNIA

Population: 678,974

In 1579 Sir Francis Drake, in his ship The Golden Hind, *landed somewhere in Marin County.*

The original name of the San Francisco settlement was Yerba Buena, or "good herb."

Before gold was discovered at Sutter's Mill in the Sierra foothills, San Francisco had eight hundred residents; two years later it had grown to twenty-five thousand. In that period the vast majority of San Francisco's inhabitants were young men.

Henry Thoreau warned men who would join the Gold Rush: "Going to California? It is only three thousand miles closer to hell."

The cable car was introduced in 1885 to negotiate the city's hills; the steepest street is pitched at 31 degrees.

In 1885 twenty-six opium dens were counted in San Francisco's Chinatown.

After the 1906 earthquake, which left seven hundred dead and 250,000 homeless, signs were put up saying EAT, DRINK, AND BE MERRY, FOR TOMORROW WE MAY HAVE TO GO TO OAKLAND.

Twenty percent of San Francisco's population is gay; 28 percent is foreign-born. The area has the highest income per capita of all major metropolitan areas, and San Francisco proper has the highest housing prices of any major city.

Some 1,125 people are thought to have jumped off the Golden Gate Bridge since it was built in 1937.

There have been 405 earth tremors in San Francisco since 1850. Much of the city is built on the unstable rubble of the 1906 quake. There is a 15- to 20-percent chance there will be a major earthquake here by the year 2000.

The Fine Art
of Mountain *Tummling*

Joyce Wadler

This is what it was like, in the Borscht Belt, from a survivor: full of noise, full of Jews, and the jokes grew on trees.

You have perhaps in some long-ago supper club seen Myron Cohen; you think perhaps this is the way it was, five dozen over-the-hill comics wandering around the Catskills shouting, "Cut velvet!" But this was only part of the mountains, rich and lunatic and green.

"The mountains": a collection of wood frame boarding-houses and farmhouses, already collapsing when acquired, with names like the Palace and Paradise and Little Budapest and more often than not a cow on the lawn and some chickens in the back. "The season": that period from Memorial Day weekend to Labor Day weekend—for the hotels are never heated—during which the guests arrive and the family, if business is good, gives up its own rooms and pitches a tent on the front lawn. "The lemosene":

JOYCE WADLER's hometown, Fleischmanns, was "the least successful notch of the Borscht Belt."

an ancient vehicle—usually an Oldsmobile, with the name of the hotel painted on the side—that goes to the train station to pick up the guests. "The casino": the dining room, after dinner, when the tables have been pulled away to make room for a show.

The jokes. All over. Yes, really all over. You do not now believe it, but such was the surreal and marvelous nature of the mountains, of the extraordinary combination of Jewish refugees in the American mountains, that everyone, from the busboys in the kitchen to the ladies around the pool, had the timing of Benny, the delivery of Berle.

"Her mink coat don't keep me warm," sings Gussie Arono-
witz, in the bakery shop in Fleischmanns.

"What you knowed in your whole life about garments, I
already forgot," an old lady actually says at the Lebowitz Pine
View in Fallsburg.

Or maybe she does not.

There are no footlights, you see, separating the amateurs from the professionals in the green Jewish mountains.

In the mountains, it will always be difficult to tell the players from the fans.

Which reminds me, in case there is someone who *doesn't* know the "Cut velvet" joke: Business is going bad at the factory of Schwartz and Ziegel. It gets so bad, Schwartz finally can't stand it. He goes to the window. He jumps. On the way down, he passes the shop of his archrival, Fierstein: hundreds and hundreds of racks of dresses. Schwartz checks out the fabric. Then, with the last words he'll ever speak, he hollers up to his partner.

"Cuuuuuut veeeelvet!"

How do you like your definitions, by the way, geography or state of mind? Geography puts the Borscht Belt three hours out of New York City, in Sullivan and Ulster counties. State of mind could put the Borscht Belt, or Borscht Belt humor, in Bensonhurst, Brooklyn, or in pockets of Lakewood, New Jersey, in the thirties, or in Miami Beach in the fifties. Though of course if you wanted to get to the root of Borscht Belt, you would dateline it Minsk.

Minsk. Feb. 23—Rabbi, give us a prayer for the czar.

Rabbi: Keep the czar well . . . and far away from us.

Time? Maybe the turn of the century. A hilarious time for

the Jewish people. My own great-grandfather, for instance, takes medicine to make him sick to keep him out of the Russian army. He dies from the medicine, but not in vain, giving me, four generations later, the material to make him the punch line of a Jewish joke. My father's father, a tailor, comes to America and buys a share in a boardinghouse in the Catskills so he can enjoy the country air. He enjoys it for approximately twenty years before being clobbered to death by a falling tree, thus making his own contribution to Jewish humor: the absurdity of Jews in nature, which you see running so often through Woody Allen's work. Nonetheless, by this time my grandfather is part of a trend. The Catskills are scattered with boardinghouses. Grossinger's, in 1914, begins as a seven-room farmhouse, with cow. By 1942 in Sullivan and Ulster counties alone there are literally hundreds of small boardinghouses, and more than five hundred of them use entertainers—even if it's only once a week.

They called them *tummlers,* Yiddish for "noise" or "merrymaker," and what they liked to pay them, in the late thirties, early forties, was room and board, and maybe fifteen dollars a week. What the guests generally paid in a boardinghouse was perhaps twenty or twenty-five dollars weekly, all you could eat. They would lie around the pool, with maple leaves on their noses, and in the afternoon they gathered on the lawn to wait for the social director—who in the case of our establishment, the Maplewood House, was cousin Bernie, an English teacher from the city —to give them cha-cha lessons on the porch. Wood frame boardinghouses around them; the shadow of Hitler behind them; but everybody on the floor when the social director hollers, "CHA-CHA-CHA!"

You ask me my memories of the Borscht Belt. I can tell you, again, the first thing is noise. Noise at canasta; noise in the dining room; noise (this is only theory) at the astonishment and joy of being alive. They dried the silverware in the kitchen by putting it in pillowcases and shaking it, to give you an idea.

The second thing—it cannot be repeated often enough, and repetition is the signature of the worrisome Jewish soul—it was funny in the mountains. The bosses yelling at the help were funny. The busboys spitting in the soup were funny. The social directors chasing the weekday widows were funny. Morris the goddamn *butcher* was funny. You want to know the essential spirit of the Borscht Belt, I give you Morris the Butcher, philosopher and refugee, who never saw the stage.

Morris the Butcher on life: "Anyone can sell a steak. To move hamburger, that's something."

Morris the Butcher on the hotel owner who sent back an order of eight dozen eggs because they were green: "When business is slow, they got time to look at the eggs."

What the crowd in the mountains really liked, by the way, was comics throwing themselves, fully clothed, into the pool. Once, after bombing at the Nevele, Jan Murray warmed up the crowd during the day by sliding down the hill on his *tuchis,* and that night, sure enough, he knocks 'em dead.

What can you say—it was very broad humor. Jerry Lewis in the main dining room pouring soup on his head to get a few laughs. Buddy Hackett, doubling as a busboy and comic, scratching his ass through supper all week to provide the setup for one lousy joke. *(Waiter, in front of the guests: "Busboy, I noticed you been standing with your hand on your ass all week. Do you have hemorrhoids?" Hackett: "We only have what's on the menu.")* Crude stuff, rough stuff. Humor of the working class.

Also—and this is perhaps why so many people these days turn away from it, want to make you believe they were never a part of it—it wasn't just crude humor, it was Jew Humor. Shtetl Humor. Unassimilated Humor. Them-and-Us kind of humor. Humor that made fun of the affectations of Jews trying desperately to become part of the middle class. Humor that pointed out the barriers between Jew and Gentile rather than making believe they did not exist. Humor that not only addressed itself to the Jewish long view of the universe (briefly put: Always keep one eye on the exit) but also dealt with areas that some Jews did not want to look at: aggression and self-hatred and overstriving and pain.

Jewish man gets a boat, gets the outfit, gets the captain's hat, takes his mother out for a spin. "So, Ma," he says. "Whattaya think of the captain?" His mother checks him out. "Son," she says, "by me you're a captain. By your father you're a captain. But by a captain, you're no captain."

Have I mentioned, by the way, how many comics who came

out of the Borscht Belt refuse even to discuss that life? I believe it is because of the aforementioned lowbrow nature of the joints. Also because *borscht* is a buzz word for "Hebe"—that is to say, for a comic who can play only to Jews.

"Dah premise is insulting," says one man who made his career in the mountains. "I consider myself a *univoisal* comedian."

"Borscht Belt? Rodney was never in the Borscht Belt," somebody else's publicist says. "He played a few *dates,* but they never went for him. His background was strictly the clubs in New York."

What a pity, to remove oneself from a scene so rich and wild.

Consider: in two counties alone, 524 hotels that require entertainment, which translates into new material *seven nights* a week—guests stay on the average at least two weeks. What a lure for comics, what a pressure cooker, what a pull!

And the excitement, in those days before Beverly Hills. Henny Youngman and his band getting into food fights in the dining room or turning a fire hose on a guest. Gas rationing, during the war, when the comic who had a decent car could get himself a job—provided he schlepped along a few other acts—and when Jack Carter, going to the mountains, would pray, *"Please,* not another dance act, to have to sit five hours under a pile of dresses; *please,* not another magician, to have to sit in the back with the goddamn birds."

Picture it: Singer's Restaurant, which is still there, where Dick Shawn and Jackie Mason and Jerry Lewis and Myron Cohen and Don Rickles and Red Buttons and Joey Bishop hung out after a show and you could always tell, according to Milt Ross, a veteran mountain comic, who was doing good and who was not according to what was on their plate. ("If they were eating a sandwich which was not so expensive, they were not doing so good; if they were having Chinese, which cost, they were doing okay.")

Their acts, within Borscht Belt parameters, are varied, though perhaps it is best to let Ross, who began his career in the Yiddish theater in New York City and now works out of Miami, call the shots.

"Jerry Lewis, whose father, Danny Lewis, was a comedian and his mother was the accompanist, did a mime record act, Jerry in those days wasn't so great," says Ross. "Dick Shawn didn't do any Jewish at all except he sang 'Roumania.' Eddie Schaeffer did a good mountain act, but a good mountain act isn't that good; always talking about fire escapes, and what did people not from New York know about fire escapes? Jack Carter did just jokes, one after the other; he'd either kill them or he'd die. Myron Cohen was a wonderful storyteller, wonderful; the Yidluch *loved* him," he says.

The *Yidluch*—the first generation; the Jews just off the boat. But the majority of Borscht Belt comics were second-generation, and they were a restless crew. They ripped off hit movies and Broadway shows, writing their own versions. (*"Awake and Sing!, The Informer*—we'd take a play and chop it up. . . . Imagine how ridiculous it must have looked," says Murray. "We had the nerve of burglars in those years.") They tired of doing the same old gags from burlesque and worked up their own material. Sid Caesar begins doing his double-talk routines; Milt Ross picks up some social satire from Max Liebman. And of course there are the mountain classics, some of them very painful, born who knows where, on the stage or around the pool.

Two Polish Jews, captured by the Nazis, are about to be executed. Very smooth SS officer approaches. Asks the first Jew about to die if he can offer him anything: a blindfold, a brandy, a cigarette. First Jew starts cursing him out. "Nazi Pig," he begins, "I spit in your face. I spit on your blindfold and cigarette and brandy. You are mindless scum now. You will be remembered as scum by history. You—" His friend grabs him and interrupts him.

"Abie," he says, "why look for trouble?"

With the fifties, the area is changing. The New York State Thruway is making the mountains more accessible, and comics are coming up for one-nighters and weekend dates rather than for the whole season. Air travel is becoming available to the middle class, and small hotels are folding, and the large ones, such as the Concord, Grossinger's, the Nevele, and Brown's, can make a Zero Mostel, an Eddie Fisher, an Alan King.

And there is something else that is going on and that is important: television. It will, as it disseminates everything, spread the mysteries of the Borscht Belt across America. Sid Caesar, with producer Max Liebman and former Borscht Belt social director

Mel Brooks, will score a television hit in 1949 with the *Admiral Broadway Revue* show, then really make his name with *Your Show of Shows*. Milton Berle, a Borscht Belt comic in spirit, though he comes out of the burlesque houses of New York, will spread New York Jew into everyone's living room—will, according to some, be the fellow who makes Jewish humor safe and takes it into the mainstream.

"Jewish humor didn't change. The country changed," says Alan King.

"Mel Brooks," he says, "The Two Thousand Year Old Man, that was about as Borscht Circuit as you could get, and it was a terrific success: *'How many children do you have?' 'Sixty-five hundred and forty—four hundred doctors.'*

"And the Two Thousand Year Old man talks like an old Jewish man, y'know," says King. "He didn't talk like John Gielgud."

And so, in its old incarnation, the Borscht Belt is finished. Perhaps a half dozen big hotels remain in the Catskills, with stars flying in for dates the way they'd go to Vegas. The old hotels were burned down for insurance money; the young comics are getting their start in comedy clubs and their break on TV.

And you ask some of the people in comedy today about the mountains, they sound pained.

"I don't even think of it as show business," says George Schultz, the owner of Pips in Brooklyn. "It's an anachronism, a closed-shop kind of thing; none of these guys could go anywhere with it . . . go, say, on *The Tonight Show.*"

Likewise, some of the people who came out of the mountains see little of value in comedy today.

"Today everybody's doing the same act," says Jack Carter. "They have no performance value. In the Catskills they demanded more showmanship—to dance, to sing, to do improv. . . ."

"You had to *give* to an audience up there," says Joey Adams. "Woody Allen would die there. . . . He just hasn't got the warmth. A Berle is a giver; a Jackie Mason is a giver. . . ."

But you know, this is really superficial, a confusion of content and style. Woody Allen wouldn't play in the mountains, maybe. *Maybe.* His style is more the third generation, the college-educated professional, while most of the Borscht Belt veterans were of the working class that came before. But when you look at the content of the thing, the attitude, they are not so far apart.

Jackie Mason, a brainy and traditional Borscht comic, doing his routine on the bad nerves of Jews in boats, is not so far from Woody Allen's Broadway Danny Rose faced with a trip across the Hudson. "I don't travel by water," says Danny. "It's against my religion. I'm a landlocked Hebrew." Shtetl humor.

Jackie Mason doing his bit about the eating and drinking habits of Jewish people—"Ya see a Jew in a bar, he's lost; ya see a Jew in a bar, he's looking for a piece of cake"—is not so far from Allen's hero in *Annie Hall* trembling at the sight of lobsters on the loose. "Talk to him," Alvy says to Annie. "You speak shellfish." And Carson, in his timing, in that look when he misses a joke, is pure Benny. And Benny, though he only played the mountains later, was Borscht. And Pryor, when he does his bit about the heart attack, when he clutches his heart and falls to the floor and starts hollering, "You didn't think about it when you was eating all that pork," is, in his attitude (expectant of disaster: Keep your eye on the exit), pure Borscht.

It's style, often, that separates Allen from Mason—a figure of speech, a veneer that comes from education, a gloss. The basic attitude of Borscht Belt—which is to be an outsider with all the conflict of the outsider; which is to expect the worst because the worst is what outsiders often get; which is to be funny because funny is the only strength the powerless have—remains.

A great part of it does not translate to other cultures, is True-blue Jew, making performers fear it; but the heart of it, should you change an ethnic detail here and there, can be made universal, translating to any alienated outsider group:

Two old Polish ladies sitting on the stoop talking. "Ya see what happened with Solidarity this week?" asks one.

"I don't see nothing," the other one says. "I live in the back."

A continuum, you see. Borscht has always been a continuum; an attitude that began, most likely, when the first Jew, at about the time of the destruction of the Second Temple, looked up and said, "Y'know, I think I'm beginning to see a *pattern.* . . ."

And if there seemed a golden time of Borscht in the thirties, forties, and fifties in the Catskills, it was not because these were the decades when Borscht was invented; it was because the number of small hotels, the coming together of the comics at that time, made the mountains such a conspicuous, fertile field, a seeming mother lode.

With the disappearance of the hotels, it seems diminished. Though, if you are curious, some of the essential flavor remains. Go to Kutsher's on a weekend: the same busboys will be hustling for tips on the floor; the same gang will be on the lawns, playing gin; the band will play the same goddamn music—"Yellow Bird," "More," "Matilda"—and when they play "Matilda" they will make the same ("My Zelda") awful joke. And when the master of ceremonies, somebody's moonlighting cousin, surely, hollers "Merengue," the same crowd of Jews will thunder to the floor. And you, outcast hoodlum, whatever the specifics of your great sorrow, you, the next time they shout it, will get up with the people, and show your joy of the mountains, and shake it, shake it, shake it across the floor.

Bearings

MONTICELLO, NEW YORK

Population: 6,306
Manuel Gonsalus settled Sullivan County in 1730. The county's flagstone was used to pave New York City sidewalks. During the Civil War 80 percent of the shoe leather and leather products used by the Union Army were treated in Sullivan County tanneries. Monticello's tannery specialized in producing leather for bookbindings.

The county became important as a resort in the 1870s, when farmers began taking in summer boarders from the city. An early innkeeper judged the success of a season by the number of times the outhouse had to be moved.

In the 1890s one hotel's advertising stipulated, "No consumptives or Hebrews."

Monticello's first Jewish boarding house, the Beauty

Maple House, opened in 1904.

The Fallsburgh Hotel, a kosher establishment, was cited by a state commission on discrimination for not hiring Jews, a practice that resulted from the Talmudic prohibition against working on the Sabbath. Grossinger's circumvented Talmudic laws against entertainment on Saturday by leasing the hotel to a Gentile from sundown on Friday to sundown Saturday.

In 1962 Grossinger's instituted the singles weekend.

Today there are thirty-two resort hotels in Sullivan County, 80 to 85 percent of which have kosher policies. There are two Italian establishments and one Polish.

The Concord has more tennis courts than Wimbledon and is one of the ten largest hotels in the world.

Keepers of the Flame

David Quammen

R emember the part about *Give me your tired, your poor, your huddled masses yearning to breathe free?* Remember *I lift my lamp beside the golden door?* Don't be fooled. Today you could go to prison for believing too fervently in that ideal. Jim Corbett and Sister Darlene Nicgorski, for a pair of instances, seem to be well on their way.

Their offense has been to welcome that category of huddled masses of whom the U.S. government particularly disapproves: Guatemalans and Salvadorans in flight from murderous chaos at home.

Jim Corbett is a wiry Quaker with a vandyke beard and a bad case of rheumatoid arthritis who lives in a small house on the north fringe of Tucson, Arizona, venturing out into the severe hill country of the Sonoran Desert whenever necessity demands and his health permits. Darlene Nicgorski is a Catholic nun, a mem-

DAVID QUAMMEN lived in Tucson for two years and has written extensively about the Sonoran Desert.

ber in good standing of the School Sisters of St. Francis, who does social-service work out of her office-apartment in Phoenix. In the view of the U.S. Justice Department, these two are parties to a criminal conspiracy. On January 10 they were indicted—along with twelve other Arizona residents and two church people from just over the border in Mexico—by a federal grand jury. The crimes charged against this group include smuggling illegal aliens into the U.S.; abetting and counseling such illegal entry; transporting, harboring, and shielding such aliens once they entered; as well as conspiring with one another to smuggle, abet, harbor, shield, et cetera. The indictment runs to seventy-one counts. Each count represents a felony worth at least five years in prison. Clearly Corbett, Nicgorski, and the others must have done *something* provocative to draw such a redundancy of official wrath.

That much they freely confess: Yes, no question, there has been a lot of harboring, shielding, abetting. A lot of smuggling, yes. Jim Corbett admits to having helped hundreds of Salvadorans and Guatemalans sneak over the border from Mexico—he has even occasionally allowed reporters, photographers, and, once, a television crew to come along. In most respects it's a very public conspiracy, this latter-day underground railroad that carries displaced Central Americans to sanctuary in the U.S. The aliens are generally kept hidden for fear they will be arrested and deported, but Nicgorski and her collaborators do their work in a glare of publicity. The point at issue, they argue, is not who drove a car, who offered shelter, who held the strands of barbed wire apart while a young widow and two kids climbed into America. The point at issue is whether the people being aided are *illegal aliens* (as the Immigration and Naturalization Service sees them) and *economic migrants* (as the State Department contends) or, alternatively, *political refugees* as defined by U.S. law.

The distinction is more than semantic. "We're *not* committing civil disobedience. We're *not* fighting against unjust laws," says Jim Corbett. "We're fighting for the *observance* of just laws." He cites the 1980 Refugee Act, among others. By deporting these Central Americans back into mortal danger, he explains, it's the U.S. government that is breaking the law.

Corbett has been the most visible of the humanitarian smugglers and he was one of the first, but he insists that he is in no sense the movement's founder. "What has come to be called the sanctuary movement started with many thousands of people in this country who decided to help fugitive Salvadorans and Guatemalans," he says. "It happened everywhere along the Mexican border and wherever else the refugees arrived in large numbers." The border town of Nogales, an hour south of Tucson, was one of those places.

On May 4, 1981, driving back from Nogales, a friend of Corbett's picked up a hitchhiker, a man who turned out to be Salvadoran. Before they reached Tucson the car was stopped at a border-patrol checkpoint and the Salvadoran was taken away. When Corbett heard the story, he began wondering what would become of the man. At that point Corbett was still ignorant of immigration law and deportation procedure, but he knew that El Salvador was a dangerous place. He had heard about the civil war that was killing hundreds of civilians each month. He had heard about *los escuadrones de la muerte*, the right-wing death squads that were enforcing political orthodoxy by means of kidnap, torture, and murder. He had also heard rumors that a planeload of deportees had been massacred right at the San Salvador airport in December 1980. "So we were concerned about what might happen to that hitchhiker," he says. "The next morning I woke up having decided that, somehow, I ought to find out."

He traced the man to the Santa Cruz County jail. Within the next few days he had learned of fifty other Salvadorans (including one woman with a year-old child) who were being held in the local jails and detention facilities pending deportation. They were confused and terrified people with little or no legal help, ignorant of their right to apply for asylum. And the Immigration officials seemed determined to keep things that way, so that these folk could be expeditiously freighted back south. In a letter he sent to other Quakers that month, Corbett wrote, "I can see that if Central American refugees' rights to political asylum are decisively rejected by the U.S. government, or if the U.S. legal system insists on ransom that exceeds our ability to pay, active resistance will be the only alternative to abandoning the refugees to their fate." So he embarked on his own active resistance: smuggling in refugees through the mountains of southern Arizona.

Corbett knew the terrain and how to survive in it, how to travel fast and light along the brushy dry washes that offered cover, how to dodge the border patrol cruisers and low-flying planes. He had ranched cattle in this country for some years, all up and down the steep hills and washes by horseback, until his arthritis made it impossible for him to continue. Compared with those physical demands, leading Central Americans on one- and two-day hikes through the border zone proved to be relatively easy. He also began making trips into Mexico, meeting with refugees there in dingy hotel rooms, briefing some for the back-country trek, advising others how to pass through official ports of entry by masquerading as Mexican visitors. In the border towns along the Mexican side he found people who would help by offering their homes as final staging points, feeding the fugitives, letting them rest for a few days before the crossing, even lending identity documents that were enormously useful at the ports of entry. When it was a matter of bushwhacking overland through the hard country for a fence climb, beating the Immigration patrols and then beating the desert too, Corbett himself usually went as guide. Dressed for one of those ordeals in an old cowboy hat and jeans, he could pass for a dotty archaeologist just wandering in from six months at Olduvai Gorge.

Last July Corbett made a crossing that (as reported by Carmen Duarte in a fine series of articles for *The Arizona Daily Star*) stands as roughly typical. In this case he was bringing across just one person: a Guatemalan woman too traumatized by her recent experiences to have much chance of bluffing her way through a port of entry.

Back in Guatemala, the woman's husband had been involved in a labor union, which in itself is considered subversive activity, threatening to the army-supported oligarchy. One night at 4:00 A.M. strange men barged into the house, beat him with gun butts, and took him away in an official-looking car. The husband was never seen again. She was warned not to report his disappearance. She searched for him at a body dump, where the hands and heads had been cut off many of the corpses. After a year there was still no news, no evidence of his fate, and now strangers had begun stalking *her*. So she fled to Mexico City. A few months passed before she was detained and interrogated by men who seemed to be Mexican immigration agents; they held her without charge in a private house, tied her to a chair, untied her only when they wanted to rape her. Finally she was deported by bus back to Guatemala. Not daring to go to her home, she returned to Mexico City. This time she was lucky enough to make contact with Jim Corbett, who escorted her by plane and then automobile up to Nogales, Mexico. From there they would continue by foot.

On the day of the crossing, they were driven out of Nogales on a road that runs parallel to the border. The car stopped briefly in a remote spot while Corbett and the woman climbed out. Very quickly they were off the pavement and down a steep bank into the dry wash below. Mesquite and creosote bush gave them a little cover, but for the first half hour they could still be seen from the road. It was the day's longest and most delicate half hour. They picked their way downward along the bed of the wash, over rock ledges and sand, through the thickest vegetation—a path that made progress slow but left at least some chance of concealment. When a truck rumbled into earshot on the road above, they skittered out of sight in the brush. Then they continued to walk. After only an hour they came to the border fence. Nothing elaborate here, not the ten-foot-high chain link barricade that divides the town of Nogales—just five strands of tightly strung barbed wire. They climbed it. As the woman stepped down onto U.S. soil, according to Carmen Duarte, Corbett greeted her with a hug.

The crossing had been made, but the hike had only begun. Mosquitoes and gnats harried them as they went, and the air was full of flying ants. The sky was overcast, a blessing because it held the temperature down, even more so because it made aerial surveillance amid the steep mountain canyons less likely. Four miles of hard walking brought them to a remote shelter, far enough for one day. The woman's feet were blistered. Raisins for dinner and only a tarpaulin for a blanket. They spent a chilly night. The Sonoran Desert, so rocky and bare, gives heat back to the atmosphere quickly; it can be a cold place after dark.

The next day was clear and beautiful, destined to be fiercely hot. After a breakfast of tuna, cold coffee, and crackers, they started walking again, passing down the canyon amid yucca and manzanita. The last mile was a hard climb uphill, then along another dry wash, to the point where by prearrangement they would rendezvous with a vehicle.

The vehicle was where Corbett expected it. An innocent-looking picnic was in progress. Jim Corbett introduced the Guatemalan woman to his friends, who offered her a ham-and-cheese sandwich and an orange drink; for the ride up to Tucson she would hide on the floor of their rig. She had entered the American sanctuary network.

That was last July. But with three years of this sort of thing behind him, Corbett has lately been forced to shift his focus. He can no longer accompany anyone through the ports of entry, and even his presence among a group of borderland picnickers can be a giveaway. "My notoriety is now a problem. Every border-patrol agent knows my face," he says. A mild, bashful smile flickers across his face. He gestures gently with his arthritic hands, which look as though they were run over by a backhoe. "I've used up my ability not to be noticed."

For Sister Darlene it began in a different way, in a different place, at almost precisely the same time. She went to Guatemala in 1981 to work at a village parish near the Honduran border. Guatemala at that time (as now) was in effect ruled by its army; there was a fierce campaign of suppression conducted both by the army and by plainclothes death squads against anyone considered subversive; and teaching the gospel, like union involvement, was often judged an act of subversion. When Sister Darlene arrived, she knew barely any Spanish; she had been asked to Guatemala to set up a child-care program for small children. "But I was only there six months when our pastor was shot and killed," she says. "And people from the village came and told us that we would be next if we didn't leave. We did not wait around." Though this was supposed to be the *less* violent region of the country, she and her fellow nuns had already discussed what they would do if conditions got really perilous. "We had all decided we would stay till the *último momento*—the last minute. But that comes very quickly." She moved down into Guatemala City for a while, then back up into Mexico, and eventually found her way to the string of refugee camps in Chiapas, Mexico's southernmost state, just over the Guatemalan border. Those camps were filled with thou-

sands of fugitives from Guatemala. She stayed in Chiapas for ten
months. Her Spanish improved, and finally, she says, the people
began to trust her.

They began to tell her their stories; they wanted her to
understand why they had left their villages for such a woebegone
place as this. She made some tape recordings, and, she said, their
"stories kind of melted into one: 'The army came and killed. The
army came and burned our crops, our animals, our people.' "

Sister Darlene went back to Phoenix for a short visit with her
parents, which instead turned into a month in the hospital. During that time she started hearing about Guatemalan refugees right
there in the Phoenix area—hundreds of them, hiding from Immigration in overcrowded motel rooms, living out under the trees in
the citrus groves south of the city. Like those in the Chiapas
camps, they needed food, housing, clothes, medical care; most of
all, they needed to avoid deportation. "That's when I learned
about sanctuary," says Sister Darlene. "I didn't know before that
it was considered illegal to help these people."

She became a collaborator with Jim Corbett and many others. She began supplying shelter and other material aid to refugees
brought in by Corbett. Most importantly, she made Phoenix a
way station and herself a dispatcher for the underground railroad
that moves Central Americans to havens among church communities across the U.S. She also began talking—patiently, and
with a distaste that is evident but politely controlled—to journalists. Like Corbett, she feels compelled not only to help the refugees but to make America hear why that help is necessary.

In a Phoenix kitchen, over a bowl of chocolate-chip cookies,
she says, "A lot of those people are never going to be able to get
out. So what's needed is somebody to speak the truth. That's
obviously why we're a threat."

Who are these people that the sanctuary activists call refugees and the State Department calls economic migrants?

Francisco R. is representative. The name has been changed
for his own protection, but he is a real person. Francisco fled north
from Guatemala because some of his relatives were active in the
labor unions and—as with the woman helped by Corbett last July
—that involvement put the whole family in jeopardy. One uncle
disappeared, according to Francisco, and fifteen days later was

found dead. He had been tortured, tied up with barbed wire, mutilated, and finally strangled. The skin of his face, says Francisco, had been peeled off. A cousin of Francisco's was also taken away, tied up with barbed wire, tortured. The cousin's eyes were gouged out, Francisco says. The body was burned. The family identified it by its teeth.

Santana Chirino Amaya is representative. His name has not been changed, because it's too late for that to help. Santana came north from El Salvador, entered the U.S. at Laredo, Texas, but was eventually picked up by Immigration. In June 1981 he was deported back. On August 29 of the same year his body was found at a crossroads not far from his home. Cigarette burns. Legs tied with wire. He had been decapitated.

Roberto J. is representative. Again the name has been changed, and again he is real. He taught history and literature at a high school in San Salvador before it became necessary for him to flee. He is also a poet of some reputation, published in Brazil and Peru, with a book forthcoming in Belgium. The poetry may have been part of his problem; Roberto himself says that some of his poems could be described as "political." His wife is a nurse. She worked at a children's hospital in San Salvador and saw hundreds of kids newly orphaned by the civil war—many of them sick or injured, and dying for lack of medicine. Roberto and his wife and their own two small children crossed into the U.S. in May last year, along a desert route very much like the one Jim Corbett used in July. They were guided by two sanctuary activists, an intense young man and a tall, placid young woman. The seventh member of the party was a craven but curious journalist, who shall remain nameless. During a long day of hiking and climbing, as he watched Roberto's family cross a strange desert into a strange country, carrying their remaining possessions in two leather bags, cowering under mesquite bushes when a light plane passed low overhead, taking care to avoid snakebite and scorpion sting, leaving behind their language and their culture, it occurred to the journalist that this was a very inconvenient way for a teacher and a nurse to turn themselves into economic migrants. Roberto told the journalist his story.

He had been picked up by the Salvadoran National Guard in June 1983. Possibly it was because of the poetry, though

Roberto never found out. In the course of searching his house, the Guardia discovered books that were judged subversive: a volume entitled *The Fight of the Campesinos,* one novel by a Cuban, several works by the Brazilian priest and educator Paolo Freire. For a week Roberto was held in solitary confinement, kept blindfolded, beaten, interrogated. "What group are you in?" the Guardia wanted to know. "Who are your comrades?" No group. No comrades. He was transferred to Mariona Prison, the main men's prison in El Salvador, where he was apparently forgotten. At Mariona he was put in the "political section" and so had a chance to talk with other prisoners jailed for suspicion of subversion—doctors, professors, and many illiterate campesinos. He collected their stories, from which he intends to write a book portraying the persecution of the Salvadoran people. "Where are your notes?" the journalist asked him. Smiling, Roberto tapped his temple. The journalist thought: I'm sitting under a mesquite bush with the next Solzhenitsyn.

For seven months Roberto was held without charge. Finally his wife, having pushed the case through legal channels, won his release. But the release did not mean he was out of danger. "After release, often, is when the death squads come," Roberto told the journalist. As soon as it was possible, Roberto and his family fled north. In Mexico City they were put in touch with the sanctuary network.

Did Roberto want to go back to El Salvador when it was safe? "Yes. Very, very much," he said. "There is so much I can do to help in the reconstruction of the country." Right now though, for him, returning sounded distinctly unsafe. Yet, if the border patrol had captured him during that hike in the desert, he would have immediately faced deportation—back to the San Salvador airport, perhaps back to Mariona Prison, or worse.

The U.S. grants asylum to less than 2 percent of Salvadorans who apply. Last year nearly four thousand were deported. The numbers for Guatemalans are even less encouraging.

To an outsider looking at the sanctuary movement of which Nicgorski and Corbett are part, three facts stand out.

First, the movement is not a political phenomenon most essentially but a religious one. That is literal fact, not rhetoric.

Religious people are doing these things—smuggling, harboring—
for religious reasons. The proportion of secular humanists, agnos-
tic liberals, political radicals of the Old or New Left variety, is
startlingly low. What you find are nuns, priests, ministers, devout
Quakers, rabbis, serious Unitarians, church assistants, church
volunteers, and all sorts of other churchly people, most of whom
sound quite convincing when they explain that abandoning the
refugees would be equivalent to abandoning their own faith. It
has been this way since March 24, 1982, when a small Tucson
congregation known as Southside Presbyterian Church (joined by
a handful of other congregations in California, New York, and
Washington, D.C.) made the public declaration that they would
henceforth be providing sanctuary, in the Judeo-Christian tradition, to refugees from Central American violence. Today there
are about two hundred churches across the U.S., accounting for
fifty thousand members, that have made the same declaration.
But it happened at Southside first because there the need was
most immediate: Jim Corbett had been bringing refugees to their
very door. The pastor of Southside Church, a lanky man named
John Fife, had been active in weekly prayer vigils focused on the
Central American situation, as well as in legal-defense efforts for
refugees who faced deportation. "We had tried all the other
avenues we could possibly think of and had taken some risks," he
says. "But none of that had made a difference. So we decided that
sanctuary was appropriate." Now Reverend Fife is also among the
indicted.

A second fact: Corbett and a few other highly visible males
notwithstanding, this movement is dominated by women. Over-
whelmingly. Of the original sixteen indicted in Arizona, eleven
are women, and in the informed view of Sister Darlene, that
proportion correctly reflects the national numbers. Why is this so?
One of the defendants, a young woman named Wendy Le Win,
told me, "We're taught in a lot of ways to take risks in taking care
of people." Another, a nun who was indicted but then saw her
charges dropped (because she has Hodgkin's disease; she protested, arguing that she is healthy enough to stand trial for her
beliefs), said on the same subject, "Women tend to get at the
heart of a matter more quickly."

The third intriguing fact is that this movement—like so

many other religious upheavals throughout history—came out of
the desert. Tucson and Nogales; Calexico and El Centro in California; San Benito and McAllen in Texas: the first battles were
fought, the first commitments were made, and the first wave of
federal prosecutions are now being coped with in these hot, red-
rock places. One reason for that pattern is obvious: to Central
Americans arriving in dusty buses and on the tailgates of trucks,
those desert borderlands are the doorway, golden or not, to America.

Several other reasons are not quite so obvious. The Sonoran
Desert of southern Arizona, the Chihuahuan Desert of south
Texas are lands of extremity and denial. Too hot, too rugged, not
enough rain, not enough fuel, not enough food. When rain does
come, nothing holds back the flood. The environment offers no
respite—the physical ecology is merciless. The moral ecology
must therefore compensate, or a species so ill-adapted as human-
ity couldn't survive. Desert tribes like the Papago understand
that. People like Jim Corbett understand that.

And there's one other reason, I suspect. People who live near
a border, unlike the rest of us, see human faces on the far side.

████████

Bearings
TUSCON

Population: 330,537
*In 1692, a Jesuit, Eusebio Kino, came upon the Indian
village of baked clay buildings called Stjukshon, "the dark
spring at the foot of the mountain." Tuscon was settled
under Spain in 1776.*

*Mission San Xavier del Bac, the "White Dove of the
Desert," was completed in 1797 by the Franciscans, and
is the most photographed building in Arizona.*

*Known as the "Old Pueblo," Tuscon has lived under
four flags: Spanish, Mexican, Confederate, and United
States. More than two inches of rain falls in June and
July during the time of the "summer monsoons."*

*Tuscon and Phoenix account for half the state's
population.*

████████

The Rockets' Red Glare

George Plimpton

Every once in a while I wonder vaguely what I will do very late in my declining years—when just sitting in a chair may be all I *can* do. The notion has kept recurring that (being a fireworks enthusiast) I would delight in being retained (at a nominal fee, mostly for travel) by Oriental fireworks manufacturers to be assisted out to a field and settled into a chair, possibly with a headrest attached so that looking up into the night sky would be comfortable, where my function would be to decide on names for their new aerial shells. I would be known as "The Shell Namer."

May I hasten to explain. Aerial shells (or bombs, as fireworks people call them) from Japan, China, Taiwan, Korea, and so forth were always imported into this country, or listed in their catalogs, with wonderfully fancy descriptive names attached. A shell would be labeled "The Monkeys Enter the Heavenly Palace and Drive

GEORGE PLIMPTON is the author of an historical appreciation, titled *Fireworks*. New York City's Fireworks Commissioner, he choreographed the Brooklyn Bridge Centennial pyrotechnics and Ronald Reagan's inaugural fireworks.

Out the Tiger." Or "Running Cur Violates Heavenly Clouds." The importers felt this was all too farfetched and imaginative (and difficult to discern in the sky, anyway), and so in the American catalogs the Oriental nomenclature would be simplified to something like "Sky Monkeys" or "Frolicking Dogs," and they would have done with it.

But one day that is what I have in mind to do—to get out there to the Orient where the new shells are being tested. I would sit out in the fields in my small bamboo chair (cushioned) with a note pad. I would watch a shell soar up, open above the rice paddies, and perform, and I would write down "The Blue Ox Comes Down the Turnpike," or perhaps "The White Parrot Escapes from the Yellow Wicker Cage," whatever, and if my imagination failed, I would call down to the pyrotechnician by the mortars and ask him to send up the same kind of shell for a second viewing: sorry, but I was not inspired.

I had always assumed that I would be very much a loner at this—a solitary figure with a small suitcase, stepping slowly down to the platform of a dusty RR station in Yunnan Province. It seemed improbable that I could find anyone else who would like to tag along—it is a somewhat specialized retirement program, after all. Very recherché.

Indeed, I could think of only one candidate who might be interested—a shoe-store owner in Norfolk, Nebraska, named Orville Carlisle. First of all, he is a fireworks expert. In fact, off in a side room of his shoe store he has a fireworks museum, surely the only one of its kind in the world. Then, coming from a small mid-American town, he would provide a fine balance and perspective to our nomenclative choices. He would keep me in check. And besides, he is a fine phrasemaker. He says things like "It's colder than a well digger's nose."

I went out to Nebraska to see him not long ago. He is an old friend, and I wanted to see his museum. I thought that during my visit I'd ask him whether, if things got slack around Norfolk in years to come, he would be interested in going to Japan or China with me as a shell namer. Equal status. He would have his little bamboo chair, and I'd have mine. We'd confer. Perhaps we would not agree. We would call down to the pyrotechnician and ask for another shell of the same variety. The sky would blossom.

Norfolk is 112 miles from Omaha and eighty from Sioux City, serviced by a commuter airline called AAA. No one at the ticket counter seemed to know what the initials stood for—if anything. Carlisle and his wife, Mary, met me at the little airport, and we drove into town.

Carlisle is a thin, spare man, lively of manner, who seems slightly surprised by just about everything, so that his speech is sprinkled with mild expressions of wonder such as "jiminy crickets," "heck," "criminentlies," "jiminy krautz," et cetera, the sort of words one remembers from the balloons in comic strips. His wife has a hearing problem, but she can read lips remarkably well. In the car at red lights Orville would turn on the overhead light and, speaking directly at her so she could follow his lips, give a quick synopsis of what we had been talking about.

First we chatted about the town. Long-time residents, I was informed, pronounced the name Nor'*fork*—because the original German settlers established a community on the north fork of the Elkhorn River that they wanted, not unsurprisingly, to call North Fork.

"The people in Washington, who are about the same now as they were then," Carlisle explained, "got it bollixed up somehow, and the postal authorities gave us the name Norfolk, like the place in Virginia. In fact, last year a couple came through who were *looking* for Norfolk, Virginia."

"Oh, come on, Orv!" I said.

"Well, that's what they were saying around town. You've got to remember that the squirrels are not always up in the trees. The point is that the old-timers say Nor'fork."

"What's that business about the squirrels in the trees?"

"That there are a lot of nuts on the ground."

I thought for a bit. "Oh, yes, I see."

"There are other ways of saying that someone's not quite with it," Carlisle went on to explain. "You can say his elevator doesn't go clear to the top. Sometimes I say that he or she is a bit light in the conk."

"Oh, yes."

He switched on the overhead light and turned to his wife.

"I was telling George about the pronouncing of *Norfolk.*"

"Oh, yes," she said, nodding.

Carlisle wanted to show me his shoe store (Carlisle's Correct Shoes, it's called) and the fireworks museum before we turned in. As he unlocked the store I remarked on the extremely heavy traffic on Norfolk Avenue just behind us. "Is something letting out?" I asked.

"It's Saturday night," Orv told me. "Those are the kids cruising out there—four or five of them to a car. It's the big ritual in these parts. I suppose there's some kind of communication between them—where the action is. Sometimes it's such a parade of cars the building here shakes."

Inside it was quiet. It was apparent from the long rows of shoe boxes that Carlisle's business consisted mainly of work shoes and children's shoes. "Not much high fashion in here," he said. "We stay out of it. Our slogan is 'How do they feel?' not 'How do they look?' A big seller in here is a Red Wing Pecos with a steel toe . . . so your foot will survive when behind the barn you're stepped on by a critter. The soles on those shoes will wear like a pig's nose. After all, when the shouting's all over, that's what we are: agriculture."

Overhead was a long wire for a puppet bicycler carrying a balancing bar to run up and down, to amuse the children. "Kids come into a shoe store thinking they're going to be vaccinated," Carlisle explained. He manipulated the puppet for me. It soared down the length of the store, and then back.

If that did not calm the children, there was always the huge cast of Robert Wadlow's bare foot to awe them. Wadlow was the most renowned of the world's giants. The Musebeck Shoe Company supplied its retailers with an aluminum cast of his foot to reflect its slogan, "We fit all sizes."

And then, of course, if the children were still distracted and broody, there was always the fireworks museum with *its* treasures. It is not large as museums go (about twenty-four by twelve feet), but it is chock-full of memorabilia, all defused and harmless. Very little in Carlisle's museum is not of interest—at least to me, a fireworks buff. Most of the items on display induce pangs of nostalgia for the days before World War II, when all kinds of fireworks were available to the public. My particular favorites in Carlisle's museum were the cardboard novelty devices made to resemble fire engines, or ocean liners, or animals, or various kinds of buildings, all of which after varying performances (usually the emission of smoke and a piercing whistle) would blow up in a sharp report. Perhaps the most original of those Carlisle showed me was a representation of a cardboard outhouse, which he told me performed by pouring smoke out of the half-moon ventilator and then slowly destroying itself in a series of small, flatulent explosions.

Carlisle, who is going to be sixty-eight in July, has been collecting fireworks, cap pistols, and various noisemakers (including exploding canes that *bang!* when you hit the ground with one) for sixty years and has had them on display in the shoe store for twenty.

His involvement with fireworks was due largely to his father, a "traveling man"—a rather more glamorous descriptive than "salesman"—who sold Palmer Candy out of Sioux City and eventually settled in Norfolk. Norfolk was the jumping-off place for his sales territory, which extended from Rushville, Nebraska, to the west, up to Winner, South Dakota, to the north—a "wild and woolly part of the West in those times," as Orv noted. His father was a generous man, the more so because his own childhood was relatively deprived. *His* father was a Methodist preacher who kicked his son out into the world after the boy turned down an ultimatum to give up playing baseball on Sunday ("Go, and never darken my doorway again!").

"So the result was," Orv said, "that our father was always very openhanded when it came to his three sons. He brought us back things from his travels—and always, on the Fourth of July, fireworks . . . piles of them, horrifying the neighbors, and on the Fourth he'd take the stuff out on the front porch to parcel it out to us. He'd sit in the swing and from time to time he'd sing out in that big voice of his, 'Spread out! Spread out!' to keep us from getting too close to each other.

"Then, of course, heck, we got the Gilbert chemistry sets at Christmas. Those sets had a lot more in them in those days— potassium nitrate, barium nitrate, strontium nitrate, with which you could make colored flares. We could make chlorine gas, and we tried it out on grasshoppers to find out if it was lethal. It was. Later in high school we had the components to make nitroglycerin, but we got scared halfway through, cold feet, and we flushed the stuff down the drain."

Carlisle's more formal education with pyrotechnics was with the Readers, an Italian fireworks family up in Yankton. He learned enough from them to help with the big fireworks affair of the summer (besides the annual Fourth of July festivities), which was the sham battle arranged by the Lyck Company out of Omaha and sponsored by the American Legionnaires. Orv would help prepare the "battlefield" with ground bombs, small sticks of dynamite, flares, and so forth, through which the old soldiers, bursting out of their uniforms, and pretty well "snookered up," as Orv described them, would caper, miming the actions of the Battle of St. Mihiel, or the Marne, or Château Thierry (the battles changed every year, so no one would feel slighted by having one's battle not included), while their families watched from the hill. "Roman candles would be shot back and forth," Carlisle said, "though I don't remember any Germans. No one wanted to play them. Everything was started by a large choir singing 'Just Before the Battle, Mother.' Very stirring stuff."

As the town specialist in pyrotechnical matters, Orv, or "Oz," as in *The Wizard of*, as many of the townsfolk know him, is on call for many more occasions than simply the Fourth of July. When the high school orchestra plays Tchaikovsky's *1812 Overture* in the City Auditorium, Carlisle stands backstage and, on the conductor's cue for the cannon barrage called for in the score, fires a pistol through a hole into a fifty-five-gallon drum. One year a thunderstorm happened by, and right on the button, following a terrific lightning bolt, a thunderclap lifted everybody in the auditorium out of his seat. Carlisle laughed. He said, "You haven't heard a thunderclap until you've heard one that comes out of a Nebraska thunderstorm. A lot of folks there thought I was responsible and that it was my finest hour."

Almost any loud noise in Norfolk is attributed to Orv. Back in the 1950s when sonic booms from military planes were more common, Carlisle would hear a particularly loud clap, the phone would ring almost instantly, and whoever was at the other end would inquire anxiously, "Orv, you all right?"

Carlisle's reputation in the fireworks field extends far beyond Norfolk. He is a consultant to the National Fire Protection Association. Five years ago the Smithsonian Institution got in touch with him to find out if its windows were going to stand up to the concussions of the massive fireworks display organized on the

Mall (which the Smithsonian fronts) on the occasion of Ronald Reagan's inauguration. "I told them there were two very reputable fireworks companies involved, and they had nothing to fear."

Not long ago Orv got into a phone exchange with a striped-bass fisherman from Atlantic City who wondered how a rocket could be best used to carry his lure out beyond the surf. Did he need a permit from the authorities to do such a thing? "We worked on it," Carlisle told me. "He didn't need a permit, but an awful lot of rockets. He was going to lose one every time he got the lure out there in the ocean. The notion didn't seem to bother him. Fishermen are crazier than duck hunters."

"Lighter in the conk," I suggested.

"Yes, lighter in the conk. Exactly." He turned to his wife. "I was saying that fishermen are light in the conk."

"Oh, yes," she said.

Of course, the Fourth is Orv's big day. One time he actually fired three shows on the Fourth: the first one at the country club in the early evening, the aerial shells against a sky still tinted with the sunset, so the members would have plenty of time for dancing later; then at the Drive-In; and finally a few blocks away at Memorial Field, where just about everybody, according to Orv, had gotten "sloshed" from waiting around.

More recently, Carlisle shoots his show—fireworks, which he carefully choreographs, provided by Rich Brothers from Sioux Falls—at Skyview Lake, where between fifteen thousand and twenty thousand spectators turn up to watch. He has been doing that show since 1976, "knocking their socks off" each time. Last year, though, the Jaycees, who raise the money for the event, got offered a big deal by a discount store for putting on the show under its sponsorship. They asked him to be involved, but Carlisle didn't want to be part of a commercial venture. "Lots of love and trouble goes into my fireworks show. I can't dance, or sing, but I can shoot fireworks."

His wife interjected: "The thing is, Orv was born only two days after the Fourth. He asked his mother why he wasn't born on the Fourth, and she said, 'Well, son, you were a firecracker with a slow fuse.'"

"That's right," Carlisle said, laughing. "That's absolutely right."

The next morning Orv Carlisle gave me a tour of Norfolk. We
went by the steel mill, which stands on what Orv says was the best
coyote and jackrabbit hunting area in the country. We drove by
Skyview Lake, where he does the fireworks shows, and down by
the plant where they make disposable hypodermic needles. We
went past Mary's Cafe, which is the truckers' favorite spot in
town, and out into the countryside. Rolling fields. Tree lines of
oak and maple. Orv said that these had all been planted by the
early settlers. "Gee whiz, there weren't any trees here at all,
except the cottonwoods and willows down in the creek beds. Just
the roll of the Great Plains, horizon to horizon. They planted the
trees to keep the farmland from blowing away. [The wind] whistles down from Canada in the winter—colder than a well digger's
tool."

"I thought it was 'nose'—'colder than a well digger's nose.' "

"Either one," Carlisle said. "They're interchangeable."

It occurred to me I had yet to ask him about coming to
China and Japan as a shell namer. I was going to, but it did not
seem appropriate while he was showing me through his hometown.

We were driving by a swimming hole called Silver Hole. "It's
a good name," Orv told me. "The cottonwoods give off this silver
fuzz, which layers the surface of the water so thick that when a
kid dives in, he makes a hole right through the stuff."

We went over to Highway 81, which runs from Canada
down to Mexico and in its brief passage through Norfolk turns
into Thirteenth Street. We passed by the house in which Johnny
Carson lived as a teenager. The house, an upright white clapboard
structure with a rather scruffy lawn in front and a lone rocking
chair on the front porch, was up for sale.

"Oh, I remember him," Carlisle said. "There was a young
man's club in town that was organized to keep us from getting
mixed up in dens of iniquity. Local older men showed home
movies. Carson, who was in junior high school at the time, turned
up every once in a while with his ventriloquist's dummy. Edgar
Bergen and Charlie McCarthy were very big then, and every kid
starting off in show business had his dummy to help him. Carson
did magic tricks. He had that old one where you put a cigarette
in your ear and it looks like it goes right through your head and
comes out your mouth. You could tell he was on his way."

At one point, Carlisle told me, some people in town wanted to change the name of Thirteenth Street to Carson Boulevard, an idea Carlisle did not warm to. "After all," he said, "we have some other Norfolk people who have gone out and made a name for themselves."

"And who are they?"

"Well, there's Don Stewart, who was the surgeon on the soap opera *The Guiding Light.* He's a Norfolk boy. And then we have Thurl Ravenscroft, or at least we have his *voice.* It's his real deep voice that comes out of Tony the Tiger and says '*Gree-e-e-a-a-a-t!*' in the Kellogg's Frosted Flakes ads."

"Oh, yes," I said. "Of course."

Carlisle himself had one great chance for renown and fortune. In 1954 he invented a solid-propellant motor for lightweight rockets and a parachute recovery system so the rocket could be reflown—thus pioneering the industry of modern model rocketry. Carlisle's first two models, the Mark I and the Mark II, sit on display in the Smithsonian Institution in Washington.

The return from his invention could have been considerable had things gone as planned. Officials in the industry estimate that a million hobbyists in this country, most of them teenagers, have bought various kits to fashion rockets that soar up and float down in parachutes from heights that vary from several hundred to a thousand feet. Some of the more complex kits contain two- or three-stage models; some, rather than use parachutes, turn into gliders at the apex of their rise and sail back to the ground. One company actually sells a miniature rocket-camera that snaps a single picture of the earth below when it reaches the top of its climb.

All of these are propelled by what Carlisle contributed: a round tube of slow-burning propellant that fits into the bottom of the rocket and is disposable after use, meaning that a single rocket can be used indefinitely.

For complicated legal reasons (he spent three years in court), Orv lost his exclusivity-of-patent rights ("A patent is simply a license to fight," he complained to me), specifically for failing to give a completely adequate notice of infringement to a competitor.

"What if it had all worked out?" I asked him. "What would

you have done differently with your life? Would you have left Norfolk?"

"Oh, I don't think so," Orv said. "My friends are here. I grew up in Norfolk, and it's a good place. I don't think much would have changed. I might have done some more duck hunting and goofed off more."

I had once seen Orv off his home turf. He came to New York to help me celebrate the publication of a book I had written about fireworks. The city, as he put it, "boggled his mind," and one morning he stayed all by himself in his hotel room.

"Did you go out to see the Statue of Liberty?"

"Well, I saw it from the airplane. Trouble was, I felt hemmed in. No place to run to. More people were on the street than there are in all of Nebraska, all going everywhere but straight. Guess what? I came to the conclusion that it's a great place to visit. It's no big deal for most people, but it was for this old dog. I'm a country jake at heart. Going home, I felt I was on my way to be decompressed."

Hearing all this made it seem unlikely I was going to get Orv to China for our retirements. But I asked. I told him about naming fireworks. We would go to the Orient with our little chairs and sit in the testing fields. He brightened visibly. He knew a lot about the Oriental fireworks nomenclature. "Ogatsu," he said (naming a famous Japanese fireworks firm), "had a catalog with almost two thousand items listed in it. Some of those names threw me clear out of the wagon: 'Dragon Skipping a Ball with a Report.' "

"That's a good one," I said.

" 'Spring Wind Makes the Willow Grow.' "

"Excellent!"

"How about 'Five Dragons with Flashlight Parasol'?"

"I would travel many miles to see such a thing in the sky."

"Or 'Celestial Maiden Welcomes Heroes with Encircling Dews.' "

"We can hardly do better," I said. "So you're with me. You'd go?"

"Of course," he said. "Taiwan. Macao. I'll be there." He seemed a little wistful. "We'd have to come back from time to time. Wouldn't we? To get refreshed and do some duck hunting?"

I thought for a bit. Then I told him I had a better idea. "We'd establish *such* reputations as shell namers that the Orient would have to come to us. They'd come to Norfolk."

"Now, there's an idea," Carlisle said warmly. "We'll cut those shells loose from Skyview Lake. I'd like that just fine. Just *fine!*"

———

Bearings

NORFOLK, NEBRASKA

Population: 20,230
Norfolk was first settled in 1866 by German farmers who migrated from Wisconsin. They wanted to name their town North Fork, because it is located on the north fork of the Elkhorn River, but when they applied for a charter, the Post Office Department amended the name to Norfolk.

Each of forty-four families was given 160 acres of land, but in the first winter they lived more or less communally.

From 1874 to 1877 the major farming problem was a plague of grasshoppers. The Indians mashed them up and ate them, but the farmers often went hungry.

Norfolk's major crops are corn and beans. The Elkhorn River is muddy and unnavigable, but the river bottom is considered some of the best farmland in the state.

Norfolk has a steel mill that relies on recycled boxcars for some of its raw material. The Norfolk Livestock Market is one of the largest livestock auction markets in the country; last year some seven hundred thousand head of cattle, hogs, sheep, and horses were sold to the highest bidders.

PART **5**

FAITH
AND
BOUNDLESS
OPTIMISM

PENSACOLA, FLORIDA
Industriousness

HOUSTON, TEXAS
Opulence

WASHINGTON, D.C.
Pragmatism

BIG SUR, CALIFORNIA
California Dreaming

RHYOLITE, NEVADA
Survival

The Good Life and Long Hours of Nguyen Nguu

Joe Klein

Pensacola Bay was absolutely calm. The sun was sinking behind a fringe of cattails, the air clear with a slight edge to it. A perfect evening—for almost anything but shrimping. Shrimpers like it hot and dark and rough. They love hurricanes.

Nguyen Nguu, a tiny thirty-six-year-old Vietnamese man, was alone on the aft deck of his boat—the *Janice G*—darning his net. His hands seemed much older than the rest of him, but they moved with the frantic precision of a sewing machine. Nguu noticed my admiration; he smiled, massaging the net. "Big fish make hole," he said. "I fix."

"Nice night," I said, to say something.

"Yeah, no good," he shrugged. He was sitting like a rag doll, legs straight out, shoeless, the net a green nylon mesh over him. "No good fish. Too cold."

Too cold . . . and yet, you never can tell. A month earlier,

JOE KLEIN was born and raised in Rockaway Beach, New York. He is the author of *Payback,* a book about five Marines who returned from Vietnam.

on a very similar night—a little warmer, windier perhaps—Nguu
had struck gold in the bay. He and his wife, Phan Thang, were
out alone (working harder than the others, as always); there was
no chatter on the CB, no blips on the radar, no other boats out.
It was about 10:00 P.M., a slow night—maybe a $200 night, little
better than break-even—when he pulled in his tri-net and found
a hundred shrimp: big, fat ones. He put them in a pail and showed
Thang, who was up in the cabin steering. She turned the boat
around, and they trawled the stretch again. He set his timer for
fifteen minutes, waited, then pulled in the tri-net once more.
Another hundred or so plump, perfect shrimp. "It was cold," he
would recall. "My wife wear four coats, but she not cold. She so
excited." Through the night, they trawled back and forth over the
same stretch. Every four hours they would haul in the big nets.
What were all those shrimp *doing* out there on a cold December
night? Nguu and Thang did not stop to talk, although they
sometimes laughed as net after bulging net came in. They worked
all night, and through most of the morning, sorting the catch,
removing the heads from the larger shrimp to increase the price
per pound. When it was done, they had more than seven hundred
pounds, which they would sell for a near-miraculous $2,454.60.

This cool, perfect Friday in January would be nothing like
that. The season was very much over now. There would be little
serious shrimping till spring. Nguu was taking me out for a brief
run, to show off his boat and his work; he swaggered about proudly
in a blue baseball cap from Johnson's Diesel, Biloxi, Mississippi.
Thang, a very attractive woman in civilian clothes, was distinctly
Buddha-like in her layers of sweaters and coats and a Baltimore
Orioles knitted cap pushed down over her eyebrows. She was busy
in the galley, cooking a small feast—chicken, Chinese sausage,
shrimp, tomatoes, noodles, and vegetables.

At dusk, Nguu started the engine. He and Thang pushed off,
and we slid into the bay, coasting easily across the black glass
surface. Just past the breakwater, Thang took the wheel and Nguu
winched the two big nets—22.5 feet long each, the legal limit—
to the outriggers. For a moment, as Nguu lowered the rigs—
prodigious wings, heavy with netting—on both sides aft, the boat
seemed a great prehistoric bird skimming the bay; then the nets
hit water and the boat slowed. When they submerged completely,

the boat nearly stopped; the engine strained against the drag, the bay now molasses. We crawled toward deep water.

"Need more big engine," Nguu said. "This six cylinder. I like V-8. Here, this," handing me a pamphlet advertising an impressive piece of machinery. "Fifty-two thousand dollar," Nguu said. His English is fluent . . . when it comes to numbers; *words* are, obviously, less important. He can remember the price of every major item he has bought since coming to America five years ago and will recite each, given half a chance.

The latest acquisition—radar—is especially pleasing. "Only two other Vietnamese have," he said, turning on the screen, which glowed a luminous, high-tech green. "Very good. I can go work when foggy. See: big ship there, go to Gulf . . . Gulf there . . . shore there . . . four thousand dollar."

The attitude was somewhere between reverence and adoration. Nguu, a Taoist, placed machinery in the same pantheon as did his ancestors—a gift from God. Machinery was the force that most differentiated America from his homeland. "No machine in Vietnam boat. Hard, hard work," he said. "America machine number one. Everything machine. I like that. America too easy."

"He caught all that $2,400 in one night?" said Allen Williams, who owns the wholesale fish house where Nguyen Nguu sells his shrimp. "Jeez, I thought it was a *week's* catch. Well, I can't say it surprises me. . . . *Nothing* that little guy does surprises me anymore. I sold him his first boat a few years ago, gave him two years to pay. He paid for it in one. Next thing I know, he's sold that boat and bought the one he has now, which is twice as big. . . . Next thing, he'll have a fleet. You can't work much harder than he does. He was out there for about a week after all the other boats came in at the end of the season. Of course, *none* of these people are exactly lazy."

"Do they work harder than the Anglos?" I asked.

"Well, I wouldn't want to say that. But . . . well, these Vietnamese are like your grandparents. They're like Americans used to be. They work like devils and pour it all back into the business. When the engine breaks, they fix it themselves. They make their own nets, and that keeps the overhead down—just gas, oil, and ice. The night Nguu brought in the $2,400, his overhead was probably only a hundred dollars or so. Of course, he won't have a night like that very often, but look here . . ."

Williams led me out to the docks. "See these boats over here on the left: snapper boats. Americans own them. Over there on the right: shrimpers," he said, pointing toward a picturesque tangle of nets and rigging. "Every last one of those boats is owned by a Vietnamese. In the past four years they've pretty much taken over shrimping on this bay."

Williams's rival, Sam Patti of the Joe Patti Seafood Company, goes even further: "I'd say they revolutionized our business, and not too far down the road they're going to *control* the fishing industry on the Gulf Coast. They're going to own big steel-hull boats and wholesale houses. Why? 'Cause they believe in the old stuff: if you work hard enough, you can be anything in America. You should see some of these little guys shucking oysters—man, I've never seen anything like it. It's like Snow White and the Seven Dwarfs."

All of which hasn't gone down too easily with many *real* Americans who've been shrimping Pensacola Bay leisurely for generations. In the old days, a shrimper might go out four or five nights a week during the height of the season, stay out till midnight, then amble on home in time for last call. Often, shrimp boats were run as a sideline by people who had regular day jobs. The idea that you could actually make a full-time living at it seemed absurd. Why, you'd have to go out all night, seven days a week, for months on end. . . . Who'd ever want to work that hard, anyway?

When the first Vietnamese arrived in the mid-1970s, the Anglos were outraged. Rumors swept Pensacola Bay: The Vietnamese used mile-long nets, sometimes strung from boat to boat. They traveled in packs, picked bays clean. Vacuum cleaners, dredging barges, *anything* seemed possible. The Anglos threatened to bring in the Klan. A grand jury convened to investigate Vietnamese fishing practices. It was discovered that they were guilty of rampant industriousness.

In response to the threats and rumors, the Vietnamese stayed cool and blended in. Their presence had surprisingly little impact on Pensacola. There was no quaint, colorful Vietnamese neighborhood to provide a ready target for frustrated patriots. There was no social club, or hangout, or church: when the newcomers opened restaurants, they tended to camouflage them as "Oriental." They weren't exactly *hiding*, just trying not to make waves. "We've tried to blend in," said Mike Nguyen, who works for the Catholic Social Services refugee program. "The idea was: stay quiet, work hard, and there won't be any trouble." The only places where the Vietnamese seemed to congregate were the Williams and Patti fish houses, and out on the bay, where they kept each other awake in the deep night, chatting back and forth over their CBs.

By the time Nguyen Nguu arrived in Pensacola in 1981, the controversy had ebbed some. Nguu bought his first boat—a little thirty-four-footer—from Allen Williams a year later, after doing his best to avoid fishing for a time. He'd had enough of *that* in Vietnam; America was supposed to be different. He dreamed of becoming a diesel repairman. He had some of the skills but lacked the language to learn more. "I too old learn good English," he said. He didn't have to learn many words to fish, though—just numbers.

Nguu comes from a long line of fishermen in Da Nang. His family owned a hundred-foot boat—a good boat, but certainly not equipped for the trip he would make in 1979 with his family and a dozen or so relatives across the South China Sea to the Philippines. Nguu is reluctant to talk about the circumstances that made the trip necessary: politics is not his favorite topic. During the war he served—not very enthusiastically—in the South Vietnamese army. "I cannot express my feelings about the war," he said, through an interpreter. "But *many* people were happy when it was over. They wanted only peace and did not know anything about the Communists. But soon these people realized that peace was not as they had expected."

Peace, for a fisherman in Da Nang, turned out to be rules and regulations and quotas and gas rationing, and a preponderance of their catch—at times, as much as 90 percent—had to be turned over to the government. Nguu heard that many fishermen in the south were leaving; he decided to try it himself, even though his wife was pregnant with their fifth child. The crossing didn't look to be particularly difficult if the weather held—a week, at most. "But on the third day there was a terrible storm and we lost most of our food and all our water," he recalled. "I thought then that very few of us would survive—certainly none of the children. But we came upon a large ship, which gave us food and water, and we made it."

Sponsored by Church World Service, they came to New York, where Phan Thang's brother—a former pilot in the South Vietnamese air force—was working as an electrician and living in a small apartment on Forty-second Street, just two blocks west of Times Square. Nguu and Thang were perplexed by the size of the buildings and by the weather . . . and by the other things they saw. "It was a very sinful place," Nguu recalled. "And very cold. My children had nosebleeds from the cold. We look on the map for someplace warm, and there is Pensacola."

Catholic Social Services was running an aggressive refugee resettlement program in north Florida; Vietnamese who had found places such as Chicago and Minneapolis and New York too cold were flocking south; some had been fishermen in Vietnam, but most not. The large fish wholesalers like Williams and Patti, in need of cheap, industrious labor, were happy to sponsor families. The women were given jobs in the fish houses, shucking oysters and heading shrimp; the men went out on the boats. "When they could scrape together the down payment for a little boat," said Allen Williams, "we'd give them a low-interest, sometimes a no-interest, loan. We gave them dock space free. In return, they agreed to sell us their catch."

Nguu avoided the bay for as long as he could. He searched for a diesel-repair training program. Meanwhile, Thang worked as a waitress and the family received welfare. Soon, though, Nguu began to sign on as a deckhand for other shrimpers—watching, learning (he had never shrimped in Vietnam). After a year, he borrowed $6,000 from his brother-in-law for a down payment on a boat; Allen Williams loaned him the rest of the $21,000 purchase price, interest free.

Nguu still keeps the purchase agreement for that first boat with his other important papers in a small, zippered plastic pencil case. "Mr. Williams trust me," he said. "He American father to me."

"What," I asked, "do you do for fun?"

Nguu laughed. It was a Saturday morning in January. Most of his six children were huddled around the Sony, lost in cartoons. The living and dining rooms were covered with the nets; Nguu spends the off-season cutting and sewing for other fishermen. Although it sometimes takes as long as a week to put one together, he charges only a hundred dollars per net—which pays the utility bills and is better than doing nothing. Nguu could not imagine doing nothing.

"Do you go out to the movies?" I pursued. "Do you go to restaurants? Is there some sort of Vietnamese social club?"

Nguu laughed. His oldest son, Binh, who is fourteen and speaks perfect English, explained: "My parents don't go out very much. Sometimes they may visit friends, but usually there just isn't time. Most days, during the season, they leave here about four in the afternoon, stay out on the bay all night, spend the morning sorting the catch, having it weighed, and cleaning the boat. They get home by noon."

"They get only four hours' sleep?"

"Well, sometimes you can take turns sleeping on the boat, getting an hour here or there."

Binh said that he takes charge of the younger children while his parents fish. He cooks dinner and puts them to sleep. Sometimes, during the summer, his mother will stay home and he'll go out on the boat with his father. "I don't like it very much," he said. "It's too hard. I want to be a doctor."

"Do you ever go on vacations?" I asked the father, who had been straining to keep up with what his son was saying, nodding with pride at the word *doctor*.

"Oh, no," Nguu said. "No time."

Still, it wouldn't be quite accurate to say that Nguyen Nguu never enjoys himself. Evidence of his pleasure is all about the modest, rented, five-room brick house. There is an elaborate stereo system ("One hundred dollar, I got from friend," Nguu said) and a videocassette recorder ("My brother-in-law, he give"); out front, in the yard, is a nearly new Ford Econoline van with plush interior, CB radio, and stereo system ("Thirty-eight hundred dollar") and a shiny black Ford pickup truck ("Not mine," Nguu said unconvincingly, "friend's"). Nguu, it seemed, is as much an equipment junkie on land as he is on the bay. Food is cheap. Clothes are unimportant (he and his wife still wear sweaters and jackets the Baptists gave them five years ago). Machinery is all.

He dreams of larger, better boats; he is dizzy with the contraptions that could be bought. A V-8 engine, perhaps a whole new boat with a steel hull . . . with a steel hull, he'd no longer be imprisoned in Pensacola Bay . . . he could go out and fish the Gulf. He could buy the hull for $70,000, the V-8 engine for $52,000. He could do the rest of the work—the carpentry and electronics—himself. Alone on the bay in lonely morning hours, he dreams of these things; it is how he stays awake.

"I also make nets to not sleep," he said, standing on the bridge the night he took me fishing. "I never sit down. I sit, I sleep. Sometime, I sleep like this. . . ." He slumped over the wheel. "But I wake up quick. You like this work?"

"It seems hard," I said. "Do you make much money?"

Nguu shrugged. "Thirty thousand dollar, more or less," he said, artfully inexact.

We'd been out on the bay for little more than an hour. Nguu pulled in the small seven-foot tri-net several times and gauged the catch. The results weren't very encouraging: a dozen or so shrimp, which looked like chubby grasshoppers with startling Day-Glo eyes; assorted squid and crabs, the crabs doing their antic sideways shuffle across the deck; lots of useless baby croakers and other small fish; a can of Diet 7-Up. "See," Nguu said. "No good. We go home now."

He stopped the boat just outside the breakwater and hauled in the big nets. Suspended above the aft deck, the catch looked like two giant green beach balls. Nguu loosed the ropes at the base of the nets, and the haul spilled onto the deck in a silverine cascade. Immediately, Thang was squatting over it with a metal hand rake, culling the shrimp and squid from the baby croakers and other fish. "Too many fish," Nguu said. "Not many shrimp. Twenty-five pounds, maybe. We stay out all night, maybe $200. You see?"

Thang was working furiously now, picking out shrimp, putting them into a plastic laundry basket, sweeping useless fish aside. She looked up at us and smiled, ineffably exotic in her Baltimore Orioles cap.

"My wife work good, yes?" Nguu asked.

"Does she like it?"

"I don't know," he replied. The question was superfluous, irrelevant. "But lots of shrimp, she very happy. She like make money."

Bearings

PENSACOLA, FLORIDA

Population: 60,584

Tristan de Luna led a Spanish expedition to Pensacola in 1559. A hurricane struck soon after they arrived, destroying most of the supplies; the colony struggled on for two years before being abandoned.

Rediscovered by the Spanish in 1686, Pensacola was ceded to the British along with the rest of Florida in exchange for Cuba; it came back to the Spanish, along with West Florida, so the British could retain Gibraltar.

The first shots of the Civil War were fired in Pensacola when, on January 8, 1861, Lieutenant Adam Slemmer ordered his troops from Fort Barrancas to fire on a Southern reconnaissance patrol. Fort Pickens, in the bay, remained in Union hands throughout the war.

The military is Pensacola's biggest industry, employing 23,371 people and paying $583 million annually in wages. The carrier Lexington, *based here, has served as the set of several films, including* Tora! Tora! Tora! *The city is known as The Cradle of Naval Aviation.*

Pensacola's aspirations to importance as a commercial port have been thwarted by hurricanes, notably in 1906 and 1916, and by fire, but today the port handles more than 50 percent of all U.S. exports of bagged food.

Pensacola Bay was closed to swimmers in 1951 and reopened only in the late 1970s. In the last two years, pelicans, which are a sure sign of clear water, have reappeared in the bay.

Flaunting It

C. D. B. Bryan

I have come to Houston to see Vince Kickerillo, who doesn't want to see me.

All I know about him is that he is in his early fifties, is deeply religious, doesn't drink or smoke, was one of fourteen children of a sharecropper living in the Bryan, Texas, area, that his mother died when he was eleven, and that he ran away from home at fourteen because, although he didn't know what he wanted to do, he did know he didn't want to chop cotton for the rest of his life. I know that he worked for Hughes Tool until he was old enough to join the merchant marine, and that while in the merchant marine he learned to play poker and eventually won enough to build his first house.

Vince Kickerillo is now worth hundreds of millions. One of Houston's major real estate developers, he owns more than a dozen banks, a security company, and a recording studio; he travels between his fifteen-acre Nottingham Country estate out-

C. D. B. BRYAN lives in a modest home in New England.

side Houston and his twenty-fourth-floor penthouse office atop his burgundy-colored granite downtown Unitedbank Plaza building in his private helicopter, flies regularly to Palm Springs and Aspen in his own jet, has four Rolls-Royces and a classic Mercedes Coupe, and is married to a formerly very successful Vegas opening-act singer, Mary K, who has just completed an album for which their good friend Paul Anka wrote and/or arranged thirteen songs.

The parking lot of the Remington, the hotel in which I am staying, on Post Oak Park, is wall-to-wall Rolls-Royces and Mercedes-Benzes. The Remington was built two and a half years ago by Caroline Hunt Schoellkopf, H. L. Hunt's daughter and reportedly the second-richest woman in America (her sister, Margaret Hunt Hill, is reportedly the richest). Each room cost $200,000 to build. The bed and couch are massive; the cable TV is hidden within a huge armoire; original art hangs on the walls. The bathrooms have marble walls, all-brass fixtures, mirrors on three sides, and a telephone next to the toilet; a little basket containing various unguents and Ralph Lauren shampoo rests on the marble counter next to the sink.

Like every hotel, the Remington has its characters: the lady who comes in once a week for a breakfast of deep-fried potato skins, a glass of milk, and an eight-ounce can of caviar. (Her breakfast check is approximately $650.) It has the man who goes through two to three bottles of Louis XIII brandy a night. (The brandy comes in a Baccarat crystal decanter and sells at the bar for fifty dollars a shot. It's $850 if you have the bottle delivered to your room.) And it has the woman who stayed in the Presidential Suite with her parrot and dog for forty days at $1,200 a day while her River Oaks house was being refurbished. Not long before I arrived there was a phone call for a couple having dinner in the Remington bar, a favored meeting and dining spot modeled cunningly after the bar at New York's "21." The telephone was plugged in at the couple's table, and the husband said to his wife, "You answer it." She did, listened for a moment, then turned to her husband and said, "Guess what, darling, we just had a gusher."

The evening I arrive Robert T. Sakowitz, of the Sakowitz department stores, is receiving a decoration signifying his nomination to

Knight of the Order of Merit of the Italian Republic from Dr. Nicola di Ferrante, the honorary consul of the Italian Republic. I have been invited to the reception being given at the house of Bob and his new young wife, Laura Sakowitz, in River Oaks. The guest list includes his mother, Ann Sakowitz; George and Annette Strake (he's an independent oil operator, chairman of the Republican party of Texas, and a former Texas secretary of state during Governor Clements's administration); Steve and Doug Wyatt and their lady friends (Steve is in the oil business, Doug is an attorney; both are sons of jet-set socialite Lynn Wyatt); Joe and Sally Russo (banking and real estate); Jennard and Gail Gross (building and real estate); Aaron Farfel (financier); Lois Stark (NBC documentary film producer); Mark and Jerry Westheimer (he's a corporate attorney); "Racehorse" Haynes (criminal defense attorney) and his wife, Naomi; John and Minnie Daugherty (he's Houston's top residential realtor, dealing primarily in multimillion-dollar homes); and, supposedly dropping by just for cocktails, *Vince and Mary K Kickerillo.*

Robert Sakowitz is handsome, dark-haired, elegant, self-assured. We are standing together near the entrance to his comfortably cluttered living room with its wine-red walls, golden Japanese screen, collection of Toby mugs, country-chintz-covered sofa and stuffed chairs, all of which lend an ambience one Houston wag describes as "early divorce." There is a De Chirico oil over the fireplace, a few Kandinskys scattered about, a framed George Price *New Yorker* cartoon.

"Texas isn't just a state, it's a state of mind," he tells me. "We have that certain independence, that vibrancy and entrepreneurship that has a certain amount of style and creativity to it. People are very creative in their fun here. They like to have fun, they like to enjoy where they go and what they do."

"And how do they have fun?" I asked.

"Saturday we're going up in a hot-air balloon," Laura Sakowitz says. Like most of the women I will see during my visit to Houston, she is very blond and very pretty. "It's for Valentine's Day. A belated valentine. Bob asked me what I wanted to do and I said, 'Let me think about it.' I was thinking, 'Do I want to do dinner?' and nothing really sounded good. And then I said, 'I want to go up in a hot-air balloon.' I haven't ever done it, and I've always wanted to do it. . . ."

"And we're going to have champagne at the start and a chaser and champagne at the end," Bob adds. "But to answer your question, people here like to entertain in their homes or have small dinners. Although there are thousands of 'disease balls,' all the charity parties, the cultural events, and things that are supported—and everybody supports them—that's really not the key. People have a tendency to think Houston people are tremendously ostentatious in their display of wealth. But that sort of showiness probably died fifteen years ago. The only real ostentation today might be doing what the Germans call *auf-geputz*, 'too much much.' People who are being over-elegant, putting on the dog too much. But that doesn't happen today as much as it used to. People are really conscious of *not* wanting to do that."

"But aren't there some left who still *do* want to do that?" I ask.

"Sure," Bob said. "Sure there are. Someone like the Di Portanovas, who are trying to live a very flashy kind of life-style. You might walk into their house on River Oaks Boulevard and find a three-and-a-half-foot-high tier of malossol caviar to be enjoyed before dinner—Enrico di Portanova's mother was a Cullen who married an Italian baron, and Rick grew up in Italy and came back here and really loves to celebrate his wealth, although it was not of his making. Now I'm not saying that much caviar is bad, if you want to enjoy it. And it could be considered a celebration of wealth more than an ostentatious display."

Baron Enrico di Portanova and his second wife, Sandra, will come up again and again in conversations I have in Houston. His grandfather, the legendary oilman Hugh Roy Cullen of Quintana Petroleum, hit it big enough and early enough to leave his children's children's children each $60 million in trusts. Twenty-plus years ago when Maxine Mesinger—the witty, popular gossip columnist for the *Houston Chronicle*—first met Rick, he was living in Rome, was a jewelry designer, didn't have any money, and was married to his first wife, Ljuba, a beautiful Yugoslavian basketball star. Several years later, in 1968, he sued to gain greater control of his trust by having its guardianship removed from his Cullen aunts' embrace and placed instead within the impersonal but accessible confines of a bank. And he won. He came back to Houston, where he bought a large house on River Oaks Boulevard and nearly doubled its size. The Di Portanovas then built an even larger, grander house, which hangs on a cliff in Acapulco and makes the Houston house look like servants' quarters. The Acapulco house has, I was told, thirty-two bedrooms, twenty-six bathrooms, and turrets with armed guards to "keep out *banditos* and unwanted guests."

Baron di Portanova subsequently went to court again, and at the moment of this writing, his appeal for an even larger share of the Cullen estate is pending. At stake is one of the largest settlements in U.S. judicial history—larger even than the settlement of the Howard Hughes estate.

In addition to the Houston and Acapulco houses, the Di Portanovas currently own a huge suite at the Hotel de Paris in Monte Carlo and a similarly large one at Claridge's in London. Even though his money comes from Houston, and even though Sandra, whom he married in 1973, is a Houston native with money of her own, many of the people I spoke with in Houston consider them "foreigners" because of the flamboyance of their life-style. It is as much for that reason, perhaps, as the fact that they spend only three months a year in Houston, that the De Portanovas have put their River Oaks house on the market. For $10 million.

More guests appear, and as the Sakowitzes go off to greet them I ask a gentleman near me if the Kickerillos have arrived. They have not. I learn I am speaking with John Daugherty, whose realty company handled the sale of a River Oaks home in 1982 for just under $6 million, which is believed to be the highest price ever paid for an estate in the southwestern United States. Another property Daugherty handled was Rienzi, described in the offering brochure as "an Italian Contemporary in design, distinguished by Palladian accents." The house contains about eleven thousand square feet of living space (the average supermarket covers ten thousand square feet) and includes four bedrooms, five baths, five half-baths, a 28' × 20' living room, an 18' × 28' dining room, an 18½' × 20' library, an 11½' by 15' breakfast room, a 15' × 22' Mexican room, a 17' × 43' gallery, a 33½' × 43' ballroom with 16' ceilings . . . need I go on? Rienzi was listed with John Daugherty Realtors at an asking price of $10 million, but was taken off the market after eighteen months when the owners decided to stay. Both houses were designed by John Staub, who is probably Houston's most famous architect.

Daugherty asks me if I would like to drive around River Oaks with him the next afternoon so that I can see Rienzi and some of the other houses there. John Daugherty's firm handles more than 70 percent of all the sales of million-dollar homes in the River Oaks area—and in outlying areas as well. He's third-generation Houston; his mother played in a poker club with the wives of Ed Scurlock, John Mecom, Sr., and Jim "Silver Dollar" West. If I was to be shown River Oaks, I could not imagine a better guide.

Bob Sakowitz interrupted our conversation to ask if I would care to see his wine cellar before the honorary consul presented him with the medal. While we were there I had the opportunity to ask him if the Kickerillos had come. If they had, he said, he hadn't seen them yet. *Damn*, I tell myself, *I'm going to miss them*, because after the wine-cellar tour I have to leave for a dinner party being given by Maxine Mesinger in honor of her friend Dr. Natale Rusconi, managing director of the Cipriani Hotel in Venice and the Villa San Michele in Florence.

Maxine's dinner is being held at Tony's, Houston's answer to New York's Le Cirque. I arrive as Maxine's other guests are threading their way past the diners in the handsome, dark-green-walled main dining room with its brilliantly spotlighted paintings (one, I see, is by Paloma Picasso's mother, Françoise Guilot, who, I later learn, hung it herself), past the huge urns containing hundreds of fresh tulips and anemones, until reaching the half dozen or so tables in the restaurant's private dining room.

Maxine has seated me at her table with Joan Schnitzer on my left—an absolutely lovely, warm, gregarious, and elegant lady wearing a very feminine tuxedo: black trousers and a white jacket over a white lace blouse with a floppy bow tie. Joan is a Weingarten; her family owned not only the Weingarten supermarkets, which were all over Texas and Louisiana, but the real estate upon which the strip shopping centers surrounding the supermarkets were built. The seat on my right was still empty, but I stole a glance at the place card. It read MARY K KICKERILLO.

Be still, my beating heart!

A few moments later Vince and Mary K arrived. I've thought a great deal about how to describe Mary K. She wears her dark-brunette hair short, uses a gel to slick it back, but that doesn't come close to making it sound as attractive as it really is. Her eyes are dark, too—dark brown? dark blue? I could not tell which, because when I looked into them they were so deep I could never think to check on their color. And her eyebrows were dark, thick—though not as thick as, say, Brooke Shields's. Maybe all this sense of darkness is because her skin is so pale, so translucent-white, so clear. She was wearing a $3,000 to $4,000 dark-blue— or was it black?—sequined Fabrice outfit from Giorgio on Rodeo Drive and a pair of brilliant pear-shaped flawless white diamond earrings, each the size of a robin's egg, but, damn it, there was nothing flashy about them or her; one had the sense that she might rather be in a running suit. And there was a shy quietness about her, an aura that surrounded her, so that when I would turn to talk with her it was as though the air stilled and the voices of the others at the table seemed muffled. And yet I can't for the life of me remember what either she or I said! I remember how her husband looked at her, the absolute adoration in his eyes, and I remember how attentive and considerate of her he was at the table. And I remember talking to him and how suddenly and surprisingly he changed his mind and agreed to speak with me for this piece, said all I had to do was call his office the following morning to set up a time.

Then there was a charming toast by Maxine's husband, Emil: ". . . because we're so glad to have 'Miss Moonlight' back with us from the hospital," which wrung from one of the guests the cry "Emil, you're so *cute!*" To which Maxine responded, "Why do you think I married him twice?" Then Maxine rang on her wine glass and said, "Listen, may I make a couple of toasts? Because of my back brace I'm not going to get up, it's an ugly scene to see me stand up." Then she welcomed Natale Rusconi of the Cipriani to Houston, and Billy Hamilton from London, who does P.R. for the *Orient-Express,* and Alex Trebeck, who hosts the TV game show *Jeopardy* and has a wonderfully wry sense of humor, and Houston hairdresser Lyndon Johnson, who had opened a new store; and then Natale Rusconi gave a short and eloquent and absolutely perfect toast, and not long after, with our bellies full of Whole Snapper and Crab Fines Herbes, Pheasant with a Red Currant Sauce, *Côte de Boeuf au Poivre, Bombe Glacé,* and three different wines, we went out into the night.

Mirabile dictu several of us ended up back at the Remington bar for a nightcap: Natale Rusconi, Billy Hamilton, Paul Zuest (the Swiss-born managing director of the Remington), Hal Foster (president of the Callas & Foster public relations firm), "Contessa" Betsy Parish (a former Sakowitz V.P., now with Callas & Foster, who is famous in Houston for—among other things—her line "Old Money in Houston is yesterday's; New Money is today's").

My favorite story that came out of that evening was the one Hal Foster told about the Houston grande dame married to a very wealthy oil man who maintained, in addition to a large estate in Houston, a pied-à-terre at the Pierre in New York. Because he was so busy she traveled alone through Europe after their marriage, having a wonderful time with all that money, but eventually she tired and in London decided to take the *QE2* home. So she cabled her husband the date and time the ship was to arrive and said that she would meet him in New York. The boat docked early in the morning, she disembarked, there was no one there to meet her. She realized her husband had not received her cable and figured what the hell, she'd take a cab to the Pierre. When she entered their suite she found a flower arrangement that covered an entire side of the living room with a card attached that said, "My darling, what a fabulous weekend! So many wonderful things happened, I will remember it for the rest of my life. Love, Mary."

The wife read the card, plucked it off the arrangement, took it into her dressing room, freshened herself up, and marched down to Harry Winston, the jeweler, and said, "I would like to see the largest marquis you have in the vault."

They brought out a tray, and a magnificent marquis diamond was presented to her that pleased her very much, and she said, "Thank you and now will you take this card and place it in the case with the diamond and have one of your nice young men deliver it to me at '21.' I will be there with my husband, who lunches there at 1:30." She handed the clerk the card off the flower arrangement, took a taxi down to "21," and greeted her husband, saying, "Darling, surprise! Here I am! You obviously didn't get my wire."

He said, "No, darling, I didn't, but it's so nice to see you! Let's have lunch."

They were seated, having their first cocktail, when the young man from Harry Winston arrived with an elaborately gift-wrapped package and placed it on their table. "What a wonderful surprise!" the wife said as she undid the ribbon. She made a fuss over carefully unwrapping the paper, opened the box containing the diamond, and gushed, "It's *lovely!*" Then she passed the card over to her husband, saying, "Darling, you *shouldn't* have!" and paused long enough for him to read it before adding, "Thank you so much!"

The husband put the card away. "My dear, you're welcome," he said.

According to Hal Foster she wears that ring every day and "it's a real klunker!" The following morning, Thursday, Vince Kickerillo agreed to meet with me at his office at 1:00 Friday. "Would you like to go up in my helicopter before that to take a look at the city?" he asked.

I said I would. He told me he would arrange for someone to pick me up at my hotel and drive me out to the helipad.

At lunch Thursday at the Tivoli, Maxine Mesinger told me how, because of her two back operations, she had had "one year of hell, but both times this year after my two operations, when I woke up, there were Vince and Mary K with Emil easing the way: Was there something I wanted? 'Is there anything I can do?' " I asked how Vince and Mary K had met.

"She was working in a very fine men's clothing store in the Galleria, which is Houston's most chic shopping area," Maxine said. "Vince walked in, took one look at her, and he flipped! She had been in showbiz, she'd started when she was fifteen or sixteen —she was and is one helluva singer! She was not star status, but she was very good, she would be the opening act in Vegas hotels for people like Jack Benny, Rowan and Martin, and Phil Harris, and she was under contract to Sinatra's record company, Reprise. But she was just so young when she went into it and didn't ever love it, so she came back to Houston, which is where all her family is from. Her father was a very fine chef in one of the big restaurants. She and Vince started going together and he married her. I said to him the other day, 'You know, you've got all this money, but I bet you've never enjoyed it like you do now!' He is *so* in love with her. And Kelli, their three-year-old, is the first child he ever had in his life. He said, 'Anybody who can give me a baby can have anything they want.' He adores that child. He's a typical Italian: if he loves you, he'll kill for you."

Speaking of Italians, Maxine told me her favorite Di Portanova story: "Emil and I were in Monte Carlo at the same time as the Di Portanovas, and early one morning we were getting ready to leave for Venice. Everybody had said, 'Take the train, it's so beautiful,' so we were in the lobby early, 8:00, and saw Ricky, who likes Dom Perignon and pink champagne and never goes to bed before 3:00 or 4:00 in the morning. But there he is in the lobby with the driver of his Rolls-Royce, which is in Monte Carlo, and I said, 'What in the world are you doing up? What is the matter with you?'

"Ricky said, 'Well, my driver's talked me into flying to London this morning because he saw this vintage Rolls-Royce, and I guess I'm going to have to buy another Rolls.'

"I said, 'Why?' " Maxine continued. "I mean, he had that Rolls limo there, and I don't know how many he has in Houston.

"Ricky said, 'Because I'm sick and tired of Sandra's luggage and we have to get taxis and it's not easy and I can't stand it! So if we have two Rolls-Royces, we can put the luggage in one and us in the other.' "

Maxine also talked about Lynn Wyatt, whose huge house on River Oaks Boulevard has a Lalique crystal banister, whose name is always in the society columns, and whose photograph—taken at events like the opening of Diana Vreeland's antique costume collection at the Met or the New York City Ballet, at charity balls with the Rothschilds, or in Monte Carlo with the Grimaldis— appears constantly in *Town & Country* and *Women's Wear Daily*.

"Lynn Wyatt does the kinds of things people here want to get into," Maxine said. "They want to be part of the international travel set, to be able to say, 'I was in London and St. Moritz for the season'—'San Morritz,' they call it. And what gets them there is money, which very few people turn up their noses at in this town—or if they do, they're so old nobody pays any attention to them.

"Lynn thrives on being in the newspapers, in *WWD*, in magazines—and she's *everywhere*. Whatever the season is, she's there," Maxine continued. "And you have to *work* at these things! Lynn Wyatt's life is devoted to working. You have to *work* to become Princess Grace's close friend. Lynn throws fabulous parties and will have everyone from Princess Margaret to Mick Jagger at the same time—Princess Margaret as a house guest. You have to work to have your house ready at all times if Princess Margaret comes. Lynn works so damn hard I often wonder if she has that good a time."

About five years ago Lynn Wyatt's husband, Oscar, bought her W. Somerset Maugham's house at Cap Ferrat for her birthday. Until then they had been renting in St. Tropez or around Monte Carlo.

Maxine told me, "The Wyatts threw a birthday party with a cast including David Niven, Johnny Carson—he was still with Joanna in those days—Princess Grace and Rainier and Prince Albert, all kinds of celebrities, and a smattering of that older, boring, pseudoroyalty that are all over Europe because they have a title. Incidentally, people in Houston drop dead at the sound of a title. It could be a princess selling perfume, they don't give a damn: 'Let me have the princess over.'

"But for this party," Maxine continued, "Oscar has a very large airplane, like a commercial jet, which he has had done over with a bedroom and a shower, easy chairs, and so on—he also has smaller jets—but Oscar flew over bringing his cook from his home in Corpus Christi with chickens, because he didn't even want to buy the chickens in France, and she stood and she cooked southern-fried chicken probably all day for this group, which was a seated dinner for about 150 people around the pool. And Lynn wanted this band from outside of Aspen and so Oscar flew the band over along with the cook and the chickens, and he had his other cook in Houston make Texas chili, which they froze in blocks, and Oscar flew that over. . . . So the opening course was buffet—all the French delicacies, like caviar, pâté, smoked salmon, the usual. And then, my dear, when they brought out the

fried chicken and the chili and beans those people, the Euro-
peans, went crazy!

"And afterward," Maxine said, "they had a fireworks display,
and David Niven said, 'My God! Lynn has never seen the streets
here! If anything catches fire, all our houses are going to burn
because the fire engines can't get through!' And the police came
and gave them all tickets, and Rainier went out and said, 'I'm
Prince Rainier, please don't do this.' And the police said, 'We
don't care who you are, this is not your province,' and ticketed
them for the fireworks display. . . . And afterward they all went
to Regine's in Monte Carlo because the Colorado band had never
been there. I think that was at about 6:00 in the morning."

If, as it appears, Houstonians are rather proud of the swath that
Lynn Wyatt cuts through Europe's royalty (who credit her with
making Texas more palatable), they also notice that in five
months Lynn Wyatt helped raise nearly $1.5 million for the
Houston Grand Opera. To Houston, Lynn Wyatt is not "just a
jet-setter"; she works hard and gives back to the town.

Back at the Remington after lunch, Hal Foster introduced me to
Caroline Schoellkopf, who was attending a tea party given in the
hotel ballroom to raise money for the Casa de Niños hospice for
terminally ill children. Schoellkopf may be the second-richest
woman in America, but there is nothing in her dress or manner
that would lead one to think that. She was very simply dressed in
a black suit, a white silk blouse with some sort of thin red-ribbon
trim, and she would have looked no more out of place offering the
tray of champagne than she did being offered it.

A great many of the women at the tea party were wearing red
dresses, and I learned that they had come from the Valentine's
Day luncheon Warner Roberts had given earlier that day.
Warner Roberts, who has her own TV talk show in Houston, had
asked all the ladies to wear red. Alex Trebeck had attended the
lunch with Joan Schnitzer; Ron Stone, another local TV personality, had read Elizabeth Barrett Browning's "How do I love thee?
Let me count the ways." Heart awards were given to people who
had been "loving and kind and dear," and everyone was asked to

look underneath her chair. The person whose chair had a little
pink heart stuck beneath it would win the door prize. It was won
by the sixty-five-plus-year-old wife of Eddy Scurlock of Scurlock
Oil. The prize was a little heart-shaped G-string and pasties.

And Alex Trebeck had stood up and said that since he drives
by Frederick's of Hollywood every day on his way to work it would
give him a good reputation in that town if he could stop in and
place an order for four hundred Texas women. And then, as he'd
surveyed the crowd, he'd said, "I really do feel Texas has the most
beautiful women in the world. But," he'd added, "I hear they kill
the ugly ones when they're born."

Someone then had sung "My Funny Valentine."

That afternoon as Hal Foster and I drove around the River Oaks
section of Houston with John Daugherty, John kept up a running
commentary on each house as we passed: "That one behind the
serpentine brick wall is John Blaffer's; his father was one of the
ones who started Humble Oil. . . . That was J. S. Abercrombie's; he
founded Cameron Iron Works; his daughter lives in River Oaks
still. She's into boxing. Our Olympic boxers trained at her gym. . . .
That one there our company had on the market for four and a half
million. . . . This one on the corner, with the iron gates and stucco
posts? That was John Connally's. We had it on the market for one
and a half million and sold it several years ago to a man who moved
here from France. It's one acre on River Oaks Boulevard. . . . And
that one is Baron Ricky di Portanova's house. They did a major
renovation. It was one-quarter the size it is now."

The Di Portanovas took what had looked like a southern
antebellum mansion and turned it into what someone described
as a "green Italian palazzo." The neighbors were not pleased.
During the renovations a fire broke out in the back of the property, and as the neighbors gathered at the wailing of fire-truck
sirens one neighbor was heard saying, "What bitch called the fire
department?" The Di Portanovas' most recent addition was a
two-story glass-enclosed Olympic-size swimming pool, which includes three crystal chandeliers that hang over the pool. "I'm the
only one concerned about who changes the light bulbs," one
person familiar with the house told me. "I'm concerned because
in order to change them you'd have to stand in the middle of the

swimming pool on a ladder." The two-story interior is totally marbled up to the glass roof. It's all air-conditioned. And they have seated dinner parties for 150 to two hundred people around the pool. It's landscaped with trees and shrubs as if you were outside in the garden, and although my informer told me, "It's an incredible, fabulous place," a friend of hers stated, "If they were to add one more baroque artifact to the house, the house would topple over." Another neighbor has resignedly said, "Well, it won't be so bad once the ivy grows."

"I like the Di Portanovas," John Daugherty said, "but they make some people angry because they're too flashy. They don't do anything much with their money except spend it."

But, as Hal pointed out, "although a lot of people get annoyed with the Di Portanovas, if the Di Portanovas give a party, by God, those same people will be there!"

We continued down River Oaks Boulevard toward the country club. "Jim 'Silver Dollar' West lived on that property," John said, looking at a large house on our right. "He had a magnificent Mediterranean home. Bob Lanier bought the house, tore it down, and built a new home. He was known as 'Silver Dollar' because he used to give away silver dollars. I used to dive for silver dollars in his pool as a kid. Houston has a very gumbo-moist soil because it's so close to the sea. It's only fifty feet above sea level, and after Mr. West's death, when they went to take the silver dollars out of his basement—there was several hundred thousand dollars worth of them down there. When they took all that weight out of the basement, the house lifted up a couple of inches.

"That's Caroline Farb's house there," John continued as we reached almost the end of the boulevard. "She and Harold had a very stormy marriage always. They were always very open about it to their friends. He likes to sing Al Jolson and George Gershwin songs, and he would sing to her from the stage of his restaurant, the Carlyle. I can remember going to seated dinner parties where he'd get up and sing to her and they'd make up. But then eventually they did divorce, and she wound up with more than $20 million in real estate, cash, jewelry, automobiles. . . . It didn't make that big a dent in Harold. He's probably worth, what do you think, Hal, three hundred million?"

"At least," Hal agreed, then added, "You've probably read about her closet."

"Of course when Caroline bought it she enlarged the house, nearly doubled its size. It had been originally built by H. L. Hunt for his girlfriend. Edgar Brown III lived there next. His grandparents were in the timber business. They were worth a hundred million back at the turn of the century—back when a hundred million was *really* worth something—and then, and *then* oil was discovered on their timberland! I remember Edgar Brown, Jr., used to come to the Houston Livestock Show wearing a bow tie made of a hundred-dollar bill—and that," John laughed, "was when a hundred-dollar bill was really worth something, too! And then after Edgar Brown, Millie and J. Collier Hurley moved in there. Collier was an independent oil operator who hit an oil field and was rich overnight, and Millie was a hooker from Tennessee who used to work the old Shamrock Hotel on weekends—the Shamrock was Glen McCarthy's. He was one of our well-known wildcatters. He married into the old Lee family, the old Yount-Lee Oil Company. They were among the group who discovered Spindletop out by Beaumont. Glen McCarthy married Mr. Lee's daughter, and he himself hit a big oil field, and the first thing he did was build the Shamrock Hotel. Back in those days, the late 1940s, the Shamrock was the cat's meow. Dorothy Lamour, Sophie Tucker, Frank Sinatra all played there. The James Dean character in *Giant* was modeled after Glen McCarthy. Anyway, the Shamrock was the hotel Millie used to work out of on weekends. She made no bones about it. She was very open.

"Well, Collier met Millie and they got married," John continued, "and they were very visible. He had her draped in the most beautiful clothes and lots of diamonds and big emeralds, and she was a very buxom lady, so all those jewels looked just great sitting there. They had many wonderful parties at that house, which I was fortunate enough to attend. . . ." We had pulled over to the side of the road by the house, and John just sat there looking at it for a moment, and then he said, "After that, Frank Briscoe, one of our well-known district attorneys, bought it at an auction. I think Collier Hurley had some financial problems. . . . It was the first auction ever held at River Oaks, and they set up a big tent in their side yard and sold the furniture and jewelry and auctioned the house off. Frank Briscoe lived there until we sold it to Harold and Caroline Farb."

"If those walls could talk . . ." Hal mused.

Millie called Collier Hurley "Daddy." When they flew to New York, the maid would travel in tourist with the dog and Millie would reserve seats in first class for herself, "Daddy," and the jewelry. Armed security would meet them. The maid and the dog would go in a cab; Millie, Collier Hurley, and the jewels would travel in a limousine with the armed security. A Houston woman who knew them well told me, "When we'd go to '21,' Millie would walk in with the chauffeur, who was carrying a case of diet Dr. Pepper. We'd sit right down there in the left bank where everybody would sit, and Sheldon Tannen would come up to Millie in her little Norell suit and say, 'Mrs. Hurley, are you ready for your drink now?' And they'd bring her dietetic Dr. Pepper and bourbon."

On Lazy Lane, outside the huge house owned by Mr. and Mrs. John Mecom, Sr., Hal told me how when the Mecoms were redecorating the Warwick Hotel, which they owned, Mrs. Mecom walked into the lobby and found the interior decorators taking the Aubusson tapestry back down. "What are you doing?" she asked.

They said, "Mrs. Mecom, the tapestry is eight inches too long. It hangs off the end of the wall."

She said, "Cut it."

"*Cut it?*" they cried. "Mrs. Mecom, you can't *cut* it! It's an Aubusson. It's an *antique!*"

"It's mine," she said, "I bought it. Cut the damned thing off."

And they went up the side with pinking shears, and afterward she said, "Now doesn't that look better?" and she took the piece that was left, had it framed, and hung it going up the staircase.

There had been a bit of talk the previous day about the posting for foreclosure by the Metropolitan Life Insurance Company of John Mecom, Jr.'s, I. M. Pei–designed Warwick Post Oak luxury hotel. John Mecom, Jr., is the owner of the New Orleans Saints football team. No one seemed terribly concerned—the Mecom family has always had its ups and downs. John Mecom, Jr., probably takes more oil and natural gas out of the state of Louisiana than anyone else, and as someone said, "It's two hundred million one day and only fifty million the next." John Mecom, Jr.'s, wife, Katsy, has money; her family's ranch in Oklahoma borders on three states.

John and Katsy Mecom's house, across Lazy Lane from the house of John's parents, contains a room made out of Tiffany windows. The elderly lady from whom they purchased the windows said her husband had bought them out of a bordello in France he used to go to and had wanted the windows because he'd had so much fun there. But the lady would not permit him to install them in their house since, they'd come from "where he'd gone to see his lady friends."

Two more notorious residents of River Oaks were Dr. John Hill and Candace Mossler.

Dr. John Hill married Joan Robinson, an attractive, well-liked, socially prominent young woman, and allegedly gave her some injections that, an Old Guard Houstonian told me, "hastened her demise." When Dr. Hill was brought to trial for the murder of his wife and won an acquittal, his wife's father, Ash Robinson, whose house was only a hundred or so yards down Kirby Drive from where Dr. Hill lived, was accused of hiring someone who successfully gunned down Dr. Hill. There were no convictions in that case either. Tommy Thompson wrote a best seller about it, *Blood and Money*.

We had rounded a curve on Willowick and pulled over, and John said, "That's where Candace Mossler and her estranged husband lived." I remembered Candace Mossler's sensational murder trial in the mid-1960s. She and Melvin Lane Powers, her nephew and supposed lover, had been accused of killing her husband. Percy Foreman had been their lawyer, and they were acquitted. Many years later she married a younger man, who, while trying to climb up to her bedroom, fell, suffered brain damage and a collapsed lung, and became a paraplegic for the rest of his life. There were a lot of rumors flying around about what had happened: Did she push him or have someone push him? But no charges were filed.

A handsome couple trotted past our car and waved at John. "That's Roy Cullen right there and his wife, Mary," John said. "They're both big joggers."

Roy Cullen and his brother Harry are Baron di Portanova's first cousins. Roy and Harry Cullen's father died on an oil rig when they were very young, and the boys and their mother went to live with the boys' grandparents. When Harry was ten or eleven years old the boys' grandfather, Hugh Roy Cullen, thought Harry ought to do something and arranged for his grandson to have a paper route. The chauffeur drove Harry in the limousine up and down River Oaks so the young boy could toss the papers on the lawns. "Harry didn't love it," I had been told, "so mostly the chauffeur threw the papers."

John Daugherty turned back to the Mossler house and said, "Right after Candace Mossler passed away, the bank that was managing her estate asked me to go through the house, look at it, and try to help them determine its value. It was in a pretty bad state. Throughout the house the walls were *singed!* She kept it so hot in there—apparently she was a very cold-natured person— the walls were literally brown, burned from so much heat in the house over so long a period of time.

"And another thing," John continued, "she had two doors going into her bedroom, one that opened only out into the hall, and the other that opened only into her bedroom. And each door had between six and eight dead-bolt locks on it. She must have been a very paranoid lady. . . ."

I asked where Vince Kickerillo lives.

"Mary and Vince live way out on the west side of town. Vince, lately, has become more active in social circles than he has been. Most all of their friends live here in River Oaks, and although it's not necessary to live here, it's important. Eventually they will probably want to move into River Oaks to a big house on Lazy Lane."

When I got back to my room at the Remington there was a message saying that Margaret Zambrano, Vince Kickerillo's secretary, had called: a car would pick me up at the hotel at 10:30

the next morning to take me out to the helipad, and my appointment with Mr. Kickerillo was confirmed for 1:00.

Bill Dryden, a vice-president in commercial lending at Vince Kickerillo's Unitedbank, drove me to the helipad on the east side of town. On the way I asked him to tell me about his boss.

"To have no larger education than he did, 'Mr. K' is probably the most astute businessman I've ever seen or listened to," Bill said. "He's just amazing. When you sit in meetings with him and you're talking X millions at an interest rate of such-and-so percent, he can quote you within one hundred dollars what that interest rate is going to be at any time. You know about him running away from home and joining the merchant marine? Well, he played a bit of cards, and when he came back he got into the building business. He didn't do well on his first house, so he went out and got some more money and built several more houses, and they made it. He went from house building into huge developments—the most famous down here is Nottingham Country, which he started on the west side of the city—and after that it just multiplied.

"He bought himself a little bank," Bill continued as we drove, "cost him maybe four million, approximately, to buy that bank in some small, little town down here in Texas, and in a short time he ran it up to eleven, twelve, fifteen million, and that was the start of his banking career. He went from there to two or three other small banks and by this past year—that's his bank building right over there," Bill said, pointing through his windshield at a wine-colored skyscraper in the middle of downtown Houston, "that granite one in between those others? Anyway, over the last twenty years or so he acquired a lot of small banks, and this past year he formed Unicorp, a holding company, and put them into this large bank here, Unitedbank. And in addition to Unitedbank he has banks in College Station, Victoria, Orange, Paris, Texas, and some outlying banks in town."

"How many banks do you think he now owns all together?" I asked.

"He owns maybe . . . he owns maybe . . ." Bill paused while he thought, then he shook his head and said, "I honestly don't know. I doubt if anyone back at the office could tell you how many. Nobody ever sat down and counted them. And then, of course, along with the banks there's the Kickerillo Company, which is only real estate—the development and sale of lots and the land area—and there's the security company, his Inergi recording studio . . ."

We arrived at the helipad atop a multistoried garage and parked on the roof near Margaret Zambrano, who was waiting there too, with her car. A few minutes later a creamy-beige Bell 206 L-III Long Ranger helicopter with a burgundy CIRCLE K logo came in from the west, approached the parking garage, descended until it was hovering just off the lip of the roof, then inched forward and down until its skids gently touched the deck.

Vince Kickerillo slid out of the copilot's seat and went around to the side door. Mary K handed him Kelli, and Vince walked backward carrying his daughter, clutching her close to his chest, shielding her from the rotor wash until he was clear of the blades; then he turned around and saw me, looked worriedly at me as though he were not sure what I was doing there, then in an instant made up his mind who I was and said hello, that he would meet me at 1:00, and continued over to Margaret and the waiting car. I turned back from him just as Mary K hurried by with a shy smile, followed by Kelli's nanny all in white, and then Vince was holding the car door and Mary K slid in, followed by Kelli; the nurse climbed in the front, Vince and Bill Dryden exchanged a few words, Vince got in the car, and they were gone.

I sat in the copilot's seat next to Vince's pilot, Terry Glenby, who had flown with the Air Cavalry Division's 227th Aviation Battalion in Vietnam; Bill Dryden lounged comfortably on the leather seats in the back. We lifted off and headed down the Houston Ship Channel, with Bill calling out over the headset what we were looking at.

"What I'd really like to see," I said, "is how River Oaks looks from the air."

We turned back over the San Jacinto battle monument and the anchored, aged, pre–World War II battleship *USS Texas*, then flew west past downtown Houston, and a few minutes later were descending toward Di Portanova's and Caroline Farb's and Lynn Wyatt's houses, and all those others so big they took your breath away. From the air, River Oaks looks like a deeply wooded

Monopoly board upon which the players have built nothing but big hotels.

We banked over the country-club golf course, and I tried to find the house of a college classmate and friend of a great many years with whom I had spoken the evening before. He had chuckled at being told he was considered "Old Guard" and related how his grandfather had arrived in Corsicana, Texas, following the oil boom in 1890 with "about seventy cents in his pocket, some skills, and a desire to do well. He parlayed all that and a few mules into an oil and gas business, which subsequently set him in good enough stead to where he was part of the original group that founded a company called Humble Oil & Refining Company."

(Humble subsequently merged in two steps into Standard Oil of New Jersey and what is now generally known as Exxon Company, USA.)

"But," my friend told me, "this has all happened so *fast!* In the mid-1880s Houston was still just a bunch of shacks on the Buffalo Bayou, so the Old Guard is a concept I find very amusing." He paused for a moment and then said, "What you have to understand about Houston is that the medium of exchange here is not old family ties. . . . In fact, after you reach a certain point, it's not even *really* money. Houston is a *working* town. The medium of exchange is accomplishments."

As we circled in Vince Kickerillo's helicopter I looked down through the Plexiglass bubble at the mansions of River Oaks. I was thinking about what my Old Guard friend had said, and I was thinking about John Daugherty's confidence that it was only a matter of time until Vince Kickerillo and Mary K and little Kelli moved to River Oaks, too. I knew there was a certain appropriateness to that, a symmetry, an *inevitability* even, since in Houston, time and history are so compressed. Yesterday's T-shirted wildcatter is today's opencollared money baron is tomorrow's pinstriped Old Guard philanthropist.

The slap of the helicopter rotor blades changed slightly as Glenby pulled back on the cyclic stick and we began a gentle, climbing turn. Into view came a massive white house still under construction that was even larger than the Farbs' or the Wyatts' or the Di Portanovas', bigger than anything I'd seen.

I heard a low whistle over my headset. Bill had spotted the house at the same time I did. "Would you look at that castle being built!" he said. "That'd really shake your money, wouldn't it? I mean that thang has some *steel* in it!"

Bearings

HOUSTON, TEXAS

Population: 3,464,600

Houston was first settled by the Allen brothers, who came from New York, bought 640 acres of land for one dollar an acre, and advertised for settlers in eastern newspapers. The city was named for Sam Houston, whose forces defeated a larger Mexican army near the site of the city by attacking during its siesta.

Houston's population has grown 70 percent since 1960, but when Frost Belt citizens came to look for work during the 1982 recession, many had to return.

Houston has no zoning laws. Because of overbuilding and depletion of the water table, parts of the city have sunk a foot since 1973. In the summer of 1980 it had to ration water.

There are more commercial helicopters in Houston than in any other city in the country. A tunnel system connects some forty of the city's downtown buildings.

Houston's Second Baptist Church built a new building in 1983 for $34 million, $2 million more than the Astrodome cost. Said one pastor about churches of that size, "America does things in a big way, and the Lord is not going to be left in the backseat."

Houston was once billed as Magnolia City but now calls itself the Golden Buckle of the Sun Belt. Former Dallas mayor Jack Evans said of the city, "It doesn't wear well."

"Houston" was the first word uttered by Neil Armstrong when he landed on the moon.

Just Another Guy from the District

Sally Quinn

T he honorable Stanford E. Parris, member of Congress, Republican from northern Virginia, is a sludge man.

"Sludge in the Potomac," he says, "is something I can do something about. So I spend more time on sludge than I do on war and peace."

Stan Parris is a man who has learned the necessity of pragmatism.

If his constituents are against sludge, then he's against it, too. If they want to limit the use of National Airport, then so does he. And if their number-one concern in life is rush-hour traffic jams, so is his. There's no doubt about where Parris stands. He stands for his constituents.

"You concentrate," he says, "on what you have to do."

Washington, D.C.: Hollywood on the Potomac. The name conjures up power. The city inspires fiction, makes films, makes stars,

SALLY QUINN has recently returned to her job at *The Washington Post* after finishing her first novel, *Regrets Only*.

makes diplomacy. America—democratic America—loves its kings and queens.

Once, power was enough. Hard work, long hours, doing homework, paying dues seemed to be the way to get it. Fame and money were there, but they held lesser rewards. Now all that has changed. Fame has replaced power as the aspiration, because fame leads to power.

Henry Kissinger understood this. He used his limited power to gain fame, his considerable fame to gain more power. JFK understood it, too. He personified America's capital city as a city of stars.

Make waves, you get the right committee, the right chairmanship, the majority leadership. Get the right committee and you get the right invitations. You meet the journalists, you get interviewed, written about, aired. You're famous. You get the right committee. . . .

But there's another side of Washington—success on another, less visible plane. Stan Parris exemplifies it. He has quietly accepted his role as a lesser-known politician, a politician who has not made or really needed to make great speeches. He gets the job done. He holds on to it. And he concentrates on what he has to do. As one colleague puts it: "He extols the virtues of 'followship' rather than leadership. In a town full of chiefs, he's an Indian."

This is not what any self-respecting congressman wants to hear. And it's not that Stan Parris wants to be unknown. He is, after all, running for the governorship of Virginia. "To keep your name in the public eye is desirable when you're looking for votes," he concedes. "When they say 'Stan who?' it's a problem. You just can't do the same thing and stay in the public eye."

But to a large extent, Parris has done the same thing—for four terms now. You will not see him at those glamorous Washington dinner parties. You will not hear any gossip about him. "There are three kinds of congressmen," says one longtime Capitol Hill observer. "There are the kind who worry about committees, there are the hotshots, and then there are the district guys. That's about 80 percent of this place. Stan Parris is a district guy."

Parris sits back in a deep leather armchair. The walls of his office in the unkempt Longworth House building are covered with the obligatory photographs, plaques, medals, and certificates. He wears a dark-blue suit, a white shirt, and a dark tie. At fifty-five, his hair snowy white, his expression tired, he has accepted the fact that he will never be a superstar.

"I hope this doesn't sound corny," he says, "but war and peace . . . you want to do something that's meaningful . . . of all the macro issues . . . the survival of mankind . . . there's very little we could do if the Soviet Union went berserk on us. So you don't worry about those kinds of things."

What kinds of things *does* he worry about? He worries about constituent things.

Sludge isn't even the half of it, though last year Parris did persuade the Environmental Protection Agency to take action against the Blue Plains Sewage Treatment Center for dumping untreated wastes into the river that separates his district from D.C. There's also been the hydrilla problem. Last summer Parris managed to wrest a quarter of a million dollars from the Department of Defense so that the Army Corps of Engineers could begin to fight the noxious weed that's taking over the parts of the Potomac that haven't been destroyed by sludge.

"The giant green monster," Parris says with a certain passion, "will one day reach out of the faucet in the bathroom and grab you by the arm."

There have been other issues: persuading Washington to build itself a new prison rather than expand the existing one in Virginia; charging the Justice Department to investigate claims of reverse discrimination in the hiring of D.C.'s fire fighters.

Stan Parris worries about lowering taxes, offering economic opportunities. He approves of supply-side theories ("The business of government is not to be in business"). He is pro-defense ("I'm a hawk; to be second in defense is to be last"). And, he says, he is no reactionary ("I'm all right on equal rights").

Like many of his colleagues in Congress, Parris displays a loyalty—perhaps a conformity—to his constituents' views that may be the nearest thing the country has to true representation. Though his district borders the capital, he sends computerized mailings home as though they were letters from back east. Parris is part of the city, part of the process, but not part of the image.

Stan Parris was born in Champaign, Illinois, the son of a truck driver who died when Parris was fourteen. Parris was a pilot during the Korean War, was decorated four times, and was shot down. During the war he got married. When he returned, he settled in Virginia and took a job in the Senate building working the mimeograph machines.

"I will share with you a long-standing secret ambition," he will tell you. "Ever since I worked in the Senate, I always kind of wished I could be a member."

But getting into the House came first. Parris went to law school, set up a private practice, made some investments, and got involved in local elections. "I was nowhere in the sense of being party oriented or politically oriented," he admits. "But I knew where I wanted to be economically. I got involved on the Republican side. History has proven me correct."

Ideology, he says, never had much to do with it, and it still doesn't. Pragmatism has replaced passion. Voters, he says, want to know about their candidates: "What kind of guy is he, what does he look like, what impression does he make—his organization, does he have adequate financial resources?"

Fourth or fifth on the list, he says, is his position on the issues.

"If you take some far-out political position, it turns everybody off."

Parris twirls the propeller of a toy airplane on the table next to him, the large diamond ring on his finger glinting in the sunlight. "I go along one day at a time," he says. "I don't have a great scheme of things, any long-range plan."

These days, he says, he is "traditional, modestly right of center, conservative." He adds: "The majority of people are. The acquisition of material things is important to all of us. Young people are aware that where it seems to have been is not where they want it to be."

After four terms of service, he hasn't lost his sense of pleasure. "I enjoy the opportunity of having an impact on what happens around me," he says. "I don't mean to get maudlin about it, but at the inauguration I stood in that rotunda. It was an intimate, moving experience. And I thought: not too many years ago, four stories down, I was running a mimeograph machine. That's the system. That's this country. My story is not unique. That's called opportunity."

He has a few regrets, a few hopes.

Along the way he divorced twice and never saw much of his children. "They literally grew up with me coming in and out of doors," he says. "I always thought I was going to make a lot of money and be somebody and share that with them rather than my presence at home. Looking back, I would have given them more of me."

It will be worth the loss only, he says, if his constituents think he was effective, if someday they say, "Oh yeah, Stan Parris. He did a good job."

Meaning he did what he had to do.

Bearings

WASHINGTON, D.C.

Population: 623,000
Washington, D.C., was formed from sixty-nine square miles of Maryland and thirty-one square miles of Virginia. In 1791 the government and local landowners struck a deal for the land at Suter's Tavern in what is now Georgetown; the government paid twenty-five pounds an acre. Among the cities that had petitioned to be the nation's capital were Kingston, New York; Nottingham, New Jersey; and Williamsburg, Virginia.

The city was laid out by Pierre Charles L'Enfant— George Washington pronounced his name Langfang—but he was fired after a year.

Anthony Trollope called the city "as melancholy and miserable a town as the mind can conceive"; Dickens called it "the headquarters of tobacco-tinctured saliva," adding that "several gentlemen called upon me who, in the course of conversation, frequently missed the spitoon by five paces."

President John Quincy Adams was bathing in the Potomac one day and, upon emerging, found that the tide had carried off his clothes. When asked how he solved the problem, he said, "I walked along the shore until I

*met a boy, whom I dispatched to the house with a
message to Mrs. Adams, and after some delay he returned
with another suit of clothes."*

*Washington's population is larger than those of four
states, and it is the most heavily policed city in the
nation. Its citizens were given the vote in 1961 and in
1975 seated their first mayor in more than one hundred
years.*

Encounters
at the Mind's Edge

George Leonard

I f there is an American story, its central episode is the westward journey of its people. This journey, this frontier experience, forged a unique national character. Perhaps more than anything else, it made Americans different from their European forebears.

The realities of frontier life reaffirmed the original American curiosity, optimism, and distrust of established institutions and ideas. The westward journey relied on individual enterprise, ad hoc communities and social forms, and the willingness to forgo refinement in favor of results. The frontier, whether experienced firsthand or observed from a distance, engendered a belief that, given enough human effort and ingenuity, almost any dream could be transformed into reality.

But the journey had to end, and the frontier's final stopping place was a state so immense, so luscious and varied, that it was itself like a dream. The pioneers poured into California as if it truly were El Dorado, the golden land. They came first by wagon

GEORGE LEONARD, a native of Georgia, lives in Mill Valley, California. The author of *The Transformation,* he is a leading theorist of the human-potential movement.

train and sailing ship, later by railroad, and finally by automobile and airplane. And by the time the state's population passed that of New York in 1962, it was becoming clear to some observers that it was here more than anywhere else that Americans were to work out the answer to an important question: What do people shaped by the frontier experience do when the frontier closes?

Why not just stop pioneering and enjoy the rewards? Many Californians have obviously done just that. But what recurrently fascinates, bewilders, and sometimes even frightens the rest of the country is that so many other Californians have never stopped their pioneering; they have simply turned from the physical frontier to the frontiers of social and commercial innovation, of thought, and of spirit.

They have also moved on to more problematic frontiers, using their own lives as raw material to create new and sometimes extreme political and social movements. Some of the experiments failed. Others survived. But in almost every case some element of the experiment has been passed along to take its place in the rich cultural mix that gives this country an unparalleled ability to adapt to new challenges. One of the experiments that has not only survived but also thrived lies on the far side of California, beyond which there are only thousands of miles of open sea.

Stand at the edge of the cliff. Nearly a hundred feet beneath you the ocean heaves and pounds against the land: foamstreaked blue-green water rising and falling lazily, as if in slow motion. But then an incoming swell reaches one of the jagged offshore rocks, and a ton of seawater explodes fifteen feet into the air, giving you some idea of the force that eats away at the foundation of earth far down below your feet. So enjoy the view. This particular edge won't always be here. A thousand years from now you'd be standing on air. Maybe even next year, if the jet stream snakes its way south and the big winter storms come again.

Turn to the left and look down the coast, where dark-green promontories thrust into the sea like the prows of enormous ships. Keep turning and you'll see that this shelf of land atop the ocean cliffs extends for only a few hundred acres. Beyond that, the mountains loom up to four thousand feet: home of fox and deer, wild boar and mountain lion. Bring your eyes down from the peaks and spend a few moments admiring the lawns of springy grass, the profusion of flowers, the windswept cypresses, red-woods, and pines, the large organic garden bursting with lettuce and cabbage, broccoli and beets, practically every kind of vegetable and herb you can think of.

There is even something organic about the man-made structures that nestle into the contours of the land: the stone retaining wall and steps, the wrought-iron railings, the redwood lodge and living quarters. No overhead wires or antennas mar your view of the sky. High above, swallows dart and wheel and then dive down to skim inches above the surface of the swimming pool.

This is Esalen Institute, named for a tribe of Indians that once lived on the land and bathed in its hot springs: both a place and a vision. And though the vision has inspired hundreds of imitators all around the world, the vision is never entirely separate from the place. If a category is necessary in understanding Esalen, then *education,* in the original sense of "a leading forth," is as good as any. But what this place has come to offer is an education of the body and senses, of the emotions and perceptions, an education, in author Stuart Miller's words, "of the soul, of the heart, of the veins and arteries and the subtle messages and meanings of the blood."

And of the mind as well. Though Esalen has addressed itself to what Aldous Huxley calls the nonverbal humanities, it is also a verbal place, where theoretical discussions among scientists and scholars are likely to be heard until the small hours of the morning. This side of Esalen is often overlooked, perhaps because it is concerned not so much with the corpus of conventional fact and opinion as with the dynamics of a fundamental change of mind, of the very way we think.

It began in the early sixties, when the world was new and all things seemed possible. The two of them didn't know exactly how it would turn out, but they dreamed of a sort of forum for lectures and seminars on the marriage of Eastern and Western thought, the latest trends in psychology, the anatomy of personal and social transformation. They had similar backgrounds. Both were thirty-year-old Stanford graduates, both were from well-to-do families, both were athletes, and both were charming. Richard Price, reared in Chicago, possessed the chiseled features and startling

blue eyes of a Paul Newman; his smile had an ironic twist that
sometimes masked his abiding sense of compassion. Michael
Murphy, a native of Salinas, California, had dark, shining Basque
eyes and a dazzling Irish smile.

Of the two, Murphy was the enthusiast and visionary. After
Stanford and a two-year stint in the Army, he had lived for a year
and a half at the Aurobindo Ashram in India, where he had
meditated eight hours a day and coached the basketball and
softball teams. He was deeply influenced by the works of the
Cambridge-educated Aurobindo: enormous, densely written
volumes that argued for a synthesis of East and West, for revolutionary social change along with spiritual transformation.

In 1960, when both Murphy and Price were living in San
Francisco's bohemian North Beach district, the two started making plans. They wrote to people whose work they admired, people
such as Aldous Huxley, who was then lecturing on recent developments in psychology, education, and pharmacology that might
lead to fuller realization of human potential. Their letters brought
them encouraging replies. But how could these two minimally
employed young men get the wherewithal to open an institute?
Simple. Murphy's grandmother owned property on the Big Sur
coast, half of it leased out for motel operation, the other half
reserved for the Murphy family's gracious summer home. Michael
talked his grandmother into letting him and Dick Price take over
the motel and restaurant, to do with as they chose.

Price took over management of the day-by-day operations,
and Murphy, as program director, started firing off letters to some
of the most eminent thinkers of the time, inviting them to come
to Big Sur and lead seminars. And for some reason they came,
traveling sometimes over great distances to an unknown institute
that offered the most modest of fees. During the first five years
at Esalen you might have spent an intimate weekend with any of
the following: historian Arnold Toynbee, theologians Paul Tillich
and Harvey Cox, chemist Linus Pauling, bishops John Robinson
and James A. Pike, semanticist (later senator) S. I. Hayakawa,
writers Alan Watts, Carlos Castaneda, Ken Kesey, and Aldous
Huxley, futurist Buckminster Fuller, and psychologists Abraham
Maslow, Frederick S. (Fritz) Perls, Carl Rogers, B. F. Skinner,
and Rollo May. Maslow, who was to have a profound influence

on the institute, stumbled onto Esalen in a most improbable manner. In the summer of 1962, looking for a place to spend the night on a trip down the coast, he and his wife spotted a light and drove off the road toward what they took to be a motel. They were astonished to find that almost everyone there was reading his recently published book, *Toward a Psychology of Being,* and eagerly discussing his ideas.

That was one side of it. On the other was the emergence of a distinctive Esalen style or mystique. There was an elusive but pervasive promise of sensuality, a hint of danger in the air. There were tanned and bearded male staff members lounging on the bench outside the office, and long-haired waitresses in floor-length skirts who wouldn't be caught dead wearing a bra. There was a faint smell of massage oil and the lingering, sulfurous smell of the mineral hot springs. There were the Mountain Men who lived on the fringes of the law in the hills above Big Sur and who would appear without warning with their conga drums, looking for all the world like nineteenth-century western outlaws. There was Hunter Thompson, who served for a while as a guard, shot holes in the window of his room, and made his first forays into what was to become gonzo journalism. And there was music: a flute at the hot baths weaving its melody into the rhythm of the surf down below; a guitar and someone singing at the edge of a cliff, the sound of it drifting through the fog, rising and falling with the wind; the beat of distant drums; the rustle of a tambourine.

Some of the most famous minstrels of those times came to Esalen to perform: Joan Baez, who lived there for a summer before she became famous; Bob Dylan; Crosby, Stills, and Nash; Simon and Garfunkel. One day, at the height of the Beatles' popularity, two of them, George Harrison and Ringo Starr, dropped in by helicopter. Were they relieved or disappointed when the Esalen staff didn't mob them as they wandered around the grounds? Maybe they didn't know that the Esalen mystique would not permit such popular behavior.

The people who flocked to Esalen had been eager to hear the theories of Abraham Maslow. But after two or three didactic weekends they were ready for something more. If, as Fritz Perls said, therapy can occur only in the present, they wanted to experience therapy in the present. And Perls was happy to oblige. After giving a few weekend workshops, the irascible founder of Gestalt therapy announced to Murphy and Price that he was moving to Esalen and making it his base of operations. From 1964 to 1969 he not only presented his own workshops but also gave demonstration sessions during other leaders' workshops.

Those evenings were high drama. There on a low platform before a large fireplace in the lodge was a white-bearded Old Testament-like prophet in a white jumpsuit asking if anyone wanted to volunteer to work with him. To the amazement of those who wouldn't dare submit themselves to such an ordeal, fully a third of the fifty to a hundred people usually present would raise their hands, eager to sit in what Perls called the "hot seat" and have their psyches laid bare for all to see. Perls distrusted long-term therapy. Sometimes in a matter of minutes, employing a keen theatrical sense and a surgeon's skill, he would cut away every prop that his "victim" habitually used to bolster his or her neurosis, even charm and humor, until nothing was left but the opportunity for an existential leap into a new way of being. At this point, as the victim sat paralyzed on the edge of an abyss, Perls would turn to his audience and, in a thick German accent, utter a classic aside: "*Ah, ze* impasse." It was stunning. It was just what the people who came to Esalen wanted.

Lectures and talk-oriented seminars continued to be held at Esalen. In the late sixties, however, *experiential* workshops took center stage: weekend and five-day sessions during which the paying customers played active roles in the drama. Psychologist William Schutz, formerly of Harvard and of New York's Albert Einstein School of Medicine, also moved to Esalen, bringing a practice he called open encounter. Schutz believed passionately that our unwillingness or inability to tell the truth, whether to others or ourselves, blocked our path toward happiness and the realization of our potential. He was convinced that we create tragic misunderstandings by failing to communicate our true feelings, that we squander large amounts of creative energy guarding our secrets. To speak the truth, to live the truth, would set us free and lead the way toward a radically changed society.

Schutz exuded confidence. He was a soft-spoken but powerful man with the build of a wrestler, a courageous and dogged frontiersman of the psyche who was not so much interested in curing people as in creating heroes, astronauts of inner space. In

Schutz's groups, respectable, middle-class Americans were offered the opportunity to act in ways they had not previously dreamed possible. Having been thoroughly indoctrinated to distrust, repress, and conceal strong feelings and to live primarily for the past and the future, they now were urged to live intensely in the present and to reveal everything, even their darkest secrets. Men found themselves arm wrestling one another as an expression of their feelings about dominance. Couples found themselves revealing past infidelities and dealing right there and then with the emotional consequences. And some participants, after hours of wrenching encounter, found themselves telling the group about childhood episodes they had spent their lifetimes hiding away. When the sky didn't fall in, when to the contrary they were celebrated by their fellow participants, they wept with euphoric relief. If there were naysayers and even a few psychic casualties, they could be overlooked in the general sense of adventure, of boundaries crossed, of new energy released.

It was a wild time. Practitioners by the score arrived at Esalen, each bringing some new approach to the fulfillment of latent human capabilities. The scene in the dining room was tumultuous. Everybody seemed to be talking at once, and there was a feeling that marvels were imminent; at any moment someone might burst in and announce a new breakthrough. To the seekers who came there and to the thousands more who received the catalog in the mail, Esalen was a Persian marketplace teeming with exotic offerings and delicious opportunities. But it was not exactly what Murphy and Price had had in mind. There were moments during the late sixties, in fact, when they felt they were riding a runaway horse and all they could do was hold on for dear life.

You take a path that starts near the lodge and slants down along the side of the cliff where it's not as steep as elsewhere. Halfway down is a rectangular building that seems to jut out over the sea. On the roof, protected by transparent windscreens, are tables on which, if the day is warm enough, massages are given. You leave your shoes on racks just outside the door and go into the bathhouse, where there are showers and a dressing area.

Both to the right and the left are bathing areas partially

covered on top and at the sides but open to the sea in front. A
steamy smell of mineral water rises from the baths to blend with
the sea smell and the hypnotic sound of surf down below. In
either area, there is mixed nude bathing.

When the media first discovered Esalen, this one fact sometimes seemed to overshadow everything else the institute was
trying to accomplish. Most reporters were bewildered by Esalen's
aims. Mixed nude bathing, however, was something they could
understand—S-E-X. That prurience has now all but faded away,
and it is finally clear that Esalen is neither more nor less erotic
than, say, a typical first-class midtown Manhattan hotel.

The mixed bathing emerged from an impulse that was not
sexual but, again, pioneering. It was initiated not by the proprietors
of the institute but by the guests, who, in the liberating spirit of the
times, took it upon themselves to desegregate the baths. Murphy
and Price, in fact, fought against the mixed bathing for more than a
year after Esalen opened to the public. Only then, realizing the
futility of swimming against the tide, did they give in.

Today, for most people, the pioneering in this matter is over.
The baths at Big Sur simply provide one of the most relaxing
sanctuaries you can find anywhere. Whatever the weather, even
in the pouring rain, the baths retain their appeal, curative for
some, soothing for almost everyone: a place where you can restore
yourself after the sometimes strenuous interactions in the meeting rooms up above.

All Saturday morning the blacks attacked the blacks. Accusations
and demands for commitment ricocheted around the meeting
room in the lodge. "When they come with machine guns and
barbed wire," one slim, intense black man said, "all I want to
know is, baby, are you for me or against me?" The whites sat in
stunned silence. This conflict among the blacks was totally unexpected. But, then, to the best of our knowledge, what we were
doing had never been tried before, and nobody knew just what
to expect.

My association with Esalen had started in 1965 as part of a
magazine assignment to write an extensive essay on human potential. I had become close friends with Michael Murphy and had
begun donating some of my time to Esalen as adviser and occa-

sional group leader. A Deep South upbringing plus experience in covering the civil rights movement had engendered in me a passionate concern about the tragedy of racism in America. Now it was the summer of 1967 and all across America the cities were exploding. It was clear that something was needed to get at the roots of racial prejudice and the web of rationalization that held it in place. My friend Price Cobbs, a black psychiatrist, was writing a book to be called *Black Rage*. He and I had agreed to do the Esalen workshop as an experiment in black-white encounter. To give the experiment a chance to work, we had planned the weekend around a marathon session that would last some twenty-four hours. We would not sleep at all on Saturday night.

Thirty-five people of mixed race and sex had traveled to Esalen to participate. By the time the marathon began, just after lunch on Saturday, the blacks had begun to coalesce. By their very ability to fight and still not fly apart, they had developed a sense of unity and power. Now they turned on the whites. If any of these white people had come to Esalen to be celebrated for their liberal attitudes toward race, they were in for a rude shock. The blacks scorned their self-congratulations, their recitations of good works. They probed for dark racial secrets beneath the enlightened, white good-guy facades. They wanted their white counterparts to understand, really understand, what it was like to be black in this society.

"*Please*. What can I do? I'm trying. Please help me." Pam, a beautiful young white schoolteacher, had been struggling to gain the friendship of Cliff, a personable black college student. He had responded scathingly to her overtures. Now, as her eyes filled with tears, he rocked his chair back and forth, looking across the room at her with contempt.

"No, I'm not going to help you. I'm not going to take you off the hook. I want you to feel what I feel . . . what I've felt for twenty-one years. Go on. Cry."

"Please," she begged. Tears streamed down her face. Cliff kept rocking back and forth, his eyes fixed on hers. No one came to her rescue. We all realized that there were to be no easy fixes in this workshop, no shortcuts. We had a long, long way to go.

Sometimes, in fact, there seemed no end to it, no possible way through. The outpouring of bitter resentment continued through the night, reaching an intensity that was nearly unbeara-

ble. We grasped at anything that might bring relief. At about 2:30
A.M. a tall engineer with a thin moustache, excoriated earlier as
the last of the old-time white liberals, began boasting about his
numerous social contacts with blacks. Then, with a faint smile of
self-revelation, he said, "Actually, I collect Negroes." That was all
we needed. We whooped with laughter. "Do you have a good
connection?" someone asked. "Oh, yes, the very best." "What's
your source?" someone else asked between gasps of laughter. The
engineer named a ghetto near San Francisco. "I collect Negroes,
too," a black woman shouted over the laughter. "My source is my
uterus."

The laughter gradually subsided. We looked at one another
and sighed. A heavy fog had moved in from the sea; it pressed
against the windows. We resumed our task, struggling to stay in
the moment, to deny nothing, however painful or embarrassing,
to speak the truth and through the truth to get to the bottom of
the rage, the unspoken resentment, the secret fear, all of which
now seemed as vast as the ocean.

Some hours after dawn the group took another unexpected
turn: the whites began revealing themselves, baring the most
tragic and painful moments of their lives. The sun had broken
through the fog and everyone seemed strangely illumined. We
had all paid our dues during the long night, and now, in the
peculiar clarity of sleeplessness, we sensed that something mo-
mentous might be possible. In his history of Esalen, *The Upstart
Spring*, Walter Truett Anderson describes the episode that finally
broke down the barriers between black and white:

It began with a white woman who said she dated black men
exclusively. This was taken by black and white alike to be another
sleazy piece of white liberal trickery, and the members of the
group, especially some of the black men, were pressing her for an
explanation of why she *really* did this. She began to cry and said,
'Because I've given up on white men.' She sat there, weeping and
alone in a roomful of tired people, and then a black woman went
across the circle and embraced her. They wept together and everything changed in a simple, nonpolitical moment of human compassion. For some minutes there was absolute silence as a feeling
of something powerful beyond words welled up among them.
People looked around the room and saw other faces with eyes that

were full of tears. Somebody hugged somebody else. Then the whole room was full of weeping and embracing people. Tears and hugs were often in plentiful supply at encounter groups, but there was nothing facile about these: they were hard won and real. The whole development was enormous and astonishing, and perhaps the most unexpected thing of all was that blacks were weeping for whites.

The groups continued at Esalen and elsewhere for a number of years, following similar formats and generally yielding similar results. How much they influenced the national dialogue about race is hard to say. But, in Anderson's words, "few people can have passed through one of those weekends and come out the other side without some small enhancement of wisdom or compassion about that infinitely difficult dimension of American life."

It was a classic Hollywood party, one of the best: a dinner for some ninety people at the Bel Air mansion that Jennifer Jones had shared with her late husband, David Selznick. The Academy Award–winning actress had spent considerable time at Esalen and had proposed the party as a way of introducing Esalen and what was beginning to be called the human-potential movement to some of the top people in the film industry. Her guest list included directors, producers, and dozens of the most famous stars of the era, among them Rock Hudson, Eddie Albert, Natalie Wood, Oskar Werner, and James Coburn. It took a long time for everybody to get there, and cocktails flowed bounteously during the wait. I had been asked to serve as master of ceremonies, and I gave a short talk before introducing the human-potential contingent, which included Michael Murphy, Fritz Perls, Carl Rogers, and philosopher Abraham Kaplan from the University of Michigan. My presentation was politely received, though some of the audience had already had a bit too much to drink, and Jason Robards, Jr., interrupted me several times, attempting to do gorilla imitations.

After dinner, which was served with champagne, wines, and liqueurs, everyone gathered in the enormous, wood-paneled living room to watch a documentary film about an encounter group led by Carl Rogers and Richard Farson of the Western Behavioral Sciences Institute. Though destined to win an Academy Award in its category, it was a rather slow film about a rather low-key group. Some of the audience fell asleep. When the film was finally over, Carl Rogers stood and announced that he was willing to give an actual encounter group right then and there, and that anyone who was interested could simply follow him through the door and into the next room. Rogers walked across the living room and out of the door, followed by only one person, a small man in a dark suit.

By then it was around midnight and the party was taking on a life of its own. Fritz Perls set up shop next to the swimming pool and offered sample Gestalt sessions to all comers. The first person to sit in the hot seat was Natalie Wood. Five minutes into the session, Perls said, "You're nothing but a little spoiled brat who always wants her own way." At this, she got up and flounced into the house. She asked for her wrap and left the party, but not before her friend Roddy McDowall had offered to fight Perls. Perls was unperturbed. At an earlier session a woman had picked up a heavy chair and held it threateningly above him. "Go ahead," Perls had said, "kill me. I'm an old man."

Perls's next volunteer was Tuesday Weld. She, too, stormed away, her nose in the air, her long blond hair flying, and left the party. Philosopher Abraham Kaplan also took his turn but insisted on sitting in the same chair with Perls, half on his lap. Beard to beard, the two sages had it out.

"I understand the first level of self-deception and the second level of self-deception," Kaplan said excitedly. "But what about the third level and fourth level and fifth level of self-deception?"

"Shut up!" Perls replied.

Despite the defections of actresses Wood and Weld, it was a wonderful party, and quite a few of the guests were there when the sun rose the next morning. Maybe they were still waiting for some announcement, some revelation. They didn't know about a meeting that our contingent had held at a coffee shop just before the party. We had not previously had a chance to get together and decide what we really wanted from the event. After a short discussion we agreed it would be unwise to become closely linked with Hollywood. A steady stream of movie stars driving up the coast road to Esalen would create obvious problems. We would go ahead and make our presentations but would ask for absolutely nothing.

The Hollywood contingent was accustomed to lavish parties at which funds were solicited or, at the least, invitations to further events were issued. They got neither, and it followed that there was never a significant connection between Esalen and the film industry. Later, two movies came out that poked fun at Esalen. It is undoubtedly coincidental that *Bob and Carol and Ted and Alice* starred Natalie Wood and *Serial* starred Tuesday Weld.

The article in *The Sunday New York Times Magazine* of April 15, 1973, was uncharacteristically effusive. It described a large symposium that marked the opening of the Esalen Sports Center, and went on to say, "Such is the clout generated by Esalen that the occasion may be to change in sports what the storming of the Bastille was to the French Revolution."

Maybe not the storming of the Bastille. Still, it must be said that the symposium (which was attended by four hundred coaches, physical educators, and athletes) and the subsequent activities of the Esalen Sports Center contained the seeds of much of what was to grow into the historic U.S. fitness boom.

From the earliest days, Esalen's group leaders had seen that the human body, far from opposing the will of the mind and spirit, replicated it with amazing fidelity. The body, in fact, could serve as a sort of Rosetta stone, a faculty for decoding habitual behavior patterns and current psychological states. It could also become a powerful instrument of personal change, a gifted teacher of the mind and spirit. "Body work"—the analysis, manipulation, and directed movement of the body—has always held an honored place among Esalen's nonverbal humanities.

As for athletics, just a glance at sports records over the past century offers indisputable proof of the rapid evolution of human abilities. No one at the turn of the century, when the world record was four minutes and eighteen seconds, would have dreamed that a human being would someday run a mile in three minutes and forty-seven seconds. It seemed a shame, then, that athletics, this rich and varied arena of human potential, should be largely limited to school and college programs, and to a relatively few professionals and idiosyncratic adult participants. The founders of the Sports Center believed there should be a sport for everybody, and for every body type. They argued that people, if they desired, could create their own new games. They felt that, while winning and performing were important, they were not all-important. The *experience* of moving vigorously and gracefully was a human birthright, valuable in and of itself.

Going a step further, they considered the possibility that sport could serve as a doorway into extraordinary states of consciousness, and even as a path of spiritual development. Michael Murphy's 1972 book, *Golf in the Kingdom,* told a story, part fiction, part fact, about a Scottish golf pro who used his sport for just that. Murphy was amazed when he received hundreds of letters from people who had had similar experiences of heightened awareness and spiritual understanding while engaged in sports; they had previously kept quiet because they had thought they were alone. Some of Murphy's correspondents were world-class athletes who became associated with the Sports Center.

For all their emphasis on participatory, noncompetitive sports, however, Esalen leaders have retained a healthy respect for competition and the pursuit of records. At age fifty-three Michael Murphy ran a 4:35 1,500 meters, winning a bronze medal for his age class in the U.S. Open Masters track meet in Houston. And he retains the undisputed title among his friends and acquaintances as the most fanatical of sports fans, becoming so excited during close games that he sometimes has to lie down to keep from passing out.

When the San Francisco 49ers played in their first Super Bowl game in 1982, Murphy rented a large-screen television and threw a party. Outside his hillside house in a suburb north of San Francisco he erected a sign that joined the Western competitive urge with a transformative concept of the Indian philosopher Sri Aurobindo: THE SUPER BOWL IS THE SUPERMIND. His guests, who included members of the interracial encounter team, a Zen abbot, and a visitor from the Soviet Union, were greeted by an ebullient Murphy wearing a white medic's jacket with a stethoscope around his neck. If anyone passed out, he said, Dr. Price Cobbs could check on his heart, with Murphy in attendance, while they continued to watch the game. Fortunately, the 49ers won.

The renowned anthropologist-epistemologist-cyberneticist Gregory Bateson, former husband of and fellow explorer with Margaret Mead, spent the last two years of his life at Esalen Institute. Early in 1978 he was diagnosed as having lung cancer. He was rushed into surgery at a San Francisco hospital, and his cancer was discovered to be inoperable. The doctors told his wife that he would probably be dead by morning. A Filipino faith healer who was called in tapped his chest and pronounced the cancer dead. Bateson returned home and set about finishing his last book.

It was then that Esalen offered the residency. The offer was both professional and compassionate. Bateson, with his wife Lois and young daughter Nora, was given Fritz Perls's old house at the very top of the Esalen property. He was expected to lead only an occasional seminar and to otherwise simply be there, a wise elder, a distinguished presence in the dining room. At the same time, he made use of a whole array of Esalen's restorative practices, including acupuncture, massage, and deep-tissue body work. He spent a lot of time at the baths. And, day by day, his health seemed to improve.

At seventy-four Bateson was a large man, over six foot five, with a prominent head, a great shock of hair, and a shambling walk. His upper-class English birth and education were revealed in an accent so thick that it was sometimes undecipherable. But then, his ideas were so recondite that many people couldn't understand him anyway. Nevertheless, his seminars were well attended; visitors came from far and near to sit at the feet of the great man. One regular visitor was California governor Jerry Brown, who would spend hours talking ideas with Bateson. These ideas would doubtless have seemed strange two hundred years ago to the Jeffersonians, who were thoroughgoing materialists, for Bateson saw form, pattern, and information as being more fundamental than matter and energy. But they would have liked his fascination with the natural world and might well have been in agreement with his notions about the ultimate unity of what we call mind and what we call nature.

The residency was a happy arrangement for all involved. And if Bateson was living on borrowed time, he hardly seemed to show it. In fact, he apparently kept getting better almost until the time he died, on a visit to a Zen center in San Francisco on July 4, 1980. Bateson's opinion of Esalen, according to historian Walt Anderson, was that it "needed a bit more iron in its veins, was a touch too *sweet.*" But as institutions go, he noted, the choice seemed to be between sweet and sour. Given that, he would take the sweet. When Esalen's enthusiasm and openness to new ideas spilled over into the area of gullibility, Bateson's perennial expression of ironic amusement would merely become more pronounced.

One day during Bateson's residency, a salesman appeared with a line of lightweight pyramidal structures that, if worn on the head, were supposed to increase energy and enhance health. They were priced from a few dollars to nearly a hundred, depending upon the type of metal used. Late that afternoon, the dining room was liberally sprinkled with Esalen staff members wearing what appeared to be the skeletons of old lamp shades on their heads.

Bateson took all of this in but said nothing. Finally, someone sitting across the table from him asked, "Where's *your* pyramid, Gregory?"

Bateson pointed to his head. "Don't you see it?"

A visitor in 1985 will note that Esalen has achieved a certain maturity. The abrasive, mind-blowing experiments of the sixties are long past. The grounds are more beautiful than ever, and the food, much of it grown in the organic garden and on the farm, is delicious. The visitor will hear a great many foreign accents, especially during the summer, when up to 25 percent of the clientele hold foreign passports. The deeply tanned middle-aged man working in the kitchen might well be a government official from Sweden or a psychiatrist from Argentina taking advantage of Esalen's popular work-study program. Most of the guests, foreign and native alike, are professionals, and there are scientists, engineers, and entrepreneurs from Silicon Valley, the high-tech capital of the world, which lies between San Francisco and Esalen. Futurist John Naisbitt was one of the first to see the relationship between the human-potential movement and technological change. "Each feeds the other—high tech/high touch," he writes in his best-selling *Megatrends.* "Technology and our human potential are the two great challenges facing humankind today."

In 1980 Esalen started a Soviet-American Exchange Program aimed at opening up communications between the superpowers in the field of human-potential research. It's an approach to international relations that has been called "track-two diplomacy" by a State Department official. Esalen people have met with Moscow's small but lively counterculture, and also with high U.S. and Soviet officials, including U.S. ambassador to the Soviet Union Arthur Hartman and Senator Claiborne Pell of the Senate Foreign Relations Committee. The Esalen Institute was instrumental in setting up the first face-to-face meetings between astronauts and cosmonauts. It has arranged a live, two-way television satellite hookup, a "space bridge" between a rock concert in southern California and a group of Soviet rock musicians and young people in Moscow. And it has founded a health-improvement project with an accompanying bookfair that traveled recently to two American and two Soviet cities. The program, moreover, has created some happy moments of rare informality, whether beneath icy Russian skies or in the warmth of the Esalen baths, when it has seemed that friendship not only must, but can and will prevail over the deadly forces that pose the ultimate threat to human potential.

Overall, Esalen appears to have become somewhat more serious than it was in its early days. A regular cycle of Invited Conferences brings scholars to the institute from around the world to compare notes on everything from microphysics to shamanic practice, from political psychology to evolutionary theory. But Esalen continues to speak the universal, high-touch language of the body and the senses. It is still possible to have emotional adventure and catharsis on a weekend.

Esalen's ancestry is indisputably Californian. But in both its strengths and its weaknesses—its optimism and impatience, its pioneering spirit and failures of refinement, its focus on results at the expense of theory—Esalen lies clearly in the American grain. Its dream of human potentialities and the full development of human resources goes back to the founding of this nation. Though a cliff on the western edge of the continent extends a long way from the Philadelphia of two hundred years ago, it is a natural extension.

Only in California? Maybe. Only in America? Without a doubt.

Bearings

ESALEN

Some of the buildings now occupied by the Esalen Institute were built in the 1920s by the grandfather of cofounder Michael Murphy. He planned to build a European-style spa here, taking advantage of the 110-degree sulfur springs that flow out of the mountains, but his plans were never realized.

The Murphy family summered here, and the baths were used by Henry Miller and his entourage, as well as by people who lived in the surrounding mountains ("Big Sur Heavies") and homosexuals from San Francisco and Los Angeles.

Hunter Thompson was an early caretaker of the property and was almost pushed off a cliff by a group of young men when he tried to keep them from using the baths.

Michael Murphy and his brother are said to be the models for the young brothers in John Steinbeck's East of Eden. *Murphy once almost lost his sight by staring into the sun while meditating.*

Esalen was opened in 1962. The first seminar offered was called "The Human Potentialities."

About two hundred people stay at Esalen at any one time. Thirty-five live here more or less permanently. Only cofounder Richard Price has lived here since the institute's inception.

Esalen grows 60 to 80 percent of its own produce, bakes its own bread, and makes its own yogurt and granola. The nearest supermarket and movie theater are forty miles away.

Abraham Maslow called Esalen "potentially the most important educational institution in the world."

The cliffs on which Esalen is built have eroded at a rate of up to five feet a year.

Desert Dreams

Bill Barich

My earliest memories of the desert date from a time before I ever laid eyes on the American West. I was a boy growing up in New York, and I became fascinated with the rugged, otherworldly country I saw whenever I went to the Meadowbrook Theater on a Saturday afternoon and paid a quarter to get in to a cowboy double feature. The movies were shot everywhere from Arizona to Baja California, but the locations all blended together in my mind and turned into an archetypal landscape, so that the first time I drove through a real desert, near Elko, Nevada, back in the 1960s, it seemed utterly familiar to me. This was on a warm summer evening, and I can still remember the rich smell of sage, the luxurious dryness of the air, and the shifting play of light on battered house trailers and rusting hulls of automobiles.

The image of wreckage in the midst of serenity surprised me

BILL BARICH grew up on Long Island and now lives in northern California. His story collection *Traveling Light* was published in paperback by Penguin Books in January 1985.

then, but I have since learned that the desert is a place where things that function bizarrely, or not at all, have a habit of turning up. Its central metaphor is one of abandonment. To be out on the Mojave at sunrise, with nobody else around, is to be informed in some absolute way that your existence is random and tenuous. You're forced to recognize that you, too, will eventually be left behind with the beer cans, hubcaps, and cattle skulls. This is a powerful vision, as disconcerting as it is liberating, and it tends to attract fifty Charlie Mansons for every Georgia O'Keeffe.

I met a man once in Lathrop Wells, Nevada, on the fringes of Death Valley, whose passion was collecting marbles. He described his collection to me over several beers, told me how it was stored in mason jars and displayed throughout his home. At first I thought he was certifiable, but later I realized that he was no more nor less sane than a general from nearby Nellis Air Force Base and Nuclear Testing Site talking about ICBMs. The desert is an extreme environment, and in order to survive in it, you need a bizarre strategy, some means of coping to carry you through. This is true of plants and animals as well as people. The common mesquite bush has fifty- or sixty-foot taproots, while the kangaroo rat dribbles saliva onto its breast in an effort to keep cool.

The deserts south of Lathrop Wells, in Death Valley National Monument, are among the most austere in the world. They are bleak, beautiful, and hostile to life for six months of every year. The temperature on the valley floor rises to an average daily high of 116.2 degrees in July, but the winters are temperate and permit hikes into the backcountry. I once walked for hours through the land beyond Salt Creek, and as I was returning I bumped into a Japanese tourist on a well-marked nature trail. In halting English, he asked me what I'd found out there. Without thinking, I said, "More of the same." This must be the classic desert exchange.

Only once in history did the deserts around Death Valley flourish. That was during the nineteenth century, when prospectors combed them for gold, silver, copper, lead, and other precious metals and minerals. In the wake of any significant strike a boomtown went up, sometimes overnight. These cities could be quite sophisticated, offering everything from gourmet cuisine to cultural entertainment, but few of them lasted. Fortunes were made, fortunes were lost, and the wave of speculation moved on.

All that remains from those halcyon years are ruins—a lone chimney, a roofless house, a main street down which the tumbleweeds blow.

Rhyolite, Nevada, is a ghost town. It's situated just across the eastern boundary of Death Valley, about five miles from Beatty, near one of three sites in America that have been selected as a potential nuclear-waste dump. In 1908, four years after Shorty Harris sank his pick into a chunk of green-speckled ore and called his strike Bullfrog, it was the third-largest city in the state, with a population of about sixteen thousand. It had electricity, indoor plumbing, telephones, three railroad lines, nine banking firms, an opera house, and countless whores. There were more cars in Rhyolite than in any comparable city, but by 1914 it had already surrendered itself to spirits.

Rhyolite has a population of forty now. The man who owns it, Jim Spencer, lives there, along with John Lupac, a former site security supervisor of Tolicha Peak electronic warfare range, and Evan Thompson, whose house is made of beer bottles. Spencer is in his early forties, and he has floppy blondish hair and a scholarly manner. There are times when he wonders why he ever invested in 3,700 acres of greasewood and sage, but then he reminds himself that he has always been something of a misfit, out of sync with the age, a person whose sensibility is Victorian. In Rhyolite's dry climate his allergies don't bother him. He doesn't feel trapped. At night he can see the stars.

Spencer is a gambler. He's gambling on the future of the desert. He knows that the population center of the United States is moving west, that people are pursuing sunshine and clean air, and he hopes to bring some of them to Rhyolite. His dream is to restore the town to its original pristine condition. He wants every building to look the way it looked around 1908, with the same sort of facade and the same period details. The houses in this new Rhyolite will be located on exactly the same lots they were located on back then, and there will be exactly the same number of banking firms, bakeries, and saloons. Rhyolite will be a working community—a historically accurate re-creation of the Old West, not a Disneyland operation.

There are those who think that Spencer's plan lists toward the utopian, but at eighty cents an acre why shouldn't he be allowed to dream? The deserts of the West have always been a region in which eccentricity is not only tolerated but sometimes rewarded. If you visit Las Vegas now, you assume that it's been around forever, but Bugsy Siegel actually put it together from scrub and dust fewer than forty years ago. As recently as 1957 you could buy forty acres on the Strip for $4,500. Then there's the example of Palm Springs, another godforsaken piece of real estate that suddenly blossomed into a colony of silver-haired golf-course people. The truth is that anything can happen out on the cutting edge of the weird.

The only restored building in Rhyolite is the Depot Bar, a fine example of turn-of-the-century Spanish-style architecture, and I sat at a table there and listened to Jim Spencer explain how he'd come to own a ghost town. Every now and then we were interrupted when a group of tourists from Death Valley wandered in. They were mostly retired people, the kind of people Spencer hopes will settle in Rhyolite (when there is a Rhyolite), and they would buy postcards or beer before wandering out again. They didn't seem particularly interested in the history of the town, and Spencer made no move to interest them, which made me think that if he was a hustler, he was a reluctant one.

Spencer prefers to think of himself as a historian manqué. Descended from prestigious colonial families and educated at Culver Military Academy in Indiana, where his father taught math, he got involved in the mythology of the West when he was a child. He read Bret Harte and Mark Twain and spent summers on a Wyoming ranch. By the time he was a teenager, he was writing stories free-lance and selling them to the *Tombstone Epitaph* and the Virginia City *Territorial Enterprise*, newspapers that cater to western buffs. He attended a Trinity University extension program in Dallas, but he wasn't happy there and left in 1963, when he went to Arizona to help a young couple who were running the *Epitaph*.

He stayed in Arizona for a year before moving on to Idaho. It was his intention to use the Mormon solitude of that state as a spur to writing a major history of the West, but instead he wound up buying the *Owyhee Avalanche,* another paper for buffs. He was publisher, editor in chief, and the only registered voter in the town of Silver City. In spite of circulation difficulties

(Spencer always had more copy than advertisements), he stayed on for ten years, acquiring several other weeklies and dabbling in politics. In 1972 Senator Frank Church asked him to be part of a thirteen-state commission whose purpose was to address the issue of historical preservation. The idea was to establish a set of criteria for choosing a town that could become the "Williamsburg of the West."

Spencer was an ardent preservationist, so it was relatively simple for him to serve. In the end, the criteria he proposed were adopted and incorporated into the committee's report. Others believed that the criteria were really too stringent ever to be met. Spencer suggested that the property in question be singly titled, of true historical significance, not a government seat, accessible year round, close to major population centers, and so on. A regular ribbon of red tape.

Meanwhile, Spencer moved again. He lived in Los Angeles for four years, serving as a consultant to TV networks on matters of western set design, and he had a construction business on the side. When L.A. finally wore him down, he headed for Las Vegas. A friend convinced him he should go into real estate, and Spencer, ever eager, gave it a shot. One of the listings he got was a strange 3,700-acre property in the desert, near Death Valley. It belonged to the Heisler estate. Spencer tried hard to market it, aiming for a big commission, but the only person he sold on the town was himself. Rhyolite, Nevada. It met all the criteria.

One morning, while we were sitting around the Depot Bar, John Lupac, the former Tolicha security supervisor, came in, took off his parka, and proceeded to lecture me on the state of things. He was wearing camouflage trousers, jungle boots, and an olive-drab Beirut Multinational Force T-shirt. He said he was concerned about all the crap that had recently been written about the West. The only author he respected was Louis L'Amour. He said that America wasn't what it used to be. He'd discovered, for instance, that Patrick Henry's patriotic cry, "Give me liberty or give me death!" wasn't even in school textbooks anymore. He said that he could tell that I lived in a city, because I had a beard and shuffled around with my hands in my pockets. When the economy collapsed, Lupac said, and all the citified people ran like rats for the hills, looking to pillage towns like Rhyolite—the new Rhyolite—

he'd be there to drive them away with a baseball bat.

I had no idea what Jim Spencer made of this, whether he found it sincere or amusing or merely familiar. It resembled the monologues I'd heard on KDWN Talk Radio, in Vegas, where callers carried on about chelation therapy and Bernhard Goetz, offering carefully considered opinions that didn't necessarily stand the test of reason. It was possible that Spencer was simply preoccupied with his weekly history column for the *Death Valley Gateway Gazette,* which he was typing on a manual typewriter. When he was finished, he gave it to Lupac and asked him to deliver it to the *Gazette's* offices, in Beatty, and then he and I went for a stroll through the ruins.

It was cold and windy outside, and the light was intense, illuminating the clefts and ridges of the distant Funeral Mountains. A wild burro was braying in the hills, and Spencer's dogs took off after it, chasing through the greasewood. We passed the skeletal walls of John S. Cook & Co., the first modern bank in the West—fireproof, with time-lock vaults. Spencer described the houses he wanted to construct and told me that he'd had a developer all lined up at the time he closed the deal for Rhyolite, ready to lend him seed money. But the developer went bankrupt and left him in the lurch. He felt that he was going down to the wire now. If he didn't get the utilities in soon, the town just wasn't going to happen.

We stopped outside Evan Thompson's place. There was a sign in the yard that said NUCLEAR FREEZIN' IS RUSSIAN ROULETTE. Spencer decided to show me the bottle house. "Evan?" he said, peering into the darkness, but nobody was around. A Rhyolite saloonkeeper had built the house, and its walls were made of newspaper, plaster, and about fifty-one thousand beer bottles. The bottles were almost all Budweiser. Bud was the beer of the Old West, Spencer said, mainly because the Anheuser-Busch brewmaster had figured a way to keep it from spoiling on the long overland trip from St. Louis. He'd pasteurized it and shipped it in ice cars.

That was the sort of pioneer ingenuity Spencer admired. He touched a finger to a wall and told me how he felt at home in the house, how it spoke to him of important virtues that seemed no longer to be part of the American heritage. This saloonkeeper hadn't owned much, but he'd been proud of what he owned, and he'd kept it up to the best of his ability. He probably dressed for dinner on Sundays, done up in a stiff collar and a black tie. He was a resourceful person, somebody who could make something out of nothing. He was interested in adventure, Spencer said, interested in taking risks, but if he failed, he just walked away without complaining, moving on to the next thing, riding that wave of speculation.

Bearings

DEATH VALLEY

Population: 500
The first white men to see Death Valley were members of the Bennet-Arcane party, who stumbled across it in 1849 looking for a shortcut to the California gold fields. The Indian name for Death Valley was Tomesha, which means "ground afire."

Some gold was discovered in Death Valley, notably in the Bullfrog strike, but the most promising veins, the Breyfogle and the Gunsite mines, were uncovered only once by disoriented prospectors and never found again.

In the 1880s borax became Death Valley's major industry. A twenty-mule team carried twelve tons of borax and twenty-five tons of water.

The average temperature in July is 116 degrees; in January, 52 degrees. Ground temperatures have reached as high as 201 degrees. There are more than thirty ghost towns.

Most deaths in the valley in recent years have been suicides.

Five species of fish live here, some in 130-degree water.

From a vantage point in the Panamint Range, one can see Mount Whitney, the highest point in the contiguous United States, and Badwater, the lowest point in the Western Hemisphere.